THE GOD WHO SMOKES

NAVPRESS DELIBERATE

From the very beginning, God created humans to love Him and each other. He intended for His people to be a blessing to everyone on earth so that everyone would know Him (Genesis 12:2). Jesus also taught this over and over and promised to give His people all they needed to make it happen — His resources, His power, and His presence (Matthew 28:20; John 14:12-14). NavPress Deliberate takes Him at His word and stirs its readers to do the same — to be the children of God for whom creation is groaning to be revealed. We have only to glance through the Bible to discover what it looks like to be the blessing God has intended: caring for the poor, orphan, widow, prisoner, and foreigner (Micah 6:8; Matthew 25:31-46; Isaiah 58); and redeeming the world — everyone and everything in it (Colossians 1:19-20; Romans 8:19-23).

NavPress Deliberate encourages readers to embrace this holistic and vibrant Christian faith: It is both contemplative and active; it unites mystery-embracing faith with theological rootedness; it breaks down the sacred/secular divide, recognizing God's sovereignty and redemptive work in every facet of life; it dialogues with other faiths and worldviews and embraces God's truth found there; it creates culture and uses artistic ability to unflinchingly tell the truth about this life and God's redemption of it; it fosters a faith bold enough to incarnate the gospel in a shrinking and diverse world. NavPress Deliberate is for everyone on a pilgrimage to become like Jesus and to continue His work of living and discipling among all people.

Become what you believe.
The NavPress Deliberate Team

THE GOD WHO SMOKES

Scandalous Meditations on Faith

TIMOTHY J. STONER

NAVPRESS ⬡ ®

Our Guarantee to You

For a free catalog
of NavPress books & Bible studies call
1-800-366-7788 (USA) or 1-800-839-4769 (Canada).

www.NavPress.com

The Navigators is an international Christian organization. Our mission is to advance the gospel of Jesus and His kingdom into the nations through spiritual generations of laborers living and discipling among the lost. We see a vital movement of the gospel, fueled by prevailing prayer, flowing freely through relational networks and out into the nations where workers for the kingdom are next door to everywhere.

NavPress is the publishing ministry of The Navigators. The mission of NavPress is to reach, disciple, and equip people to know Christ and make Him known by publishing life-related materials that are biblically rooted and culturally relevant. Our vision is to stimulate spiritual transformation through every product we publish.

© 2008 by Timothy J. Stoner

All rights reserved. No part of this publication may be reproduced in any form without written permission from NavPress, P.O. Box 35001, Colorado Springs, CO 80935. www.navpress.com

NAVPRESS and the NAVPRESS logo are registered trademarks of NavPress. Absence of ® in connection with marks of NavPress or other parties does not indicate an absence of registration of those marks.

ISBN-13: 978-1-60006-247-6
ISBN-10: 1-60006-247-4

Cover design by The DesignWorks Group, David Uttley
Cover image by Istock
Creative Team: Caleb Seeling, Keith Wall, Reagen Reed, Darla Hightower, Arvid Wallen, Kathy Guist

Some of the anecdotal illustrations in this book are true to life and are included with the permission of the persons involved. All other illustrations are composites of real situations, and any resemblance to people living or dead is coincidental.

Unless otherwise identified, all Scripture quotations in this publication are taken from *The Jerusalem Bible* (TJB) published by Darton, Longman & Todd, © 1966. Other versions used include: the HOLY BIBLE: NEW INTERNATIONAL VERSION® (NIV®). Copyright © 1973, 1978, 1984 by International Bible Society. Used by permission of Zondervan Publishing House. All rights reserved; and the *Amplified Bible* (AMP), © The Lockman Foundation 1954, 1958, 1962, 1964, 1965, 1987.

Library of Congress Cataloging-in-Publication Data

Stoner, Timothy.
  The God who smokes : scandalous meditations on faith / Timothy Stoner.
    p. cm.
  Includes bibliographical references.
  ISBN 978-1-60006-247-6
  1. Christianity--21st century. 2. Emerging church movement. 3. Postmodernism--Religious aspects--Christianity. I. Title.
BR121.3.S86 2008
270.8'3--dc22

                                  2007044501

Printed in the United States of America

1 2 3 4 5 6 7 8 / 12 11 10 09 08

For my parents.

For showing me four things:

There is a truth to know.

There is a way to follow.

There is a person to love.

And that ultimately these are all about Jesus.

CONTENTS

SO WHAT'S WITH THE WEIRD TITLE?

To give you a clue, I will have to back up just a little. It goes back to something I read several years ago. I didn't like it that well at the time, and, to tell the truth, I can't say I like it any better now. It will probably bother you, too. But it is the one thing that really helps make sense of this book. After all, what *is* one to expect from a book with such an incongruous title written by a guy whose last name evokes images of joints and bongs and beer?

My favorite Catholic author, Peter Kreeft, teaches philosophy at BCU, "Barely Catholic University" (sometimes known as Boston College University). He wrote this little powerhouse of a book: *Three Philosophies of Life*. It addresses three books of the Bible: Ecclesiastes—life as vanity; Job—life as suffering; and Song of Songs—life as love.[1]

In the middle of a brilliant excursion on Job's trials, Kreeft tells us that the meaning of life is about getting a face, about becoming real, about becoming yourself.[2] This sounds like pop psychology, but trust me, it's the furthest thing from it. He is alluding to *Till We Have Faces*, which is where C. S. Lewis sketches this out in a haunting myth so beautiful it burns. Becoming real is gaining substance, becoming who we were meant to be: Lords of Narnia, regal splendors, who as Lewis says, will one day shine like the stars, such that if I could see now what you will be then, I would be tempted to bow and worship.[3]

The problem, Kreeft tells us, is that it takes a bit of doing to turn a cretin like me and like you into a little Christ. "It is not easy getting a face," he says. "It is done by suffering not sinning, by saying No as well as saying Yes: by climbing against the gravity of the selfish self, not by the direct paths of self-realization and self-actualization."[4]

And then he drops the little bomb. "The meaning of life is war."[5]

This is so counterintuitive. This runs so contrary to the accepted wisdom. This is so brutally hard to hear. And it's the last thing you want to be told when you are kicking back, holding a frosty glass, watching the surf come in through your brand-new sunglasses that would do Bono proud. Who wants to hear that? So I shoved it aside until I began my private quest through the Gospels these past two years.

I was reading them like a Navajo tracker studying a week-old trail. I was taking my time. I was picking up and smelling the droppings, fingering the bent twigs, and putting my ear right to the ground. And I heard these drumbeats. I could make out the sound of swords clashing, feet stomping, mothers crying, and babies screaming. Rachel was weeping for her slaughtered infants (Matthew 2:18), and I knew Kreeft (and a lot of others) was right.[6]

Like any decent piece of literature, the Gospels use foreshadowing. We hear it in the Magnificat and in Simeon's prophecy of the sword that will pierce Mother Mary's heart (Luke 1:51-52; 2:34-35). Then Jesus tells it to us straight up. He comes to rip and tear families apart because He is bringing not peace but a sword, not unity but division (Matthew 10:35; Luke 12:49,52). He was not on vacation in Palestine but on a mission of violence that would end violently.

I don't much like it, but there it is.

It does make sense, however, of the bloody battles that soak the pages of the Old Testament. It does give a perspective to those war cries we call the Psalms. And it helps explain the ongoing suffering of thousands of sister and brother martyrs who right now are giving their lives, as Jesus did, for the life of the world. And I tend to think it places the final, cataclysmic battles in Revelation in an understandable context.

But my real dilemma was how does one write about this?

I got my answer at a sushi restaurant.

I had never before tried those pinwheel delicacies. My sons Ben and Aaron had graciously invited me to take them to a nearby all-you-can-eat buffet. I was not fond of every variety but found one I liked a lot. It was the house specialty. It was fried and, when a thin slice of salmon was draped over the top, could make your taste buds shout the Hallelujah Chorus. While savoring the exotic flavors, my sons and I were talking about my idea for a book about Jesus. They were commenting on the essay I had given them, summarizing my research. Both sons very kindly proposed that I select another writing style entirely, lest the reader fall over in a fit of exhaustion halfway through the first page.

Ben asked why I didn't just tell stories.

So I began reminiscing about growing up as a fundamentalist

missionary kid on four continents. By the time we had our fill of raw fish, I had decided to follow my sons' advice. I would ditch the essay and get autobiographical.

These stories are signs pointing to a Bigger Story that is really better called a Great Epic in which we get questions *and* answers.[7] We get hope and we get joy. We get death that bursts up into life; and it is now, and it is then, and it lasts forever, and it makes sense of all the crap and the hurt and the sometimes unrelenting tragedy of life. For it whispers and shouts and sings that it all ends up in a wedding dance where we all get drunk on joy, and it will never, ever end.

And the point of the book is not so much war—that is backdrop. What I want to say is pretty simple: despite what postmodernity (whatever you may conceive it to be) says, there is truth that can be known; there is a center that holds reality together; there is meaning and purpose; there is destiny and a calling of epic proportions (though you may never be famous).

The stories let you in on a wonderful secret: We are not only invited guests but the blushing Bride. And our Groom is a heroic King, a mighty warrior who is good and just and stunning in His beauty. He is so full of passion and blazing emotion that He burns—and yes, smokes in the ferocity of His infinite, holy love that compelled Him to give it all away for His Bride. And He who gave it all for us is worth giving ourselves completely to. We exist not to believe, and not even so much to follow, but to love. And as Luther says somewhere, love God with all your heart and do what you will.

But is the meaning of life *really* war? The final answer may surprise you. What I can say is that, according to the Creator of the world, there is an oppositional defiance disorder in the cosmos, and we are smack in the center of it. Darkness and Light are in mortal conflict. The Seed of the Woman and the Seed of the Serpent are not friendly to each other. And the very epicenter of the hostilities runs right through our own hearts. The battle rages within and it rages without. We are called to love the world and hate it. We are to lay down our lives for its blessing but cry out for God's vengeance. We are to be *in* the world and *for* the world but not *of* the world. After all, the captain of the heavenly hosts is both a Lamb who was slain and a Lion laying claim to the whole jungle. There *is* a war, but there is so much more.

For our God is a God who smiles and sings.

But He is also a God who smokes.

I

KING OF FOOLS

I think I love Jesus because I was a stutterer. The childhood pain of being mocked for an unflattering appearance has been compared to the shock of a drive-by shooting—I would say that the stutterer's suffering is more like slow roasting on the Inquisitor's rack. Whereas a bullet brings a sudden startling pain and then oblivion, fire in the hands of an expert can be protracted, exquisite torture.

Stuttering is like a vicious ghoul—with talons as long and sharp as needles—it eases up on you, luring you into irrational security, then gleefully drives its hooks into your tongue. And there you are, incoherently flailing and fumbling in a waking nightmare.

It is a constant dread and a recurring reality.

You become unusually sensitive to the conversational spotlight. Like Mexicans in the old westerns, you prefer those really big sombreros—they shield your head and face and cast a shadow over your entire body.

But I wasn't really wired to hide out under broad brims or be a complete wallflower. I had things I wanted to say. Quite a few, apparently. So time and again, I would be driven—almost insanely—to take that terrible plunge into the dangerous cataracts where the stakes were very high and the water shallow. The crazy thing was that I would crash and burn, or come awfully close, almost every time.

Stuttering may be a more cruel disability than most. While others are obvious and readily apparent, this one is not. You look, act, and at times even talk normally, so people interact with you as though you have no speech defect. Their defenses are down—until the goblin grabs your tongue and your eyes fill up with fear and you begin to stammer incomprehensibly. It is then that reality hits: They are dealing with a person with a handicap. They have been caught unaware, plunged into a situation they never invited or expected.

How well I remember the terrible coolness falling like lead. The tightening along the sides of the mouth as the warm smile turned to glass, the eyes growing wide as though staring at a car wreck, and the body inching back at an obtuse angle.

They are trapped as you are trapped.

They can't walk away. To do so would be a grievous breach of etiquette. Had they known what you were, they would most likely have avoided you. But avoidance is impossible now. They must wait nervously, embarrassed for you and for themselves, as you grit your teeth and somehow manage to pull your tongue free of the demonic tormentor. For them it is an uninvited assault, an intrusion into their calm and safe and predictable normalcy. It is as unwanted as being forced to watch an epileptic seizure when all you came for was a pair of pants at the mall.

To survive, I had to become a master of verbal whitewater

rafting. I could spin on a dime as I saw the jagged rocks up ahead. Conversation was an exhausting venture in skimming and scraping past words that could, if not kill you, destroy your boat and ruin your day. A thorough command of the *words-that-must-never-be-uttered* was required. These tend to be the ones that begin in hard consonants like B, P, or T (as in my first name—having to introduce myself on the first day of school was death by paper cuts), or with the sound of K as in *kiss* or L as in *love*.

And that puts a real drag on romantic dialogue.

When it is with Kathy, the blonde in eighth grade, the pain of it can feel like a belly full of battery acid. But when it is with Sharon, the dark-haired female lead in the high school play, when the interested look softens to pity, the acid can start to bore a hole through your stomach.

Sharon was an upperclassman, who won the lead in all the plays. She was a free spirit and, being a bit of a hippie, was also remarkably kind. We were talking over the kissing scene in *Anne Frank*. It was my first play, and I had somehow been chosen to play the part of Peter Van Dam, Anna's romantic interest. I, a ninth-grader, was *very* interested. During that tentative conversation on a subject I was no expert in, with a lady who was, I began to do the tango on the hard consonant in the word *kiss*. As the blood rushed up my face and fire blazed through me, she smiled, pretended not to notice and finished the sentence for me. I cursed myself for an idiot and vowed never to risk such a verbal gambit again. I don't recall ever having another conversation with her—that is, until the next year when I was chosen to be her romantic lead in *Tevya's Seven Daughters*.

That time I chose my words more carefully.

Glib, I was not. Funny, I could not be. So, robbed of control over that part of the body that James tells us "makes great boasts"

(James 3:5, NIV), I was forced to opt for the monastic's best friend: silence. I lived in a state of mute panic that I would be drawn into a conversation requiring multi-syllabic responses. Shame and fear followed me like bad perfume, even as I tried to melt into anonymity hiding on the fringes.

And this brings me to my love for Jesus. I get His stories. I can relate to the people He interacted with. The woman with that humiliating bleeding problem that forced her to the periphery, dragging behind her the whispers, the finger-pointing, the label "unclean." I know her. She hung out with me there at the edges. She spent twelve years on the outside looking in. Not that we were friends exactly. When you've been deeply shamed you hover alone on the outskirts—bleak, silent, and independent islands. You protect your space.

I understand the lepers, too. They hung out in the back with us. But they at least hung together. They'd somehow learned the value of being a part of a community of sufferers.

The shame-filled who teem on the fringes are like magicians who've mastered the art of becoming invisible. There is blessed safety in anonymity. Of course, it comes at the cost of slowly leaking away into a twilight zone of nonexistence.

You're there but not really there.

The woman with the blood disorder (probably some kind of hemorrhage) lived essentially as an outcast. According to the Law of Moses, she was ritually, and thus socially, unclean. She was an untouchable. Like Hester Prynne in Nathaniel Hawthorne's *The Scarlet Letter*, she also had a large letter stitched onto her chest, except it wasn't an *A* but a *Z. Zabah*. It was a designation imposed by the Torah: "unclean." The Law made it abundantly clear that not only was she dirty, but anyone who touched her, even inadvertently, would also be made unclean (Leviticus 15:25-33).

So this woman, for a dozen achingly long years, has been shunned by her own community, suffering alone. There has been no one to embrace her, no one to express comfort and grace. She has been shut out of the social fabric, the warm, inviting circle of belonging. Neither family nor friends have been able to physically communicate love or affection.

Her sickness has stolen her place and expelled her into the shadowed existence of a foreigner, a social and religious defective. Like Oliver Twist gazing wistfully through bright windows at families celebrating happy, plentiful Christmases, she could look but not touch. She might try to warm herself at a hundred vicarious fires, but these provide no cheer or relief to her lonely distress. It is cold comfort indeed to watch others laugh, holding easy hands as they dance, knowing you can never join up.

So she stands year after year, looking in from a distance until her heart grows cold and hard like a burnt gray cinder. She shrinks back and withdraws, permanently . . . until she hears that Jesus is in town.

Flinging caution to the wind, she inches her way through the crowd, trying hard to avoid notice. Her goal is just to touch, not a person, but a bit of a robe. It is the fringe of the prayer shawl. *If He is the Messiah*, she tells herself, *the Torah guarantees healing beneath those "wings."* If she is wrong, she knows she will be humiliated for befouling a nationally respected rabbi. Yet she pushes through, eventually putting the anonymous tips of her guilty fingers to the fringe of His shawl. She has shuffled her way invisibly from the fringes to the fringe. She risks it all, and she is rewarded abundantly.

From my perspective, the real miracle of these Jesus miracle stories is that fringe dwellers—these indistinct, bare smudges of existence—stood up, cried out, or stretched forward to make contact with the Real. Taking their courage in their hands, these insubstantials pressed through the veil of shame that had rendered them nonpersons, crashed through the barrier of separation that expelled them to the periphery, and connected with the only one who is truly substantial.

They crashed the party and found themselves not only accepted, but favored and blessed as well.

They got the seats of honor.

Of these Jesus would say, "Since John the Baptist came, up to this present time, the kingdom of heaven has been subjected to violence and the violent are taking it by force" (Matthew 11:12).

Blessed are the violent.

Blessed are the wild eyed, the inarticulate, the social misfits, the desperate — those who throw all caution and reputation aside so they can just get close.

Blessed are the gate-crashers who push over every restraint in their mad dash to grab hold of life and hope to find in their delirious hands joy.

Blessed are those who trample their pride to death as they cry out their longing and pain and, in falling on their faces, get not only a new face but a new name. Where once they were unloved and overlooked, they grow drunk on the sparkling wine of acceptance and welcome and home.

I also get the delicious intoxication of the first-name-basis: "Matthew, follow me" (Matthew 9:9), or "Zacchaeus, can I hang out at your place tonight?" (Luke 19:2).

Zacchaeus was short even by Jewish standards. He was the weakling who could not escape the scorching tongues and cruel fists of the village bullies. In the wolf-pack hierarchy, he was the disregarded runt of the litter — the last and least. But when he grew older, he figured out a way to power.

Both he and Matthew, despite their money, were forced by their professions to the margins. They were despised as traitors. They represented the interests of the Roman establishment. They were the FBI agents shaking down the poor blacks in Selma, Mississippi. They were the quislings, the French collaborators who sided with the Nazis. They were the representatives of big business who busted up the union and enforced sub-minimum wages on the working poor. They stood erect for law and order and profited handsomely for it.

Their consciences were rubbed down to a nub. But when they were given a chance to break free from the yoke of greed, they made a run for it. When they were given their names back—no longer "Traitor" but "Zacchaeus" or "Matt"—they were released and rushed into an embrace they never expected and knew they never deserved.

I also get the tangy sweetness of the words: "I've come to find and to save the rejects, the misfits, the overlooked and undervalued. I came on purpose to choose you, as Rob Bell writes, 'the not-good-enoughs.'"[1]

Though Jesus was not a true insubstantial, He may have grown up feeling like a third-culture kid—not at home in this country and no longer at home in the one He was born in. He was from another planet after all, but He'd changed dramatically.

He didn't look the same.

He wasn't the same.

How does a God-man fit back into the heady sweetness of the infinitely loving, interrelationship of infinite Persons?

Certainly, the perfect Son of God, the Creator of the world, found Himself not at home in the fragmented darkness and bleakness of His fallen creation. As His feet raised dust clouds on the mountain trails of Israel, was He afflicted with the pain of displacement, the ache of homesickness, the disquieting longing for His true home and His perfect Father?

I think He was.

Did He miss glory?

I think He did.

Judging by how the Pharisees threw back in His face the implicit accusation of illegitimacy, I think that there was a black cloud that hung over His head His entire life (John 8:31; Matthew 12:24; John 1:46). Did the moral minority exclude and shove Him to the periphery populated by the "unclean": the traitors, the morally and physically foul, the corrupted and corrupting, who bore the perpetual acne marks of unworthiness?

I think they did.

That was part and parcel of bearing our sufferings and shouldering our pains. And of carrying our humiliation and shame. Which is why I think there was a bit of intoxication for Jesus also when He drank in those sweet words: "You are my Son, the Beloved, my favor rests on you" (Luke 3:22). He needed to know He was inside too.

We all do.

That's why it's the poor, the weak, the needy, the bottom-feeders and cave dwellers, the expelled and repelled, the shame filled and shamefaced who run when they hear His voice. They can hear their names being called from miles away, and they can't help themselves. They lose their heads and come running from the dim fringes into the light of day and find themselves, finally, against all hope, inside.

» » »

There is a scene that sticks with me from the black-and-white version of *The Hunchback of Notre Dame*. It is Paris during the

New Year's celebration known as the Festival of Fools. In France, as in the majority of other European countries, the celebration was kicked off with the election of a Lord of Misrule or King of Fools. Historians tell us that this harlequin king went by many names: the King of the Bean in England, the Abbot of Unreason in Scotland, the *Abbe de la Malgouveme* in France. This mock ruler had the power to call people to disorder. This could include cross-dressing, bawdy songs, drinking to excess, and gambling on the church altar.

In some places the Festival of the Ass was commemorated. A young girl with babe in arms would enter a church riding a donkey. During the mock services, prayer responses that would have normally elicited an *amen* were concluded by a hearty (but hardly respectful) *hee-haw* instead.

Apparently, Parisians had a particularly infamous reputation. Such was their debauchery and disgraceful behavior that by the fifteenth century an embarrassed Catholic Church was compelled to finally clamp down on these "monstrous" celebrations.

Quasimodo is a fringe dweller. He is the impossibly ugly, deformed hunchback who lives and works at the Cathedral of Notre Dame. He has been irresistibly drawn in by the gleeful sounds, the guttering torches and shouts of delight from the crowd. He is on the outskirts spying on the revelries. When the time comes to crown the ugliest member the King of Fools, the pathetic, mentally challenged bell-ringer readily wins.

The hunchback is thrown up on their shoulders and bounces down the cobbled streets of Paris, held up by the cheering riff-raff—the inebriated, filthy backstreet dwellers. Poor Quasimodo feels thrilled and embarrassed and honored. He has never been chosen for anything before. Now, not only has he been hand selected to be inside but to be the top dog as well. He doesn't understand that the celebration is a mockery. He does not know he is being made sport of. He is the King of Fools in more ways than one.

It's the look of surprised joy and timid, hopeful delight mixed with the tiniest little question that gets to me. It's too good to be true, Quasimodo is thinking, but the shouts of approval seem so genuine.

Quasimodo cannot tell that the cheers are really jeers.

When you live on the margins, you never really know for sure. There is this needling suspicion, this carnivorous worry: Are these prestige brokers patronizing or, behind sidelong glances, quietly mocking?

When it dawned on me that Jesus came to the outcasts like me who choke on the smog of a rejection that is both real and imagined, I began to be won over. When you've given up all hope of being picked for the team, much less of hearing your name get top billing, this is heady stuff.

No wonder an avaricious, cold-blooded thief named Zacchaeus lost his grip on sanity and promised to give back four times what he'd defrauded. No wonder the lepers forgot to say thank you. They were simply too stunned at their unbelievable good fortune. Their heads reeled from the delirious thrill of being clean, being cool, being invited in by the only one who really matters.

That's why I love Jesus.

He called me by my first name, put His arm around my shoulder, and as we strolled over the luscious green soccer pitch, He told me I could play fullback on His team. And I could start, if I wanted.

But I have a feeling most of us get all this too.

Our brokenness is such that we walk around with trace levels of radioactivity from exposure to the painful blows of misfortune.

We are a band of miserable brothers and sisters — a motley crew of the shattered and battered, the bruised and broken.

We have come to Jesus, or are thinking of coming, because we have heard that He is kind and gentle and tender, that He is protective and would hold us and heal us. And it is all very true. But I worry that it is all we know. It certainly is mostly all that we read or hear or sing. It is sweet and delicious, and it is repeated and then repeated some more.

Though true, it is only partially so. And as a wise soul pointed out, a half-truth, if taken as the whole truth, is a lie. I do not for a moment want to deny or minimize the attraction of love incarnate. I join all those other fringe dwellers and shout out, "Jesus is good!" But I also want to link arms with another timid introvert, an unassuming little beaver speaking about Aslan, the King of Narnia, and say: "Yes, He is Good, but He's NOT safe!"

He is a lion, after all.

» » »

There is a Christian bumper sticker on the back of lots of cars in our town that reads: LOVE WINS. I understand the sentiment and even approve, kind of. But like all bumper stickers, its impact suffers from a diffused ambiguity. Whose love wins? Does human love inevitably win? Wins what? Wins the war, the tennis match, the poker game? Anyway, isn't it now passé to view life preeminently in terms of winning and losing? Isn't that a carryover from the modern, colonial, black-wing-tip-and-oxford-shirt era?

The big question that looms in my mind is this: If it's God's love that wins, then what *kind* of divine love wins? This may seem to be a very odd question. It may seem self-explanatory or moot — God's love is God's love, right?

And, as the Bard said, there is the rub.

The divine love we have been trained to think about is the sentimental variety. Brian McLaren astutely takes note of this in *The Last Word and the Word After That*. He calls this distortion "the divine doting auntie in Heaven full of sweetness and smiles, who sees war and corruption and violence and racism and says, 'Well, boys will be boys. Would you care for another blessing, dearie?'" He surmises that this theological caricature and others like it "probably, in some way, flow from an understandable but unhealthful overreaction against God the eternal torturer."[2] Maybe. Maybe not.

The only problem with his critique is that it provides no real alternative. Today, the cultural, philosophical, and religious flow is rushing so strongly in the direction of the Auntie God that you need to be very insistent and clear (one might even suggest a bullhorn) in proposing an alternate perspective. Otherwise, it just gets drowned out in the surge of converging waters and is dragged under. The undertow is so powerful that there is an almost numbing inevitability to its insistence that God's love is driven by a sugary sentimentality, not something more solid and substantial and dangerous.

When the flow of culture (the Germans called it *zeitgeist*) is rampaging along the same narrow channel, it is the voice of wisdom that insists, "Take a step away from the stream. Take a step away from the stream." One step sideways is usually all that is needed to catch your breath and clear your head.

If the church has a higher calling than being the world's chaplain, baptizing its wars, its social and political agendas, as some still believe — if it exists to do more than pronounce approved religious blessings on culture — then stepping outside the prevailing stream is not only wise but essential. This is the only way to provide the prophetic counterpoint that brings a perspective that is out of this world, which, if you study the example of the biblical prophets, seems to be their exclusive literary point of view.

This voice will frequently, though not always, be at odds with the *zeitgeist* and will incur its hostility. The birth of Jesus was inaugurated with a bloodbath. Herod's slaughter of all male children in Bethlehem two years old and younger is merely its foreshadowing. The Messiah made it explicit: "If you belonged to the world the world would love you as its own; but because you do not belong to the world, because my choice withdrew you from the world, therefore the world hates you" (John 15:19; Matthew 10:22).

What Jesus is saying to His followers is that if they are going to be faithful to their calling to challenge the prevailing assumptions and values—the accepted paradigms of their world—sparks, at least, will fly. There is an inherent, settled antipathy between God's kingdom and the kingdom of this world. The voice that speaks for God outside the accepted stream will create an uncomfortable and eventually intolerable dissonance. Sometimes it is so intense that it may get you killed, as it did Martin Luther King Jr. and others.[3]

As C. S. Lewis puts it:

The enemy has not yet thought it worth while to fling his whole weight against us. But he soon will. This happens in the history of every Christian movement, beginning with the ministry of Christ Himself. At first it is welcome to all who have no special reason for opposing it; at this stage he who is not against it is for it. What men notice is its difference from those aspects of the World which they already dislike. But later on, as the real meaning of the

Christian claim becomes apparent, its demand for total surrender . . . men are increasingly "offended." Dislike, terror, and finally hatred succeed: none who will not give it what it asks (and it asks all) can endure it: all who are not for it are against it.[4]

What we need to make clear with our bumper stickers and culture-current writings is that the love that wins is a holy love. The love that won on the cross and wins the world is a love that is driven, determined, and defined by holiness. It is a love that flows out of the heart of a God who is transcendent, majestic, infinite in righteousness, who loves justice as much as He does mercy; who hates wickedness as much as He loves goodness; who blazes with a fiery, passionate love for Himself above all things. He is Creator, Sustainer, Beginning and End. He is robed in a splendor and eternal purity that is blinding. He rules, He reigns, He rages and roars, then bends down to whisper love songs to His creatures.

His love is vast and irresistible. It is also terrifying, and it will spare no expense to give everything away in order to free us from the bondage of sin, purifying for Himself a people who are devoted to His glory, a people who "have no ambition except to do good" (Titus 2:14). So He crushes His precious Son in order to rescue and restore mankind along with His entire creation (Isaiah 53:10-12). He unleashes perfect judgment on the perfectly obedient sacrifice and then pulls Him up out of the grave in a smashing and utter victory.

He is a God who triumphs.

He is no Auntie. He is a burning cyclone of passionate love. Holy love wins.[5]

The Jesus we love and follow reaches down to the alienated and the dispossessed. He goes to the fringe and draws in the rejected. He lays gentle hands on the dirty and the ostracized. But He does not only touch and heal, He also instructs and warns. He tells the woman caught in adultery, "Go now and leave your life of sin" (John 8:11, NIV). He tells the invalid by the pool, "See, you are well again. Stop sinning or something worse may happen to you" (John 5:14, NIV).

Our accommodation to our culture's insistence on a half-truth puts us in danger of declawing and domesticating the mighty King, whose presence made demons scream in terror and death flee in shame. He came on an invasive, dangerous, and unwelcome mission of mercy to cut open and expose what was hidden in men's hearts (Luke 2:34-35). His coming was not to be marked by peace and tranquility—He came to impose a test of absolute allegiance. He forced people into a divisive crisis of choice (Matthew 10:34-39). The peace He came to bring first triggered a war. He was on a guerrilla mission to infiltrate territory controlled by His enemy, raid his camp, and set the prisoners free (Mark 3:23-27; Luke 4:18).

That's why from His carpenter's tool belt there also hung a sword.

Which is why David, Israel's poet laureate, got it just right:

Let me proclaim Yahweh's decree;
He has told me, "You are my son,
Today I have become your father.
Ask and I will give you the nations for your heritage,
the ends of the earth for your domain.
With iron scepter you will break them,
shatter them like potter's ware.
So, now, you kings, learn wisdom,
earthly rulers, be warned:

serve Yahweh, fear Him.
tremble and kiss His feet,
or He will be angry and you will perish,
for His anger is very quick to blaze.
Happy, all who take shelter in Him. (Psalm 2:7-12)

That is why I love this Jesus—but fear Him, too. For though He is a King of fools, He is also the King of kings.

And so at the outset of this book, I begin with a blessing. It is a blessing for the outcast, for the displaced and misplaced, for the desperate and the lonely, it's a blessing for the alienated and expelled, for those who have lost hope or are hanging on by a hair. It's a blessing for you, and it is a blessing for me.

Blessing

May the Lord of the outcast, the King of fools,
the great shepherd of our souls,
come and place a kiss of peace on your cheek.
May He say to you, "You are mine and I am yours."
May He give you the embrace of the Father
that will heal a thousand wounds and speak a thousand
hopes into life.
As He takes the dry ashes of misspent passion
and gives you in its place a garland of praise,
may you rejoice.
No, may you shout with a bold, confident joy
at the dizzying delight of being chosen,
of being welcomed in by your true Father
and invited to sit with Him at the banquet table reserved

for His friends.
But,
as you celebrate your delightful privilege,
may you never forget that the one who called you His own
is friend but also sovereign King—
that He who gave everything up for you
calls you to give everything up for Him.

2

VELVET REMBRANDTS

I have this horrible memory of running down packed sidewalks along the beach in Valencia, Spain, being chased by a murderously angry, well-dressed young man. It was evening and everyone was promenading on the sidewalk by the beautiful waterfront of the Costa del Sol.

I was in my early teens. My missionary parents had left Chile and moved to Spain. I enjoyed the occasional prank, which at that time included throwing little pea-sized explosives next to handsome couples, watching them jump and publicly lose their dignity. My aim has never been the best. So, on one of these forays, the firecracker missed its intended mark. It struck, not the pavement, but the expensive high-heeled shoe of a stunning lady, strolling with her Spanish escort. The gunpowder flashed against her immaculate white pant leg.

Never in all my life have I run so fast and so hard. Gallantry is taken very seriously by Spaniards. The glossy-haired fellow whose lady I had affronted sprinted after me with bloodlust in his eyes. He was intent on revenge. I was intent on survival. I eventually outran him, but I was the one who shed his dignity like a molting snake.

I still like to shake things up a bit. After all, I grew up in Europe, where the national pastime is sitting on benches or stools at the local bar eating tapas of chorizo, tortilla, or calamares and arguing about things that matter: politics, religion, and European football (soccer, for the uninitiated) — or the politics and religion of football. This environment tends to convince you that ideas are really important — and that passionate discourse and the fiery arguments that follow are as normal as whistling to get the attention of your waitress.

It is difficult to find such fervent interchanges in these colder American climes. What makes it even harder is the postmodern penchant to view heated discussion as a sign of the fatal disease of modernity. So I like stoking the conversational fires, if only for old time's sake, and if it takes a little explosive device, well then, so be it.

» » »

So there I was with a generationally diverse group of spiritually and intellectually astute types in a suitably eclectic coffee bar. There was beer on tap, and my three oldest sons were hefting a pint or two. There were seven seated at the round tables we'd pushed together. All of us had been raised in evangelical or fundamentalist churches. We had a common theological vocabulary, and we were all working on unlearning a lot of what we had been taught. Some of us had not yet learned to be nice about it.

I had kind of invited myself along when I overheard my sons

talking about getting together with some friends who I knew enjoyed their theology on tap.[1] I tend to gravitate toward these circles, if for no other reason than to throw little firecrackers and see what lights up. On this occasion, no real trigger was required. We were discussing a book that had just hit the Christian bookstore shelves. The title was *Velvet Elvis*. Its author, Rob Bell, pastors a church in our town. It was provocative and creative and cool. It asked a lot of good questions—Rob really knows what the restless and thoughtful natives are asking. He was born almost two decades after I was, placing him in my children's generation, or close enough. Whereas he is a card-carrying member of the postmodern generation, I am ducking the AARP, which wants to mail me their little gold card. He has become internationally known through a DVD series called NOOMA, which features his teachings in hard-hitting, edgy, MTV-style format. It has sold more than a million copies.

I should be so lucky.

The book was plenty controversial in its own right. It poked a lot of holes into pet religious beliefs and raised some important questions about Jesus and the Bible. I hadn't read it yet, but the buzz was that Rob believed good questions, not answers, were what really mattered. There was no real problem getting a vigorous conversation going among this gaggle of Emergent (and Emerging) ex-fundamentalists. Still, I was propelled by this uncontrollable impulse to agitate.

"Okay," I said, "I get it that it is important to listen to other 'stories.' I get it that other points of view need to be given dignity. And I agree. But"—and here I took a breath for dramatic effect—"at the end of the day, is Rob saying that there are other stories that can lead to God? Is he just creatively repeating that old line from the 1900s that led to the split between liberals and fundamentalists? Does he believe, down deep, that those who sincerely follow other roads, who pursue justice and compassion, even though they reject Jesus, will be saved?"

There was the moment of silence that inevitably follows explosive verbal gambits. What I didn't expect was the fervor of the response.

In our small coterie, there was a young man who knew Rob personally. He had been a founding member of his church, had served in leadership roles, and so was on a first-name basis with him. After that split-second of quiet, he blurted out, "Of *course* that's what he believes!"

The statement was not meant to be derogatory. It was an affirmation and a very vehement one at that. I have to admit that I have become accustomed to the nuanced diplomacy of postmodern nonarguments, so I sometimes startle myself when I lapse back into the absolutist and categorical vocabulary of my youth. It's amazing what a little cultural pressure will do to even the bluntest of us. His candid response was therefore a bit of a shock to all of us—including, I'm sure, to him.

His wife, who also knows Rob well, began to massage and sandpaper the rough edges of the impolitic assertion.

"We really can't put words into his mouth," she said. "That really isn't fair. It's probably better for you to read it for yourself."

Wise words.

It was evident that emotions were running high, so I deflected the conversation onto calmer waters.[2]

Later, as I thought over the discussion in the coffee bar and its unexpected conclusion, I realized that what bothered me was not precisely whether or not that emphatic statement was true. And I should add, I have not been able to confirm the accuracy of that remark. But it wouldn't matter all that much since what gave me pause then and still does is that, somehow, this is what a friend who really ought to know is convinced Rob believes. That's the danger of posing too many questions. You may wind up confusing your own friends, if not yourself.

If you're a late-night talk show host, nobody really cares. If, on the other hand, you are a widely respected Bible teacher with thousands of spiritually inquiring minds tracking your every word, then it matters — a lot.

Rabbis like to ask questions too.

No problem.

Jesus asked lots of questions. He also told lots of stories.

However, He also issued a lot of instructions and gave a lot of answers. It was not all parable and ambiguity and misdirection. When asked how to get to heaven, He was so blunt with the rich twenty-something executive, that He drove him almost to despair. The young man "was filled with sadness, for he was very rich" (Luke 18:23). And so the young man walked away.

In Jesus' conversation with a member of the religious Supreme Court of Israel, He also laid it all on the line. He told him straight up that God the Father's singular purpose in sending Him into the world was to save it. But Jesus did not stop there. Instead, He tightened the screws just a little bit more:

> No one who believes in [the Son] will be condemned; but whoever refuses to believe is condemned already because he has refused to believe in the name of God's only Son. On these grounds is sentence pronounced; that though the light has come into the world men have shown they prefer darkness to the light because their deeds were evil. (John 3:18-19)

That's really not terribly ambiguous. Is it?

Pilate wanted to know if Jesus was the real deal. Jesus responds, "You said it! I am a king, I was born for this" (John 18:37).

So when asked directly about the basic core, Jesus did not duck. He made it plain what He believed about Himself and about those who refused to follow Him. The Son was sent on a mission of salvation. His intention was not to bring condemnation. Everyone who chose other paths and refused to put their faith exclusively in Him were bringing condemnation upon themselves.

When eternal destiny is on the line and the question is sincere, you get a definitive answer from Jesus, not a question. He did not want any confusion about who He was or what He was asking from people or what the consequences were for rejecting Him.

When salvation is in the balance, there is no rabbinic dodge. You get it straight—shaken maybe, but not stirred.

In *Velvet Elvis*, which I later read, the necessity and value of doctrines and belief systems are questioned. Using the metaphor of an outdated velvet painting, Rob suggests that just as paintings become anachronisms, so do beliefs about God, Jesus, the Bible, salvation, and the future. They all need to keep being repainted.[3] He uses a brick wall as a metaphor for how old-school types view theology: Take one brick out and the whole thing collapses. He views it as a harmful and rigid tool for exclusion.

Rob queries: Would the entire wall of Christianity fall down if we found out Jesus had really been the product of a secret liaison between "Larry" and a Jewish maiden? What would be lost if that "brick" were removed?[4]

As one notorious, testosterone-drenched thirty-something pastor put it: "Not to mention the incredible disrespect of this question to Mary the Mother of Jesus, if we take that brick out, well . . . we would lose—Jesus." (Pause for effect.) "I went to public school, and I know *that*."[5]

Again, while Rob states that he accepts the orthodox teaching on the virgin birth, a teacher needs to tread very cautiously in such matters, lest his broad, open-ended questions confuse not just his friends but a lot of his listeners too. The usual effect of a host of interrogatories is to weaken rather than support the brief indicative that follows them.

Rob then asks two corollary and very intriguing questions: If we found out Mary was not technically a virgin, could you still love God, and would the way of Jesus still be the best possible way to live?[6]

The question fails to ask whether we get to or whether it is wise to poke holes in any wall we want. It assumes something rather significant—that we have the right to repaint any painting we stumble across. But is my Rembrandt as outdated as your Velvet Elvis? Are the ancient masterpieces that have been regarded as priceless and timeless by centuries of experts really on the same artistic level as cheap Velvet knockoffs? Can each of us bring our bucket of Magic Markers and start repainting any canvas we think needs updating?

I ask another question. Is it not true that for every thousand gaudy velvet paintings, there are one or two masterpieces that serve as artistic standards for every generation?

I think the repainting metaphor is a bit misleading. Some paintings have to be discarded, true. Some paintings you can repaint, also true. Some just need new frames, obviously. Others are so precious and valuable you hardly dare put your fingers on them. Perhaps that is not so obvious.

Not every canvas inside a rectangular frame is a Velvet Elvis.

Theology is the study of who God is. While it can be pedantic, mind-numbing, and can start wars, it can also be poetic and inspire music and cathedrals that are so beautiful they can make your eyes sting. Theology has been the source of lots of bloody fights, angry words, hurt feelings. It has wrecked homes and churches and nations. It has probably done damage to a family you know. It has divided and killed. As a result, lots of people conclude that it is inherently evil, it is a monumental waste of time, or it is just too toxic to handle and is best left alone under thick, dusty leather covers.

The deal is this—we live in a fallen and broken-down world. This means that things around us and inside us are not working like they should. Nothing is as it should be. But this didn't just happen. It was caused. Like nuclear war is caused, insanely, cruelly, purposefully. "Fallen," as those who've read *Paradise Lost* know, implies that there lurks behind the scenes an enemy who is a master at moral, or immoral, Twister. Unlike the Milton-Bradley version, he doesn't contort himself. He pulls the strings so that everything else bends out of shape. He is not creative, so he specializes in wrenching everything meant for good into evil. The more inherently beneficial to humanity, the better he is at perverting it into something that steals and destroys life.

Take sex, for instance.

What could be more life-affirming, life-enhancing, life-producing, more fun, joyful, freeing, and exciting? Now think of how the enemy has bent it into a grotesque caricature in the sex shops, peep shows, and prostitution markets—how it perverts and debases the pornography-bound, the sadomasochist, and the child abuser. Life bent into death. The same can be said for any aspect of reality, and that includes the intellectual, the philosophical, the biblical, the theological. What God intended for blessing has been — but need not continue to be — a curse. Sex is still really good, despite its ugly distortions.

So is theology.

I encourage you to try it. You'll like it.

Good theology, like good sex, is not optional for the survival of the human race. It is not just for the religious/philosophical Geek Squad. It is essential.[7]

Without getting it right about Jesus, for example, there is no salvation. (Getting it right about Jesus is what theologians call Christology. It is one of several *-ologies* in the list of topics-that-relate-to-God. And very few of them are as crucial as this one.) As I saw on a theologically enhanced bumper sticker: No Jesus, No God. Know Jesus, Know God.

That's about right.

If you honor Him as a really good guy — an impressive martyr who showed us how to love and die well, and that's it — then you've gotten something fatally wrong. If you get your Christology wrong *there*, you lose your hope and you lose God. This is not just literalist, KJV-smoking, Michigan-militia zealot talk. This is what all of Jesus' best friends say. This is also what His hand-picked ambassador to the non-Jewish nations, Saint Paul, says. And my assumption is that they all know better than I about such matters. In legal jargon, their statements are controlling.

And let me add that a main part of wisdom is knowing when to be quiet and listen, and to whom. That's theology. That's the way it is. Good theology and benefiting from its goodness demand that we humble ourselves and admit we don't know, but we know the ones who do know.

It comes down to humility.

Jesus called it becoming like little children:

"Daddy, how do I turn on this tractor-combine?"

"Mommy, why can't I get my toy from the middle of the six-lane superhighway during rush hour?"

"Mom, look at these pretty diamonds on the back of this cute snake. And what's this cute rattley thing on its tail?"

Or, as my sixteen-year-old daughter asked at 11:00 p.m., calling on her cell phone, with panic in her voice, "I'm in the middle of nowhere. I'm totally lost. How do I get back to the main road?"

No matter how we may wish to finesse it, no matter how uncool it may sound or how stupid or culturally out of touch it may make us appear, sometimes a categorical imperative is the difference between life and death. "Stop! Don't move! Don't touch that! Turn around now! Don't get out of the car!"

Or, "Believe on the Lord Jesus Christ and you will be saved" (Acts 16:31).

Or, "Don't be deceived or confused! For of all the paths to God that have been proposed in the whole world, Jesus is the only path by which we can be saved!" (Acts 4:12).

Old-school types like labels, and as I've said, they label this type of conversation Christology or Soteriology. In theology, there are big deals and little deals, as well as big and little words. Some you shrug your shoulders at and say, heck with it, who cares whether the Millennium is actually a thousand years long? What is important is that Jesus is coming back and that He will rule. What you have to keep your eyes open for is whether this or that belief or doctrine—or "brick"—directly impacts a person's ultimate relationship with God, his service for God, and whether it enhances or detracts from God's honor.

Your salvation is not dependent upon the length or quality of the End Times Tribulation, the most accurate version of the Bible, the identity of the Antichrist, the real presence of Christ in the Eucharist, the identity of those Jesus died for, or whether charismatic gifts died out with the last charismatic apostle. There is no connection between your being reconciled with the Father or honoring Him or being a fruitful person in His kingdom and whether creation was completed in 144 hours. However, while your eternal destiny also does not hang on whether God is ignorant about the future, the suggestion does subtract immensely from His majesty and glory. Quite simply, it dishonors the Father. It makes Him just a bit dumb. Which is one reason why a current theological experiment known as Open Theism is just not terribly compelling.[8]

Some things you have to cling to fervently and others you can simply smile at, shake your head, and walk away. Some things matter; other things don't matter so much; and others don't really matter at all. Not every religious disagreement is a matter of life or death. But—and here is the big *but*—some are.

And great wisdom is needed to make the distinction.

I'm not saying it's always easy.

Like elementary mathematical concepts such as $2 + 2 = 4$, there are core issues that are nonnegotiable—they are essential and necessary and mean the difference between making it to the moon or blowing up in the stratosphere, between having fun or getting run over by a semi. These basics don't get to be repainted or reformed. They may, however, need the occasional new frame.

"Jesus is God" is one such elemental fundamental. You may disbelieve it, or want to redefine it, but it is not one of those velvet Elvis paintings you can color over. This does not belong in the basement—it goes in the living room and is passed down from generation to generation. It deserves respect from everybody, no matter what their birthday might be.

So when dealing with theology this is always a good prayer: "God grant me the humility to accept the things I must not change, the courage to reject the things I have to change, and the wisdom to know the difference."

And I will say it again because we make this mistake so frequently: Just because so many people have gotten it wrong or been so unkind does not mean that the attempt to decide what *is* big is unimportant or bad or simply a waste of time and energy.

This isn't just some pre-postmodern, white guy's opinion either. As impossible as it may seem, it comes from Rabbi Jesus Himself. It was He who laid it all out there in terms that sounded (and still sound) dangerously intolerant and absolutist and narrow-minded.

A traumatized group of Jews breathlessly reported to Jesus a recent tragedy that was also a stunning act of political provocation. While a group of zealots were offering sacrifice at the temple, Pilate sent his troops to slaughter them all and, in the process, desecrated the holy site. Rather than entering into their pain and offering comfort, Jesus said:

> Do you suppose these Galileans who suffered like that were greater sinners than any other Galileans? They were not, I tell you. No; but unless you repent you will all perish as they did. Or those eighteen on whom the tower at Siloam fell and killed them? Do you suppose that they were more guilty than all the other people living in Jerusalem? They weren't, I tell you. No; but unless you repent you will all perish as they did. (Luke 13:2-5)

These are His assertions, not mine. Jesus apparently believes some things are just terribly important, so important that they surpass the need to be nice or civil or empathetic. There *are* matters of actual life and death. Warning people in grave and mortal danger is, if we accept Jesus as Rabbi, more important than having them like you. If people are heading on a self-righteous or deluded or self-destructive path — if they are *blind* (His words) or *lost* (His words again) — they have to be warned. They have to be told of their peril and they have to be shown the one certain way of escape. And sometimes the only way they'll hear you above the roar of surging water is with a bullhorn.[9]

Sure, if we take doctrines or beliefs or bricks (or paintings, even) seriously, we will get a lot wrong. Sure, we will place too much importance on one thing and too little on the other. That is not the issue. That is smoke and mirrors. What is the key is that you know Jesus. The real Jesus, not the "Jesus-I-prefer" or the "Jesus-that-fits-my-cultural-temperamental-preference." Jesus is the one who is really insistent about that.

When His disciples were listing the current opinions that were floating around about Him, Jesus asked, "But you, who do you say I am?" (Matthew 16:15). Unlike the Law School Aptitude Test, He wasn't asking them to choose the best possible response.

There was only one right answer: "You are the Christ (the Messiah), the Son of the Living God" (16:16).

When Peter got it right, Jesus let Him know immediately that he'd nailed it. The right answer was so important that Jesus said it would serve as the mighty, unchanging bedrock upon which His church would be established for all time.

Saint Paul would later compare the family of God to a large house that is built on the foundation of the apostles and prophets with Jesus as the chief cornerstone. "As *every* structure is aligned on him, all grow into one holy Temple in the Lord." (Ephesians 2:21).

Apparently, Jesus and His chief spokesperson believed that recognizing who He really was is fundamental. Even Saint John, the disciple whom Jesus loved, known also as the Apostle of Love, minced no words on the matter: "Who is the liar, if not one who claims that Jesus is not the Christ? This is the Antichrist, who denies both the Father and the Son. Whoever denies the Son cannot have the Father either; whoever acknowledges the Son has the Father too" (1 John 2:22-23).

I think we are therefore on safe ground to say that Jesus Himself (His Person) and what people believe about Jesus (faith in His Person) is absolutely foundational.

That's why getting it right about Jesus matters — He is the whole point. Everything rises or falls on Him, not theories about the end times, or the location and duration of hell, or even about inspiration, for that matter (unless the theories undermine confidence in what the Bible teaches about Jesus).[10] Everything comes back to Him. If your theory about any of the above makes Jesus out be less than He said He was — merely a quaint, well-intentioned moralizer, a great rabbi even, who simply came to show us the preferred or even the "best" way to live — then the theory is no longer innocuous, it is deadly.

The apostles, whose teaching is the unshakeable foundation for this new architectural masterpiece, this Parthenon, this Freedom Tower Complex extraordinaire, all agree that Jesus is the central, the crucial, the optimum load-bearing wall. He is the cornerstone. Crack it at *that* point and the entire structure and all living souls inside are in mortal jeopardy (Acts 4:10-12; 1 Peter 2:7-8). While the teaching of the apostles is foundational, the bedrock beneath it all is Jesus: "For the foundation, nobody can lay any other than the one which has already been laid, that is Jesus Christ" (1 Corinthians 3:11).

» » »

I am somewhat put off by heights. I have an embarrassing memory in which I utterly failed to live up to my image of myself as a red-blooded American stud. My self-concept was not damaged in private—it was a full-scale public humiliation. It happened after my first year of college.

I spent that summer on a red-iron crew. This is the group of guys who puts up the steel framework for commercial sites of all sizes. Among construction workers, they are on the highest rung of the testosterone ladder. They walk on the four-inch-wide purlins (the joists that hold the building together), high up in the air, carrying several tons of metal on each shoulder without breaking a sweat. They drink a six pack for lunch and smoke three packs a day. They are mean and foul, and they don't think much of youngsters whose brains may very well be stronger than their biceps.

Let's just say I didn't fit in with this crowd.

After a few days at the site, I was told to haul some corrugated roofing plates from one side of the structure to the other where the roof was being bolted into place. I had seen how it was supposed to be done. There was no way I was going to walk on a metal frame the width of a balancing beam, forty feet in the air while holding a stack of metal over my head. So I did what appeared to be the only prudent thing—I sat down on my butt and inched my way along, dragging the screeching metal behind me all the way. I was good friends with the owner (that's how I got the job), so the catcalls and obscenities were somewhat muted, but they still scorched me all the way there and back. I do not recall being asked to complete that little task again.

This is why I have not gone rock climbing. I understand Jimmy Stewart's issues in the Hitchcock film *Vertigo*. Some of us are not meant to rise higher than our own heads.

I will opt for the beach over the cliff every single time. I think that the majority of the mentally healthy among us would do the same. We prefer to relax by strolling on the silky sands rather than risking life and limb clambering over ragged and dangerously high outcroppings. Sand is forgiving—rock, not so much.

But, while it is smart to build your house on a rock, it is a really bad idea to do it on sand. Jesus tells us the same thing. The problem is that both buildings will look perfectly sound from a distance or even close up. It is only when the proverbial feces hit the fan that the differences become apparent. A house built on sand will not be able to withstand the pressure of gale-force winds. It is stress that will expose the weakness at the foundational level. What Jesus is saying is that if we choose the inflexible, less comfortable bedrock, when it all starts to fly, the core of your life will not come unglued.

It is only the hard rock that will keep your house from collapsing.

So the simple answer to what's the big deal about doctrines or beliefs—or "bricks"—about Jesus is that if we get that wrong, hope and meaning disintegrate. Our personal world, resting on the flexible, forgiving sand of our own preferences, conjectures, or those of teachers we like, will not be able to withstand the battering of outrageous misfortune. If Jesus was just a good guy or simply the most impressive, self-sacrificing martyr this world has known, we're left with a bland wasteland of sentimental spirituality that will leave the addicted, the empty and wasted, in the same condition we found them—hopelessly lost. It will also leave the "well" and the self-confident, the "successful" overachievers, clinging to the empty mirage of a false hope that will ultimately disintegrate and break their hearts.

If the cornerstone of the building is out of whack, so will be the rest of it.

No matter how sincere we may be, we will put at risk the structural integrity of our souls and those of others.

What I'm saying is that there are certain things we don't get to repaint every generation. Some things just are—basic. Every generation does not get to decide whether the chemical symbol for water should be H_4O. Some things have the weighty, sobering density and permanence of authority behind them. In the church we call this heaviness, this solidness and weight, the apostolic tradition of the church.

Saint Paul refers to it as the church's foundation.

Eating meat offered to idols, wearing head coverings, lifting hands in prayer, setting aside a separate offering for the poor, kissing each other on the cheek, two or more prophesies during a church service—these are all peripherals. These we get to paint over or around. They are not essential to the basic issue at hand.

The issues we do not repaint are elemental: Is Jesus the Son of God? Did He have a sinful human nature (i.e., was His mother a virgin)? Did He die on the cross in order to pay for, atone, forgive, and effectively take away our sin? Did He physically rise from the dead and thereby defeat sin, death, and Satan? Do we need to believe in Jesus (confess, accept, trust, surrender, bow down before Him) and claim Him as our exclusive Lord in order to be reconciled with Him and His Father? These paintings were finished long before we showed up and have stood the test of time. They are the standards by which all other paintings are judged. The most you ever need do with these masterpieces is carefully and respectfully polish their golden frame.

All I'm saying is what everybody knows intuitively: You just don't mess with the Rembrandts, you keep your brush away from the Van Goghs, you can stare at Picasso's Guernica so long as you keep your hands off. But, you can do anything you want with the velvets in the basement.

This is humility.

It's just the way things are.

It's about respect, and it's also just plain smart, since those who try to paint over the old masters usually wind up in really hot water with the curator and the owner.

Blessing

May the God of our Lord Jesus Christ,
the Father of glory,
give you a spirit of wisdom and eyes wide open.
May He bring you to full knowledge of Him.
May He enlighten the eyes of your mind
so that you can see what hope
and rich glories are being reserved for you.
May you know this Jesus
who is Unique and Exclusive and Above
every other "savior" who has ever come or will ever come. . . .
And through His Spirit
may He empower you to grow strong in your inner self,
so that Christ may live comfortably at home in your heart.
And then, firmly built on the bedrock of His unyielding love,
may you be able to grasp its breadth and length,
its height and depth;
And, knowing His love, which is beyond understanding,
amazingly—
be filled with the utter fullness of God Himself.
(Ephesians 1:17-21; 3:16-19)

3

A GOD WHO LETS YOU DROP

Being remarkably inept in the navigational department, I have always been mystified by my wife's ability to know with absolute certainty that we should turn left instead of right. How is it possible for anyone to know when the sun is hidden by clouds that taking a right is wrong since that would be heading southeast instead of northwest? Since we don't have onboard GPS, I have to take her word for it. But once, just once, I'd like to challenge her on it just to be sure.

Directional deftness is something you're born with, I am told. It's a gift, like how some people know intuitively what to say next to keep the witty badinage going at a cocktail party. That would be my wife, Patty, again—not me, again. After the Big Three superficial questions are dealt with, I pretty well freeze up. Unless, of course, they like to talk about philosophy, religion, social ethics, ecclesiology, or the World Cup. (Politics, not so much.[1]) Then I get my wings and I can fly. Per capita, Americans seem to be less interested in those topics than the average European, which is why I'm still hunting for that affordable villa in Tuscany or, barring that, the three-bedroom flat in Barcelona.

Absolute certainty is under major attack these days. It's now as passé as the *MacGyver* mullets my boys sported as they contrived clever escapes from all manner of deathtraps. I gather that being absolutely sure that you are absolutely right is a sign of a fatal and terminal disease that afflicts people who handle snakes, refuse to touch "likker," and believe in a literal twenty-four-hour-day creation. These are the folk who inveigh against Hollywood and homosexuals with equal alacrity and pronounce their other favorite H-word in two elongated syllables: *Hey-yull*.

The fatal illness is that of smugness.

It is a sickness no one wants any part of. It tends to make women wear a lot of eye makeup and causes men to poof their hair. Since I do not want to be tarred with that sticky brush, I will temper what I need to say here. It seems to me that sometimes — not always, mind you, but sometimes — you just *know*. You know that this smiling man cannot be trusted, that they are laughing about you even as they nod approvingly, that there is someone stalking you, that, yes, you just knocked that question out of the park and the job is yours, or that although it is your first date and you barely know her, you are going to spend the rest of your life with this woman.

Sometimes it is weird. Like the time my mother-in-law found herself suddenly wide awake at 2:10 in the morning. With no logic but an overwhelming clarity, she knew that she must pray for John, her police-officer son. She prayed for twenty minutes then went back to sleep. Later that day, he called to let her know that for the first time in more than twenty years on the force, he had been in a shoot-out. He was pursuing a young man in a stolen vehicle who had plowed into a used-car lot. To impede a hasty exit, John drove his cruiser into the driver's-side door. He jumped out of his car, and as he did so the young man pulled out a semi-automatic weapon. In his haste, John, who had not seen the gun, dropped his flashlight. As he bent to retrieve it, the shots hit the door he just happened to be crouched behind.

After the investigation was completed, it was discovered that at least one bullet had smashed into the side mirror exactly where his head had been. Some might think this fortuitous drop-and-crouch coincidental. I tend to believe it had everything to do with a seventy-year-old mother in a mobile home, praying at that very instant. If she had been asked that morning to justify her confidence, she would have been hard pressed to give one. All she would tell you is that she was utterly certain about what she was to do, without feeling smug about it at all.

This happened to me once—just once. (Well, twice. The second time it took us to Mozambique, but that comes later.) I had ditched my polyesters and unpoofed my hair. I no longer had the slightest inclination toward smugness, being radically uncertain about nearly everything and delighting mightily in ambiguity. Kind of. So when it hit me, I was shocked at my certainty. I checked my rearview mirror just to make sure the hair was still cool. It was.

But I just could not shake the feeling.

It was the winter of 1991. I had graduated from law school five years earlier. I had been working for two and a half years as a research attorney for the Michigan Court of Appeals. I was finally making enough money to start paying off my student loan. My book-lined office in the Federal Building downtown was feeling occasionally claustrophobic. But I was finally becoming what was known in my social circles as a "faithful provider." It is terminology borrowed from the hunter-gatherer period. I was foraging, tracking down, slaughtering, and bringing home the bacon — at last. The four little carnivores and my wife — who deserves a much kinder, gentler appellation (dove, perhaps) — were starting to eat well.

Then, somehow, I knew. There was this odd confluence of events that year and they were all centering in Spain, my "home country." I had lived there during my teen years and had adopted it as my own. The World Cup, the World's Fair, and the 500th anniversary of Christopher sailing the ocean blue were all going to be celebrated there the glorious summer of '92. Now I can sense the knowing little smirks already. Had I had this irresistible urge to go to Barcelona for the World Cup championship, then one would have grounds to arch the eyebrows and smile superciliously. But that was not the case.

I had heard there was going to be an evangelical exhibit at the World's Fair and that counselors would be needed. A light went off — what can I say? I knew I was to take my family to Sevilla, where the fair would be held, to be part of this venture. It was an insane idea — utterly illogical, absurd, and quite possibly, professionally damaging as well. Firms do not take kindly to lawyers leaving the country on a whim, even if they do have this unshakable certainty that it is the right thing to do.

We were to be short-term missionaries. The process of raising support for the three-month project resulted in our being encouraged to find another church — no Baptist money for "charismatic" (noncessationist) missionaries, thank you very much. But despite that trauma, by April of 1992 the support money had poured in, passports and tickets secured, and we were ready to go.

In retrospect, I wonder at myself. I was leaving my job and transplanting my family to a country none of them knew, among a people whose language none of them spoke. My wife had taken three years of high school Spanish but had zero confidence in her communicative capacity. She is highly verbal, so this was a daunting prospect. But she had agreed with me. That is what sealed the deal and how I knew that this was not just a clever and complicated ruse to return to the climate, the people, the culture, and, yes, the food—crusty loaves baked fresh daily—I loved. She is not a risk taker. If she gives the thumbs-up to a harebrained idea, I can pretty well lean back and relax.

We arrived in Sevilla, the capital of Andalucia, in southern Spain the first week of summer. The city was broiling in a dry-sauna kind of way. You took a deep breath, and you thought that maybe your lungs would instantly dehydrate and crumble into fine ash. The yellow-gold sun pulsated down on us, and though I was not really a hat guy, I knew that a cap would probably be a really smart idea. I had no real interest in having my precious gray matter liquefy.

But I absolutely loved it.

I come from west Michigan, which has the singular curse of averaging the exact opposite number of sunny days in a year that Spain does. Apparently, when we see the sun in Grand Rapids, an unexpected and startling rain begins to fall on the plains somewhere in Spain. I lifted up my hands to the impossibly blue Mediterranean skies and drank in the waves of hot, glorious light.

I was home.

The oddest thing happened, though. We had been corresponding for months with a missionary couple. They were the ones who had encouraged us strongly to come to work at *La Feria Mundial* or, as the locals were calling it, "Expo." Our second day there, they took the elevator up to our two-bedroom, fourth-floor apartment to welcome us to España. They gave us the name of a contact at the Expo and, after drinking a Coke, left. Apparently, we were going to be left to our own devices—we did not see them again for months. Fortunately, I had remained fluent in Spanish, but still, it was just a little weird. "Great! You came and brought the whole family, too—how nice. By the way, the Feria is in that direction. Have a good time! Bye."

What actually transpired those three months was almost completely unrelated to the Expo. Within a few days, we had made friends with another missionary couple who desperately needed spiritual community. They had three small children, all younger than our own. They were burning out on their solo church-planting mission and needed to hang out with some people they could be real with. Less than a week later, the husband knocked on my door looking as if he'd just walked away from a near-fatal car accident. He had come from a conversation with his wife in which he'd confessed to an addiction to hard-core pornography and more. She was on the verge of an emotional break. It became obvious very quickly that we had been summoned to Spain to walk alongside a couple whose marriage and ministry were in meltdown.

We stayed through the hottest part of the summer and left in late August. If the money had lasted, I would probably still be there, looking much tanner and considerably more European. Alas, the funds ran out, and I had to return to less-than-sunny midwest Michigan. But I was quite confident that I would find a new position in short order. Surely, God would have a sweet spot waiting for me. I just knew that our risky adventure and my professional sacrifice would be met with an ample (read "highly compensated") reward.

I was wrong.

There was no opening. No firm I was interested in was interested in me. I wasn't sure where in the legal universe I wanted to attach my shiny star anyway, but I had to start bringing home the bacon and soon — the carnivores were making these low growling noises. I searched and interviewed, but nothing materialized.

God most definitely did not come through for me. He gave me no reward, no golden plum. He threw no lavish spread. He did not appear the slightest bit impressed with what I had sacrificed or we had accomplished that summer.

Things grew desperate. Finally, I was driven to shameful and humbling straits. I stuffed my JD degree in the drawer and went to work at a company that manufactures and prints packaging materials. I was the most educated four-color-press cleaner in the United States. My job was to breathe in noxious fumes from the astringent chemicals used to wipe off the massive rollers and ink trays on those mechanical monsters. I lived and worked inhaling the acrid fumes of shame and failure.

It lasted over six months. It was a long and bitter comedown.

God had let me drop.

It was a lesson in unlearning what I knew, or thought I knew, about God's logical predictability. I was forced to reevaluate the God I had grown comfortable with. The biblical God I had been taught about was not playing by the rules; He had let me down badly, with little grace and no advance warning.

I still have my Thomas Chain Reference NIV Bible from that time. It is a memorial, of sorts. Its black leather spine is split. I threw it to the floor in the frenzied grip of a sudden, angry terror that I would not be able to provide for my family. When it hit, a big chunk of concordance broke free. It is a quiet and, I must admit, troubling memento to a God who fits no theological box. It is a testament to a God who, whatever else He may be, is not nice.[2]

The God with whom I had become familiar while growing up fundamentalist, then evangelical, in a Baptist college and seminary was a God very much like us. The God I thought I knew made sense. He played by the rules—ours.

I had to do some serious unlearning.

» » »

As I talk to my kids (who no longer wear mullets but still enjoy the frequent juicy burger or thick steak), I find that they are also being encouraged to get comfortable with this nice, predictable God. I seem to be reading a lot about Him these days. Admittedly, this is a very likable deity.

We like Him because He is like us and He likes us. He is no dictator, no oppressor, no meanie. He suggests, not demands. He accepts and forgives unconditionally. He tolerates and includes and never speaks a discouraging word. He makes us feel comfortable and secure. He is never rude or demanding or politically out of touch. He would make a good bartender or a really smart therapist.

He supports us and comes through for us. His main passion appears to be propping up or massaging our self-esteem.[3]

That is the God we want—a God made in our own image.

But the God we want is not the God we got.

The God of Abraham, Isaac, and Jacob, of Joseph, Moses, and David is not predictable, domesticated, gentlemanly, or safe. Nor for that matter is the God of Job. What we want is nice, what we get is the Lion of Judah, the Creator of the heavens and the earth, the King of kings, and the Lord of lords. A lot of ink is being spilled on four-color presses to assist His image consultants in making Him look cherubic and presentable.

Anybody think they really understand Him? I confess I some-times do, and I will admit I'm always wrong. And here we arrive at the whole issue of God as *unsafe*—where Mr. Beaver of Narnia got it right, and where most of our current religious innovators haven't.

God—at least the God who revealed Himself in the Bible to a series of normal, proud, selfish recalcitrants like myself—fits into no crisp category, no clean box, no sociocultural niche. Try as we may, He breaks the stereotype, cracks the mold, and strides forth like a king. Sometimes He leaves behind Him smoking wreckage, carnage, groans, and wails. Without the slightest concern for how He may be scorned or vilified in the press, He does whatever He wants and most of the really awful stuff He refuses to explain. He will let famine, plague, and disasters of all sorts afflict those He says He cares for most.

And He doesn't even bother dodging behind the passive voice, for He declares in *fortissimo basso profundo*:

I am God.
    Yes, and from ancient days I am he.
No one can deliver out of my hand.
    When I act, who can reverse it?" (Isaiah 43:12-13,
        NIV)

Referring to the crushing national disaster of the Babylonian invasion, He declares, "Yes, I have struck you as an enemy strikes, with harsh punishment. . . . I have done all this to you." (Jeremiah 30:14-15).

He seems to have this infuriating God-complex.

He goes so far as to declare that He is sending catastrophic invasions and cruel oppressors to wreak havoc—to pillage, rape, and murder. He calls the perpetrators of these heinous acts "the rod of God's anger, the war club of His wrath" (Isaiah 10:5-6), and the horrors they inflict are "the Lord's work" (10:12). The brutal Babylonians are "my weapons of battle, with you I clubbed nations and kingdoms" (Jeremiah 51:20). He then has the nerve to turn around and heap judgment on His "weapons" for exceeding the bounds of propriety in carrying out His desires (Zechariah 1:14-15).

In the case of Job, an innocent, good man who we are told has done nothing to offend, God withdraws His favor and allows the destroyer to swoop in gleefully and, with unflinching blows, drive him to financial ruin. Then He gives further permission for Job's ten children to be buried alive. Surprisingly enough, these calamities do not provoke a fit of rage, a long string of heartbroken obscenities and furious fist shaking. Instead, Job falls on his knees and in utter brokenness, with childlike faith, cries out, "Yahweh gave, Yahweh has taken back. Blessed be the name of Yahweh!" (Job 1:21).

I would expect that if anything is calculated to win back divine favor and blessing, Job's humility would be it. The preaching I've heard for forty-plus years and the contemporary Christian writings I've read have me convinced that God must now come through for Job. Job's faith will be rewarded.

At this lowest point, God will not let Job down.

Countless times I have heard the affirmations that assure me breezily that "God is there for us." (I have to say that I really, really dislike that unmistakably American phrase. It smacks just a little too much of God the obsequious waiter with white linen folded neatly over the arm.) And most especially is He "there," we are promised, when against all natural tendencies we trust Him in the dark. Well, Job is in the depths of dark — the darkest dark night of the soul. He is suffering cruel and unusual punishment; frankly, it's outrageous. But he has refused to cave in, and he's chosen to worship and trust this cruel, capricious, and inexplicable God.

Does God relent?

Does God release the abundant showers of blessings we sing about?

Is God happy yet?

Apparently not.

He permits Satan to turn the flame up some more by afflicting Job with excruciating ulcers from his head to his feet. We know that Job's wife helpfully suggests the option of indirect suicide: "Curse God and die." And we also know Job declines. Instead, he meekly asks, "If we accept happiness from God's hand should we not also accept sorrow too?" (Job 2:10).

There seems to be a growing number of current writers who reject Job's premise. From what they tell us, God is kind and is the source of all good. Bad things come from other sources entirely, sources utterly disconnected from Him and utterly out of His control.[4]

Job is saying a mouthful, and he's saying the opposite.

What is so significant about this confession is that it does not let God off the hook. Job isn't scurrying around picking up after Him, sweeping up the smudges of mud He's left on the carpet or spraying lemon-scented room freshener in the bathroom. Neither is he feverishly applying makeup so God won't look like Tricky Dicky on TV nor telling Him to shave off His beard so He won't remind folks of Osama Bin Laden.

Job stares through hollow eyes at a life that has been blasted and wrecked and with stark realism anticipates Solomon's question, "Is it not from the mouth of the Most High that both calamities and good things come?" (Lamentations 3:38, NIV). Or perhaps he is paraphrasing Isaiah: "I am Yahweh, unrivaled. I form the light and create the dark, I make good fortune and create calamity, it is I, Yahweh, who do all this" (Isaiah 45:7). In any event, by contemporary standards, Job's God is neither nice nor safe.

He does not make sense.

» » »

When I'm struggling to figure out God, I have to remind myself to begin with this simple premise: An infinite mind will pose just a bit of a challenge for a finite little mind like mine. We should not be surprised if He doesn't fit into any of the tidy compartments we've crafted or the stereotypes our culture has conditioned us to embrace. Further, we are operating under an additional disadvantage—our inner moral wiring is more than a little off, so we can't fully trust even our cleverest ideas or hunches. As a result, "It just doesn't seem fair!" can't carry all that much weight. I mean, does it seem fair that a gangly computer geek should become one of the richest men in the world? Or how about the wealth of some ditzy blonde actresses?

Most Christians who maintain a solid hold on the plain teaching of the Bible believe that God is and that He is infinite. The starry, starry nights blaze out the irrepressibly joyful chant, "God exists and He is Glorious and full of Splendor" (Psalm 19:1-4). The song is so loud and beautiful that no one can really claim atheism in good conscience. Or so Saint Paul tells us (Romans 1:20).

To say that God is infinite in His glory means there is no limit to His attributes, whether of goodness, justice, mercy, righteousness, faithfulness, wisdom, or power. But what we don't usually ponder is the limitless reach of God's self-confidence as well.

He is not afraid of or paralyzed by bad press—four-color or otherwise. He does not worry about looking bad or being misunderstood or shaking (or shattering) the faith of His best friends. Look at Abraham and Sarah. Despite being way too old, God promises them a son. They are in their eighties, but what does He do? He makes them wait twenty more years. After Isaac is born and has become a nice obedient little boy, God asks Abraham to take him to the top of a mountain and kill him.

Then there's David. God tells him he's going to be king, but then for at least a decade has him running for his life, living in caves, and letting drool drip down his beard while pretending to be insane so he can avoid being slaughtered by King Saul (1 Samuel 21:13).

God promises His people a deliverer, but they are forced to wait in slavery and in exile for centuries. He raises and crushes their hopes until hope is almost extinguished. Then for four hundred years He stops talking to them entirely. We call that the Intertestamental Period—the Jews could call it "the centuries when God dropped the phone and left us hanging."

God has this total certainty that He can pull off anything He sets His mind to. And that includes ultimately gaining for Himself a people who will look like His Son, who will love Him and be devoted to Him above all things. That is, after all, what it means to be sovereign.

God has no worries.

"His sovereignty is an eternal sovereignty, His empire lasts from age to age. The inhabitants of the earth count for nothing: he does as he pleases with the array of heaven and with the inhabitants of the earth. No one can arrest his hand or ask him, 'What are you doing?'" (Daniel 4:31-32).

This unsafe God plays by a different rulebook from ours. He promises us the moon, but what we get sometimes smells like Limburger cheese.

Job, scratching his boils on the garbage dump, and a lawyer, wiping ink off a press roller, were in similar straits. They were in the middle of that bad joke about the father and the little boy. Perhaps you've heard it.

The dad tells his son he's going to teach him to trust his father, which is one of life's most important lessons. He convinces his little boy to jump off a four-foot wall. The boy does, and the dad catches him. The son jumps from higher and higher heights and each time is caught by his father. On the fifth jump, this time from a height of twenty feet, the father steps back and lets his son hit the ground. In great pain, the little boy looks up through his tears and asks his father why he did not catch him.

"Son, I did this to teach you life's *most* important lesson: Don't trust anyone."

This is precisely what I felt God had done to me.

What could possibly be the point of this humiliation? Why is God not more predictable, dependable, explainable? Why is He not more of a gentleman?

Why does He treat His best friends so shabbily?

This reminds me of a story I heard about Teresa de Avila, a sixteenth-century Catholic mystic born in Avila, the capital of a province in Old Castile. She came from a prosperous, noble family. She had more disciplined passion for Jesus in her little finger than I have in my whole body. At the age of seven she was intercepted by her father running away from home to seek martyrdom among the Moors. But she was nobility and a Castilian at that. Once, while climbing out of her carriage, she tripped and fell face down in the mud. Aghast at the stains on her clothes, she looked toward heaven and in upper-case, Castilian Spanish declared, "If *that's* how you treat your friends, no wonder you have so *few* of them!"

These questions frustrate us because we assume that God must conform to our standards of logic, justice, and fairness. We are convinced that He is a puzzle to be solved and that life is a detective story to be unraveled. But we are wrong. We are like Job's smart friends, who had life and God both figured out.

They were wrong too.

Life is not a riddle but a romance.

Have you tried to apply the principles of logic to a love affair recently?

Welcome to mystery.

Welcome to wonder.

Welcome to being humbled and becoming a child.

» » »

Job is pummeled and battered, but none of his losses capsize him. He manages to keep his equilibrium until he suffers the most cruel loss of all—He loses God. Then he pours his heart out. He makes his lament and admits his frustration. His questions gush out like a fountain. But he gets no satisfaction. He gets no answers to soothe the confusion and mend the fractures. God is nowhere to be found. "If I go eastward, He is not there; or westward—still I cannot see Him. If I seek Him in the north, He is not to be found, invisible still when I turn to the south" (Job 23:8-9). These are a faint echo of what Jesus cried out in the moment of His greatest extremity: "My God, my God, why have you deserted Me?" (Matthew 27:46).

Those words are a quotation from one of King David's most

intense and prophetic prayers, which foreshadows the Messiah's utter abandonment by His Father:

> My God, my God, why have you deserted me?
> How far from saving me, the words I groan!
> I call all day, my God, but you never answer,
> all night long I call and cannot rest.
>
> . . . .
>
> Yet, here am I, now more worm than man,
> scorn of mankind, jest of the people,
> all who see me jeer at me,
> they toss their heads and sneer,
> "He relied on Yahweh, let Yahweh save him!
> If Yahweh is his friend, let Him rescue him!"
>   (Psalm 22:1-2,6-8)

As the High Priest transferred and removed the sins of the Jewish people by laying his hands on the head of the goat who would bear their faults into the desert (Leviticus 16:5-10,21), so Jesus was made our "scapegoat." According to Isaiah, "Yahweh burdened Him with the sins of all of us" (53:6). Saint Paul tells us that "for our sake God made the sinless One into sin" (2 Corinthians 5:21). For this reason the Father had to turn away from His beloved Son.

Jesus also had to become a perfect intermediary for us, so He had to experience every level of pain and suffering and weakness His people face—the Son had to experience the wrenching trauma of abandonment.

But these cries that erupted from the dereliction of Jesus or David were not shrieks of despair. Jesus clung to *"my"* God, while David concludes,

Yet you are enthroned as the Holy One;
> you are the praise of Israel.
In you our fathers put their trust;
> they trusted and you delivered them.
>> (Psalm 22:3-4, NIV)

The sovereign goodness and power of David's inexplicable God was his only comfort in the crucible of abandonment. We need to take note. It is possible that in deleting hard-edged, colonial, oppressive words like "king" and "throne" from our God-talk, we may also be deleting the last ground of comfort in those moments of crushing loss and despair.

For most of us, the much, the plenty, the blessing can obscure the one and the only. So God removes the much as well as the only so that we can come face to face with our heart's true need. We are stripped so our true craving—what we cannot truly live without—is exposed. In the words of Saint Augustine: "Oh God, you have made us for yourselves, and our hearts are restless until they find their rest in thee."[5] So, in a hard and severe mercy, He allows it all to evaporate—even His nearness. He does this so we can become present to the quiet and ravenous restlessness of our true heart and cry out for what alone is real.

In the end, although Job's questions are all brushed aside and he gets no intellectual satisfaction, his heart and his mind are strangely at peace. He admits that he had been going on about matters that were way beyond his pay grade. He concedes that he had been prattling about God as if He were a mathematics problem, a logical abstraction, a complicated knot to untangle. And he admits, "I knew you then only by hearsay; [he sounds like a seminary student] but now, having seen you with my own eyes, I retract all I have said, and in dust and ashes I repent" (Job 42:5-6).

Job had questioned God, and all the while God had been testing Job. God does not answer any of Job's questions; God draws near and answers Job instead. Jesus learned well from His Father, for He did the same. Rather than answering the question, He answers the questioner. He knows that the real issue is not the problem but the person.

What you and I most need is not to have our intellectual issues with the problem of suffering or injustice resolved. God knows what few of us know and what frequently only suffering brings into the open—we were made for Him, and only He can satisfy. Truly, as C. S. Lewis well knew, while God may whisper gently in our pleasures, He lifts the bullhorn and shouts in our pain.

Peter Kreeft comments, "God answers Job's deepest heart quest: to see God face to face; to see Truth, not truths; to meet Truth, not just to know it. Job is satisfied with the only answer that could possibly have satisfied him, in time or in eternity, the only answer that can satisfy us in time or in eternity, the only answer that can overcome boredom and eventual 'vanity of vanities,' the definitive answer to Ecclesiastes, as to the three friends: the Answerer, not the answer."[6]

God gives Job Himself.

And that is enough.

Job's shattering questions were left unanswered, but his craving was satisfied. The sad truth about ourselves is that our hearts are idol factories. We are starstruck and mesmerized by the empty promises of a thousand false lovers. The prophets call this insanity spiritual adultery, and liken it to wild donkeys in heat (Jeremiah 2:24). What God is doing in our suffering is exposing the false, the temporary, the rivals who clamor for our love, our devotion, our allegiance. When what gave us significance, comfort, and meaning lies broken and shattered on the ground, we are given a gift—the freedom to give ourselves to Him in whom alone is real life and joy and peace that lasts forever.

Suffering is the rocky path that destroys the false within and without but that also sets us on a path toward becoming real ourselves. Being dropped hurts. But having a fake God made in your own image can destroy you. Sometimes it's only in the dropping that the fake gets broken and the real appears.[7]

God may let you cry out, "Why have you forsaken me?" but only so that you may treasure what is worth treasuring, hunger for what is worth feasting on, and embrace what alone is worth loving. His gracious severity is only a necessary part of the journey to finding our heart's true home: the One in whom our soul delights—the One who alone is the way, the truth, and our life.

Blessing

May you find in the depths of your darkest night
the bright and only light.
With tears and terrors and broken heart,
with your dreams dead and your hopes gone,
may you abandoned and alone walk toward and not from.
May you wait and wonder,
stifling the curse,
and in the silent solitude of your deafening pain
feel His hand and hear His voice.
May He fill your crushed and empty heart
with the oil of joy—the promised presence;
and on waking from your brief and restless slumber
may you receive your reward:

*the delight and the comfort, the utter satisfaction
of gazing up into His smiling face.
And, trial tested, your faith, though small as seed,
will be turned to golden praise.*

4

GOD IS AN EARTHQUAKE

For years, I was a terribly conflicted soul. There was a war raging in my head. It was a pitched battle between the logical left and the creative right. It was a hemispheric conflict. But it was one to which I was oblivious. It was sneaky. Not active combat, mind you, it was more like a cold war, where the opposing sides refused to sit down at the negotiating table and opted instead to shoot each other in back alleys. It was silent combat but one in which the "left" had gained supremacy.

How did this happen? I can't be positive, but I think it occurred suddenly and without warning when I was eight years old.

I was a skinny missionary kid in Chile, living much of the time in his own private world. Our home was in a cement-walled compound in Santiago, the capital. One half of the ten or so acres was devoted to missionary-type stuff like eating, sleeping, swimming, playing tennis and soccer, swinging on parallel bars, and other assorted sacrificial tasks. The other was leased to a farmer who cultivated succulent, deep red tomatoes year round, along with cabbage, lettuce, and carrots that were a biblical cubit long. The road that led from the large gate that protected this modest paradise parted it down the middle and was flanked by trees that bore marvelous raspberry-type fruits. In my memory, the trees were perpetually laden and the ground permanently stained with their juicy entrails.

Scattered around the missionary dwellings were a prolific assortment of trees: lime, lemon, peach, apricot, cherry, almond, the occasional mandarin and orange, and, of course, avocado. It was a harsh and deprived childhood. That is where I developed the capacity to suffer quietly with stoic fortitude. Perhaps I should explain that we were living not so much in a restive paradise as a year-round Bible camp. The pool was only filled during the months the campers were there. It was not tiled. It was just a big Spartan-like cement circle in the ground. This is a crucial caveat for those rethinking their missionary giving.

The camp half of the area was not the problem; it was the agricultural half. The hard-working farmer, who I cannot recall, had a large white horse, which I do remember clearly. I can see him now—white sides bloated with too much fresh food and not enough labor, ears and tail twitching, and mean red eyes alert to the approach of unsuspecting children. He was ornery and lazy and not overly handsome. The Lone Ranger would have taken one look at him and out of sheer mortification would have sent the ungallant steed packing to the glue factory. With confidence in the masked man's tacit approval, my brothers and I would engage in the heroic task of directing small, stony missiles his way.

On one such furtive foray, it was I with a handful of pebbles taking a stand against the angry mass of horseflesh. Now that I am opening childhood wounds, I should also admit that I have notoriously poor aim. My expertise being kicking soccer balls ("footballs" for the initiated), not throwing them. So, more frequently than not, the modest little pebbles flew far off the mark. That is what provoked my tactical error. Frustrated at making such infrequent connection with the bulging, fly-specked belly, I drew closer. Too close, as it turned out.

I cannot tell you how such a large and ungainly beast moved so quickly. All I can say for certain is that I flew several feet in the air and landed on my back as if my feet had been taken out from under me by an earthquake of monumental force. His hoof had landed a thunderous whack on my temple that exploded a myriad of comets and stars and a host of unidentified flying objects before my eyes. I'm not sure how long I lay there semiconscious.

While unable to recall much, I firmly believe that it was at that moment that the two sides of my brain began launching incoherent accusations at each other and then, in an irrational fit of resentment, swore they would stop talking altogether. While they chose to cease communicating, I chose to stop taking potshots at lumbering beasts. I'm convinced that it was at that point that the left side somewhat wrestled away the advantage and obtained what might be called hemispheric hegemony over the right. The conflict, however, went underground.

My reformation came at a high price: the total loss of two of the masculine six senses: the olfactory and the ability to know intuitively one's exact geographical coordinates at any given nanosecond. This was the revenge taken by the right in a fit of angry pique.

So I had to learn early on to suck it up and ask for directions.

» » »

Many contemporary postmodern writers seem unable to come to terms with God's stereo-depiction in the Old and New Testaments. What they write about Him bears a startling resemblance to Dr. Jekyll and Mr. Hyde—they seem to conclude that there are two distinct divine personalities: the Mean Intolerant Hebrew Deity and the Nice Tolerant Christian God.

By listening carefully, you get the impression that God is afflicted with MPD, or that there are conflicted artistic personalities in the Godhead. There is the angry, vindictive God in His bombastic Jewish period. He paints in blacks and whites. He could use a stint at an anger management clinic. And then there is the nice, benevolent, civil God in His muted Jesus period. He prefers a lot of mauve, peach, and rose hues. He's in touch with His feminine side.

The way I view it, the reality is that God is a really complicated and complex artist. He weaves both periods together because, unlike Picasso or Goya or Pollack, He does not have stages of development. He does not improve or experiment.

He Is—or He Am. (In the Old Testament God reveals Himself to Abraham as The I AM. Jesus used the same language and got a lot of people really ticked off.)

And I love this artist.

I love His complexity, His layers, facets, and sides. I love and fear the turbulence and heat of His "moods," if that is what we can respectfully call them. He blows my mind and rightfully so. He does not fit in any of our nifty boxes. He is neither Catholic nor evangelical, charismatic nor Reformed. He shatters the stereotypes of the old-school fundamentalists and culture-current Christians with equal, breezy disregard. This One-in-Three torches towns, wipes nations off the face of the earth, then crushes the very instruments of His wrath, judging them for their excess of cruelty.

He is untamed, unfathomable, unpredictable, yet utterly and infinitely good.

This exuberant, flamboyant, violent Transcendence is a blazing furnace, a percolating cauldron of molten lava ready to blow. And when you wrap your arms over your head ready to cry out in terror, He touches your cheek, whispers your name, and tells you, "Don't be afraid, I am your God, and you are my child. I will be with you always, even to the ends of the earth. I am your shelter, your strength, ever ready to help in time of trouble. Though the mountains may crack and tumble into the depths of the sea and its water roar and seethe, I am on your side, your strong citadel, your mighty God" (Psalm 46:1-3, author's paraphrase).

It's difficult maintaining your balance around this God.

He makes your head spin and your heart sing.

He cannot be taken lightly or for granted.

The God whose self-portrait we uncover in the Bible is the one who skips over the mountains, holding the nations like grains of sand in His hand. When He takes human form, He yells out to the chaotic waves, "Calm down. Now!" (Matthew 8:26). And to the belligerent demons, "Get to hell out of here!" (Matthew 8:32, author's paraphrase).

He lets the broken-hearted, shame-filled adulteress off the Mosaic hook and whispers in her ear, "Just stop what you've been doing. I saved your life now, but if you don't, you're on your own" (John 8:11, author's paraphrase one more time).

He leans back and lets the prostitute wash His feet with her tears. He does not rebuke her for breaching every social convention by kissing the feet she has washed and anointing them with perfume, or for the sexually charged act of undoing her hair so she can use it to dry them. He lets it go to shame the critical, self-righteous alpha males. He publicly honors her but not before addressing and forgiving her many sins (Luke 7:36-50).

He later pronounces dire prophesies about Jerusalem (Luke 13:34-35) and screams hoarsely at the other towns that refused to submit to Him, "Damned! You are damned, and you don't know it! If you'd only repented and surrendered to me you could have lived. Now, a worse fate than Sodom's awaits you" (Matthew 11:21-24, author's paraphrase). And to Capernaum He declares, "You wanted to be exalted as high as heaven, didn't you? Instead, you will be thrown down to hell" (Luke 10:13, not a paraphrase).

This is a God who terrifies the hell out of you.

At one moment, Jesus tells His followers, "Come to me all you who labor and are overburdened, and I will give you rest. Shoulder my yoke and learn from me, for I am gentle and humble in heart and you will find rest for your souls" (Matthew 11:28-29). Then at another, He who was celebrated by angels as bringing peace on earth says, "I have come to bring fire to the earth, and how I wish it were blazing already" (Luke 12:49), and "Do not suppose that I am here to bring peace . . . it is not peace I have come to bring, but a sword" (Matthew 10:34).

In the end of the Great Epic, Jesus depicts Himself not as an uncomplaining and compliant lamb, but as the Returning King, on a mission to reclaim His radiant bride and, along with her, the whole creation.[1]

Riding on a prancing white stallion, "He is a judge with integrity, a warrior for justice" (Revelation 19:11). His eyes are flames of fire, His head is crowned with many crowns, and, staggeringly, His cloak is soaked in blood. From His mouth comes a sharp sword to strike down the rebel armies; He is the One who will rule them with an iron scepter and tread out the wine of God's fierce anger (Revelation 19:11-15).

This God-man is impossible to categorize or defend. He bows

to no one. Rather, before Him every knee will bow and every tongue will acclaim, "Jesus Christ is Lord, to the glory of the Father" (Philippians 2:11).

I understand why some are tempted to cover their eyes (or at least one of them) to block out this depiction they find most repulsive. I sympathize with the desire to imply that what we are dealing with here are again two distinct paintings of two incompatible and incongruous entities.

How do you reconcile this antithesis?

The answer takes me back to the hoof upside my head.

» » »

Although there may be no relationship between getting smacked on my right temple and the eclipse of my subjective, intuitive capacity, the reality is, that is what somehow occurred. Nature hates a vacuum and so the left took control and decided to monopolize the entire conversation. However, in my middle thirties, the creative side won a temporary victory in a daring frontal assault.

I discovered I was a writer.

This came as a profound shock.

That brief hemispheric coup resulted in my writing a fantasy novel.[2]

Subequently, over time, bridges were built between the warring factions. Alliances were made, and then somewhere along the line, not only were there conversations, but actual linkage occurred. As a result, I can no longer tell whether I am right- or left-brained.

I feel like I am hemispherically unipolar.

It is probably this healing of the hemispheres that prevents me from swearing allegiance to either extreme in the discussion about

God's MPD. I am not as compelled anymore by false antinomies: God must be either Sovereign or Gracious, Merciful or Vengeful; Jesus is a Revolutionary or a Conservative; Republican or Democrat; Green or Red; we must become believers or followers; what matters is not what you believe but how you behave; or my favorite, you can't dance the salsa or drink sangria and be a good Christian. I can now appreciate both sides and don't feel the need to beat the drum for one or the other theological extreme. What I really believe, when all conflicting voices quiet down and I'm back in my right (or is it left?) mind, is that the masterpiece God has painted of Himself is so vast and so multifaceted that nobody can get it all just by looking up at it on the wall. It stretches too far and high and wide, eclipsing the entire horizon.

It is so subtle and yet too overwhelming.

It is overly simple yet impossibly complex.

And it changes depending on where you are standing in the room.

Like those pictures that morph into something completely different, God's painting of Himself does that too. It is not God who changes; it is just that our life circumstances flex, our perspective alters. Our brains are so very small and He is so amazingly vast that we can only catch tiny disconnected pieces of the work.

If we could stand back far enough, we might begin to make better sense of what the masterpiece depicts. However, that perspective is not available to us here on this earth. A new heaven and a new earth are required for us to start getting a real clue — till then it eludes us. What little we see is seen "darkly," like looking at a reflection in a polished plate under candlelight. And what appears to be a change or movement is just our shaky hand and the wind blowing on the flame.

» » »

Prophets are experts on bipolarity. They are also God's unwilling lightning rods.

Those individuals who are wired (or miswired) along these lines get struck with jolts that can be really embarrassing if they hit during a date, a church service, a Bible conference, or some other venue that is public, calm, and civil. Prophets have a hard time with civility. They suffer from a polarity disorder which causes them to identify with God first and humans second. You can identify them pretty easily because their hair is usually singed. These types have what is known as a prophetic electrical system.

Their God smokes, so they do too.

They've been jolted so many times that they sometimes walk around like those guys you see pushing shopping carts and wearing winter coats in summer, talking to themselves. And like those people, you can sometimes hear prophets muttering and swearing in the heat of a private, frenzied argument.

They wrestle phantoms.

They receive transmissions whose provenance we might say is extraplanetary. They pick up on signals. Maybe they're just paying closer attention than most. I will admit that I have on occasion felt the odd vibration and the unexpected shock of . . . intuition, let's call it. So assuming prophetic wiring is still extant, I may possibly fall into that uncomfortable category. This, however, may merely be another latent consequence of the horse's hoof. Additional internal fuses and circuits may have been damaged by the blow.

But the interesting thing about prophets and what makes them indispensable is that because of the smoking-and-jolting thing, they are more accustomed to the smoke and the fire than most. They can therefore look a little longer toward the consuming fire and see what many miss. And because they have sworn an oath of allegiance to another reality, because they feel the compelling weight and gravitational pull of a point of view that is not of this world, they can sometimes provide a helpful, other-worldly perspective. This is especially true when struggling with paradox, where the constant temptation is to endorse the side whose colors we prefer against the side whose colors we hate. At such times, it's a good idea to pay attention to those whose miswiring allows them to love pink and red, white and black, with equal passion.

God does not need spin doctors or marketing gurus. He has no need of defense attorneys who will emphasize only those facts favorable to his client's position. It does Him no service to cover up or ignore or modify the parts that make Him look bad (to us, or to our friends). We have not been hired as God's image consultants. It is we who need Him, not the other way around. So, though sympathetic with the desire to dress God up, to prop up His image or soften the anger lines running alongside the mouth, I say what any prophet would say, as civilly and as kindly as possible:

STOP! Just stop!

This abrupt imperative is not intended as a condemnation of moral wrongness but as a cry of warning from a motorist waving hazard lights in front of a washed-out bridge. You mean well, but what you don't know is that you're on slippery, dangerous ground. If you keep driving in the same direction, you will be swept away by the current.

» » »

All that we needed to learn we really did learn in kindergarten. The lessons are so simple and basic that as grown-ups we may tend to forget them. Two of these are don't run with scissors, and don't play with fire.

This massaging of God's public image, this painting over the portions of God's masterpiece we don't like, this "deconstruction" is doing both those activities your teacher warned you against. And both can get you and others hurt. While falling with scissors in hand may only poke *your* eye out, it is possible to burn down your own house *and* your neighbor's as well playing with matches in the attic.

What the prophets report from behind the smoke is that God scares the pants off us. And to even entertain the idea that we can improve His painting by airbrushing away some offensive "flaws" is incredibly demeaning at best. To act as though God needs our assistance to better position Himself for improved market penetration is so presumptuous and stunningly disrespectful that it is really kind of frightening.

As the tokers and stoners used to say in the sixties, "He is wild, man! Wild!" They were right and still are. He was wild with Moses and Pharaoh, and He's still wild today. He is fierce, and He acts like He owns the entire planet. No, make that the universe.

He really believes that He is the most worthy, most majestic, magnificent, glorious, stunningly beautiful being in the universe. And He is fixated on the certainty that only He deserves worship—that to Him alone belong honor, glory, and praise forever and forever. With red-rimmed, stinging eyes and burning hair, all we can say is—He is right. He is astonishingly beautiful, utterly majestic and perfect in the symmetries of justice and righteousness, knowledge and wisdom. He is as hypnotically compelling as a surging forest fire and ten times as dangerous.

He is out of control—ours, not His.

All us smoking-hair types admit that none of us imagined

we'd need biohazard suits to protect us from the radioactive isotopes emanating from the Transcendent One. However, had we taken the biblical Epic a little more seriously, maybe we wouldn't have been so surprised. After all, what do we make of a God who strikes an inoffensive priest dead just for trying to lend Him a hand? I mean, the injustice, the unfairness of it all is repellent and confusing. It's really kind of infuriating. Especially if you happen to be a king on a mission prompted by love.

» » »

King David is taking the Ark of the Covenant to Jerusalem, where he intends to house it in a tabernacle specially designed for daily cycles of continuous worship. From this tabernacle, psalms of praise and supplication, adoration and devotion will rise up before God 24/7. This is what is bursting in David's heart as he leads the people of Israel in dancing and singing "with all their might." As they process up the rutted trail to the City of Zion, the oxen stumble. Uzzah, one of the priests leading the cart, reflexively reaches out to keep the ark from tipping over. The instant his hand touches the gilded box, God kills him. He drops dead in front of the joyful throng and its dancing king, putting a serious crimp in the worship service. And David gets royally ticked.

"David was displeased," we are told (2 Samuel 6:8). That's putting it mildly.

David is so shocked, offended, and a little afraid too, that he leaves the ark at the home of Obed-Edom and returns to the safety of Jerusalem "in the fear of the Lord that day" (2 Samuel 6:9). The king of Israel had been put in his place by the King of the Universe. God had shattered a common and very natural (but mistaken) syllogism: We need God—He needs us.

In the words of Rabbi Abraham Heschel, David had experienced firsthand that "God is not nice. God is not an uncle. God is an earthquake."[3]

It is a lesson God intended that David never forget. God's hard lessons are intended to drive home a point, not for His good, but ours. He wanted His king to remember it years later when he lusted after Bathsheba's body. Sadly, for David, his wife, his children, and an entire nation, he didn't. This fiery God is always way ahead of us—millennia ahead. That is why the wisest and the safest response when you just don't get Him is to go back home "in the fear of the Lord," put your hand over your mouth, and in utter silence, worship.

If you don't, you will be tempted to say and believe things about God that are simply not true, though they may sound like they are. Things like, Jesus is the Way, He is not in the way; Jesus is not an offense, it is His followers who are offensive; Jesus is not the only way to the Father, He is the best way; God is not really in control, He is just as surprised by the choices we make as we are; history is a massive crapshoot in which God is gambling on a good outcome; He is the great cosmic risk taker who sometimes gets it wrong.

Because of my wiring or hemispheric issues, I have this sense that those who are on the right or the left (evangelical or Emergent) are getting it right while also getting it wrong. Maybe the real Jesus was a dovish-hawk or a hawkish-dove. Maybe the God of the Bible is both kind and inflexibly stern just as Saint Paul tells us (Romans 11:22) and remains absolutely strong while being perfectly loving (Psalm 62:11-12). Perhaps instead of pitting one aspect of God or His work against the other and forcing a false antithesis, what we need to do is to start listening (and reading) in stereo.[4]

Maybe it is possible to be like that brown, furry little beaver I mentioned in the first chapter who was wired more along the gentle-pacifist-Democratic lines, but having seen the Great Lion up close and personal knew what many of us are in danger of forgetting:

"Yes, Aslan is good."

Of course He is good!

He is the Benevolent Lord, the Almighty Ruler of Narnia and of the entire universe, for pity's sake!

But when He throws His head back and roars, watch out!

Your skin will prickle, your hair will stand on end (maybe also smoke just a bit) for you will know something else:

"He is not safe."

That is the God of the Epic.

That is the God of the Masterpiece.

That is a God worth worshipping.

Blessing

May the mighty Lion of Judah,
the Holy King of heaven,
the Righteous Judge,
who will weigh the nations and everyone in them in just
and perfect scales,
fill you with the true, deep, rich,
utterly delightful and comforting knowledge of Himself.
May you, childlike, kneel;
may you lovingly trust,
even when He shatters your box and singes your hair.
May you, lost in wonder, worship, love, and adore.

May the God who roars and sings
calm your fears and soothe your pain and set you straight.
And, in reverential, trembling awe
may you kiss the Son and with sturdy faith
confidently say:
I am His and He is mine.

5

THE GOD WHO SMOKES

On occasion I have been accused of having anger issues. Maybe rightly so. King David did too, so I'm not going to get too bent out of shape about it.

Jesus was not immune either, so I think I'll just relax and give my blood pressure a break.

I remember being very, very angry at God. It was at the end of 2000. What had me so profoundly ticked at the end of that year was a lie God had told us. It had to do with adopting an orphan from Mozambique.

Okay, I should probably explain. It wasn't like God wrote us an e-mail telling us to immediately leave our safe surroundings and go to a far-off land that we knew not of and there adopt a certain six-year-old African boy. It's not like He wrote it out for us in the Bible in code. It was not quite so direct. But it was still clear and unequivocal.

In June 2000, my wife, Patty, and I were at an orphanage in

Mozambique. Three cyclones had hit simultaneously and flooded nearly two-thirds of the country. The rural orphanage in Machava, forty-five minutes from Maputo, the capital, had been devastated. We had come with a multigenerational, self-contained team to help with construction and care for eighty-six children.

On our second night, we were gathered around a bonfire singing and roasting marshmallows. I was sitting on the ground holding a sleepy little waif.

His name was Bentu. I liked it immediately, especially with that marvelous Portuguese lilt: Beyn-tu. We found out later that the actual spelling was Bento. Portuguese is the language of the samba, so it turns its words into music. The flat *o* at the end of a word becomes a lilting *u*. Sometime after that, we discovered that his name was a diminutive of the Portuguese word for "blessed" from the Latin *benedito*. Apt indeed.

Patty came over and asked me in quiet tones what his name was. I told her. She looked deeply at him and then walked away. I thought nothing of it. She loves children. The smaller the better. I did not know it, but at that moment her world had tilted. It took her several days before she was able to uncover the rawness of her wound to me. What she had to say was simple. She believed we were supposed to adopt Bentu.

There was something solid and almost holy in how Patty described the basis for this utterly unexpected desire that left little room for disagreement. Before she had even heard his name, she had been arrested by his startling resemblance to our second son, Benjamin. At six, Ben was a spitting image of me at the same age. At his age I was given the endearing Spanish nickname *fideo con ropa*, which translated means "spaghetti with clothes on." Bentu was identical. Not only that, Bentu's hooded sweatshirt could have been taken from Ben's memory box.

What pierced through Patty with the shock of a knife's blade were these questions: What if this little orphan were Ben? What if Ben were the one who had lost his parents and was now among the hundreds of waifs being cared for in an institution somewhere? And what if he were longing so desperately to be held by his father that he would climb up on the lap of the nearest available man in order to breathe in the security and comfort he'd lost forever?

What if Ben-tu had been Ben-one?

» » »

Two weeks later, as we flew out of the Maputo airport, Patty's heart was breaking. All the way back to the United States, she tried to hold back the tears as she kept asking herself why she was leaving one of her children behind in Africa. After returning home, she began to pray for specific confirmation.

Still, she was holding herself back.

What she was waiting for was clear and unambiguous approval from the orphanage leaders that Bentu was adoptable, and that they were in favor of our adopting him. Patty was no stranger to deep disappointment. Her father died of cancer when she was ten. For years after his death, she felt compelled to tell her mother before going to bed, "I'll see you in the morning," believing that if she failed to do so, she would awaken to find her mother dead. Ten years later, her closest brother died from the same disease.

So she held back and waited, and as she waited she prayed — for a sign.

After two months, Katie, the adoption coordinator sent word that we should, by all means, begin the process of adoption. Patty's heart leaped. She had gotten her sign. The walls were breached, the door flung open. For all intents and purposes, Bentu was now hers. Everything else was just details. A mother's emotional bond had now been consciously and irrevocably established.

Then, almost three weeks later, with no warning, another e-mail arrived. In so many words, it was telling us, "Stop!" In cryptic fashion, it said:

"Bentu's mother has been found.

She was asked for permission to allow the adoption to proceed.

She refused.

You cannot adopt Bentu."

Had we been told this before Patty opened up her heart to the process, the pain could have been kept to a minimum. But no, it came afterward, after all the defenses were down, when the pain and disappointment could inflict its most severe and jagged trauma.

As Patty wept, I seethed.

God, I thought, *how difficult could it have been for you to wave us off at the beginning? Certainly you could have made sure the mother's identity was uncovered at the start? Why could we not have been told, "No, we don't think you should proceed with this adoption. He has a mother. We've talked with her, and she is not in favor. Sorry. Better luck next time."*

It was the unfairness and the meanness of the whole thing that made me so angry.

But what could we do? We gave up on the adoption.

Many months later, we discovered that a jealous Mozambican orphanage worker had lied about the conversation in which Bentu's mother had supposedly refused permission. On October 31, 2001, only six weeks after 9/11 and sixteen months after meeting him, we left Grand Rapids, Michigan, to finalize the adoption. We returned on Thanksgiving Day with a new seven-year-old son.

» » »

Sometimes anger is not appropriate; sometimes it is. I know that at times I have gotten angry inappropriately, as most of us have. I would bet that most of our fathers or other authority figures in our lives have as well. That doesn't make anger evil or wrong. Sometimes it is the only right thing.

When my friend Bill and I discovered the corruption in the Guatemalan infant adoption monopoly, we were angry. Baby brokers scoured the city and the countryside on the lookout for poor pregnant women willing to sell their infant for a year's wage or less, or women willing to be paid to become pregnant. "Baby farms" harvested the infants, where they would be fattened up by the lawyers running the "foster homes," for sale to the agencies that would then charge American couples anywhere between twenty-five and sixty thousand dollars. Not every infant was a part of the web of corruption, but the majority were. It was a hundred-million-dollar business, monopolized by about four hundred attorneys.

Anger is the correct response to such abuse. What pornography is doing to women in the sex trade, the "orphan" infant brokers are doing to women and babies in the corrupt adoption trade. People turned into objects and commodities. Bodies are perverted by greedy men (and women) into machinery for profit. This is what the capitalist manufacturer does to the children in his sweat shop or the women slaving at their sewing machines fourteen hours a day for pennies so we can get cheap T-shirts at the superstore.

Inevitably, this makes me think about a verse of Scripture I read once, then quickly tried to pretend I hadn't. The Lord, like a Judge, is rising up from behind the bench to arraign the leaders of Israel. He lays out the charges:

> It is you who have ruined my vineyard;
>> the plunder from the poor is in your houses.

What do you mean by crushing my people
    and grinding the faces of the poor? (Isaiah 3:14-15, NIV).

The plunder of the poor is in *our* houses? Yours? Mine?

The Almighty Judge then turns it over to His prosecuting attorney, Isaiah, who goes on listing the indictments. "The Lord expected justice but found bloodshed; integrity, but only a cry of distress" (5:7). And then he gets angry. "Woe to those who add house to house and join field to field until everywhere belongs to them and they are the sole inhabitants of the land" (5:8).

And here I thought God liked it when I made a lot of money and spent it on bigger and bigger houses.

During the course of his lengthy summation, Isaiah informs Israel fifty-two times that their God is very angry. He is furious and full of wrath. Jeremiah, the next chief prosecutor (also known as major prophet), warns Israel about God's anger fifty-five times.[1] What's more, the prophet admits having some anger issues of his own. "I am full of the wrath of Yahweh, I am weary of holding it in" (Jeremiah 6:11). Ezekiel, the last of the crew of legal eagles, hammers it home fifty-seven times. He also admits to his own issues: "The Spirit lifted me up and took me; my heart as I went, overflowed with bitterness and anger, and the hand of Yahweh lay heavy on me" (Ezekiel 3:14). On sheer volume alone, we would have to conclude that God was getting angrier. Or His spokesmen were. Or maybe both.

The Hebrews have a finely calibrated appreciation for anger. They use at least eight major words for that emotion. The Jews were not embarrassed about their anger; they come off like a bunch of Italians.

The most common word is *aph*. It is used nearly two hundred times in the Old Testament in reference to God. It is vivid. It refers to the nose and is a word picture of the snorting and harsh breathing exhibited by the utterly furious. *Zaham* is even more dramatic. Its attention is drawn to the mouth, from whence spittle and froth can fly. This is the word used in Psalm 7:11: "God is a righteous judge, a God who expresses his wrath every day" (NIV). This verse can also be translated as "He is a God who is always enraged by those who refuse to repent" (7:11-12). *Hemah* refers to the heat that is caused by poison. *Haron* speaks of the glowing and blazing up of fire. This is the word used the first time God's anger is mentioned in the Bible (Genesis 18:30). It is used exclusively for God's anger (thirty-three times). *Rogez* looks at the effects on the body (such as trembling) and speaks of thundering and agitation. *Chawas* is to be grieved and indignant and provoked. *Quesep* is to be enraged. *Asan* gives us the image of smoke and the smoldering of hot coals (Psalm 80:4).

The image of fire, heat, and smoke seems to have won out, for in the New Testament the words *thumos* (smoke) or *orge* (to swell or become agitated) are used interchangeably for God's anger. No doubt this image is drawn from the most dramatic experience that marked the Jewish historic memory.

The nation of Israel is camped around Mt. Sinai, and God shows up at the top. When He does, the whole thing reels and shakes like a drunk. There is thunder and lightning, and the summit is ablaze with fire and wrapped in smoke, so much so that "all the people shook with fear at the peals of thunder and the lightning flashes, the sound of the trumpet, and the smoking mountain, and they kept their distance" (Exodus 20:18).

I would think so.

They are so traumatized by the drama that they tell Moses they've really had about enough and he can go ahead and talk to God on his own, thank you very much. Then after God speaks to him, he can come back to report what he's heard. Moses responds by encouraging the Israelites not to be afraid (right!) and explains that "God has come to test you, so that your fear of Him, being always in your mind, may keep you from sinning" (Exodus 20:20).

This is a God who commands and demands respect.

Forty years later, when Moses recaps this event, he reminds Israel that they are to obey and serve God exclusively because "Yahweh your God is a consuming fire, a jealous God" (Deuteronomy 4:24) and will not shrink back from utterly destroying them (4:27). He then launches into a prophecy, telling them that they will do exactly what they have been warned against. They will, in fact, be seduced and will fall for other, more earthy deities, and God will thrust them out into the nations, "but at the end of days you will return to Yahweh your God and listen to His voice. For Yahweh your God is a merciful God and will not desert or destroy you or forget the covenant He made on oath with your fathers" (4:30-31).

This God smokes and rages and punishes severely.

But He also forgives extravagantly.

As He strides majestically in front of Moses, who is hiding in the crevice of a rock, God makes this proclamation about Himself:

Yahweh, Yahweh, a God of tenderness and compassion, slow to anger [aph — of the contorted nose and flared nostril], rich in kindness and faithfulness; for thousands He maintains His kindness, forgives faults, transgression, sin; yet He lets nothing go unchecked, punishing the father's fault in the sons and in the grandson to the third and fourth generation. (Exodus 34:6-7)

» » »

Because man's anger is almost exclusively and categorically evil (and is depicted as such in the Bible), we have a hard time with this language about God. Here is where our culture and temperament can hurt us. We look at God's emotions from the grid of our own emotional brokenness and painful experience. The Jews, obviously, did not share our hang-ups. They had no problem describing God's emotions in (to our minds) patently offensive terms. I mean the image of God's face contorted, nostrils distended, lips twisted, limbs shaking, and ears pouring smoke is enough to put anyone off his feed.[2]

But here let me issue a warning from a very wise Orthodox priest, Patrick Henry Reardon, who recognizes our preference for the gentler, kinder Messiah over the angry Jewish Deity: "The loving mercy of God must never be thought of or described in ways suggesting that Christianity is less morally serious than Judaism."[3]

Jesus was not less serious, nor can He be taken less seriously, than His Father.

According to the writers of the Great Epic, God gets exceedingly mad. He burns with a furious, fiery wrath. And they are not put off by this at all. They almost relish it. The first-tier writers and the second string say the same: "Yes, God holds the godless and his godlessness in equal hatred, work and workman alike shall be punished" (Book of Wisdom 14:9).[4]

They knew what we all know down deep: If God did not get angry, He would not be God.

If God forever turned His eyes away from the abuse, the perversion, the pollution, the pillaging, raping, spilling of innocent blood, the sexual slavery, the Lord's Resistance Army conscripting little children to become cold-blooded killers, the decapitating of political prisoners in the name of God Allah, and decapitating forests and jungles in the name of God Mammon, then God would not be just or righteous.

We know that.

So God rages and roars and smokes.

He thunders, shakes, and burns like this massive forest fire.

Because at the core of His being, God is love.

In allowing these terms to be attached to His emotions, God does not want us to picture the face of a deranged, maniacal, or abusive Father. He wants to woo us with the image of an aggrieved and heartbroken Husband, whose beautiful bride, after returning home from her honeymoon, has begun to sell her body on the street corner to pay her pimp for drugs.

That is why He tells us He is a jealous God.[5]

He wants to elicit sympathy by painting Himself as a Father who walks into the baby's room to see a spitting cobra coiled insolently on top of his infant's cold, blue body.

That is why He is an avenging God.[6]

He is saying something to us much more about His love than about His hate. At the deepest root of the idea of God's wrath (which fills the Scriptures from beginning to end) is the reality that it is fundamentally an expression of passion from a wounded husband and a ferociously protective father.

His wrath is about His love.

Granted, this is a difficult idea. It is not easy for us — moderns and postmoderns alike, who are very much children of our time — to put these two ideas together.[7] Our intuitive and automatic response to anger is predominantly negative. We are conditioned to feel the same repulsion for anger as for a pedophile.

» » »

God's anger is not what we think. I never put this together until seeing the movie *The Patriot.* Mel Gibson is a retired colonel in the Colonial Army. After witnessing the murder of his young son at the hands of British soldiers, Mel grabs his hatchet and musket and races off to intercept the band and rescue his eldest son, who the redcoats have captured and intend to hang. His prayer as he runs is simple: "Lord, make me accurate. Lord, make me fast." With the help of his two youngest boys, he lays a successful ambush. In the melee, Mel rushes in with his ax high overhead and strikes down the remaining British soldier. The redcoat falls, and Mel, in a ferocious, sobbing rage, strikes him over and over until the splattering blood covers his clothes, arms, and face.

He then looks up to see his two little boys looking down at him from behind a log. There is this fierce, heartbroken rage twisting Mel's face for just the briefest moment. As I watched the expression shift to a human father's embarrassment at the excess of violence, I knew I had seen something about God.

After the movie, I asked my sons, "What do you think? Was Mel's assault on that soldier prompted by hate or by love?" They thought for a moment, then they all agreed, it was compelled by both. But to be more precise, I think the answer is by a love driven to hate. Granted, Mel, as father, loses control. That is what probably clouds his eyes as he looks back at his youngsters. There is the slightest hint of shame. But there is none in God's eyes. He executes justice with perfection.

That helps me a lot as I try to put together this difficult image of God the roaring, raging consuming fire, whose nose gets bent out of shape when His anger is provoked.[8]

To allow our cultural sensitivities to force us to conclude that this picture is somehow demeaning, to dismiss it as mere hyperbole or an extravagant Hebrew-peasant metaphor, is just not terribly convincing. So what if these words are metaphors—or as the experts say, anthropopathisms (using human emotions to describe Him)? All these terms mean something—serious—and what they don't mean is that God is a doting Irish mum, clucking her tongue as she passes out cold Guinness to her IRA lads planning the bombing of a school bus filled with little Protestant children.

He is no sappy, sentimental deity.

* * *

The death of Jesus is the best window we've been given into this profound, paradoxical reality. That is where two high-pressure systems collide: God's infinite, holy love crashing into His infinite, holy hatred. At the cross, two mighty streams crash together. It is where God's zeal for His own honor, His jealous and protective love for His Son and His Bride cascade into His righteous, inflexible insistence on justice and His unfathomable abhorrence of evil. At the cross, we see love driven to hate in order that love might win over all, yet not without sacrificing or annulling righteousness or justice.

At the cross, judgment triumphs over mercy in order that mercy may triumph over all. It is only this that makes sense of the most startling and offensive of all biblical statements.

Isaiah prophesies that the Messiah will come as a Suffering Servant upon whom Yahweh will lay "the sins of all of us" (like the scapegoat in Leviticus 16:21). He will be led like a sheep to the slaughterhouse and, despite having done no wrong, will be killed for our faults. And here is where that terrible phrase comes in: Standing behind and over this awful travesty will be the Father, for we are told that "Yahweh has been pleased to crush Him with suffering" (Isaiah 54:10).

There is no way to lessen the sting and the affront of this.

The term Isaiah uses, *hapes*, describes the enjoyment a husband finds in his new wife (Deuteronomy 21:14), King Saul's pleasure at David's music (1 Samuel 18:22), or what a king experiences in the most beautiful member of his harem (Esther 2:14).

Whereas God receives no enjoyment from the Jews' ritual sacrifices, He does delight in putting His Son to death. The only way we can make any sense of this is to understand that what's behind the cross is holy love, first and foremost. There is rage and hatred and wrath against sin placed upon the Messiah. But before all, there is first of all infinite love.

God's hatred of wickedness and evil is so profound because His love is so profound. His infinite and holy love compelled Him to offer His Son as an atoning sacrifice (the older "propitiation" is much more accurate) to take away sin in order that He might redeem, reconcile, and restore the world (Exodus 30:10; Isaiah 53:4-6; Romans 3:25; Hebrews 2:17; 1 John 2:2; 4:10). That is where the pleasure came. It was the foreseen fruit of victory won, of justice vindicated, of death defeated, and of creation healed and whole that provoked the joy. It was the absolute certainty of His creatures being freed, delivered, cleansed, and restored to fellowship with Him forever that made His heart sing. His creation and His Son's bride made beautiful again. That gave Him supreme pleasure.

When Moses reminds the Israelites of what happened to them at the holy mountain where they received the Ten Commandments and were married to Yahweh, he refers to the fiery mountain fourteen times in six chapters. He also makes mention of the cloud and the thick darkness (Deuteronomy 5:22). He is making a point.

This is a fiery, smoking God. But what blazes and roars and crackles is a consuming fire of passionate love. And the smoke is a protective screen that allows us to look and not go blind, to get close and not get burned, to show us the way when the right path is far in the distance. As Rob Bell suggests, it is also mystery and question and wonder too.[9]

The smoke is fiery love toned down; it is brilliance muted and frosted.

This smoking, smoldering God is holy love aflame. And when He assumes the shape of a man, He continues to burn, for we are told that zeal (a fiery jealousy) for His Father's house consumed Him (John 2:17). What else could we expect? After all, like Father, like Son.

There are those who wish to tone down the anger, to smother the fire and smoke on the mountain. If they succeed, they will lose more than an image of a mean God—they also lose mercy and extinguish grace.

When sin is directed against God, it is unrighteousness; when it is directed against the creature, it is injustice. From man's side, these bring death and result in guilt and alienation. For God, they are an offense to His holy love and produce wrath. Holiness demands that sin be punished and injustice avenged.

God's holy anger requires judgment.

God's holy love requires mercy.

So He offers His Son to bear the full weight of judgment so that His creatures can be offered forgiveness. The death of Jesus becomes the means of forgiving the guilty, reconciling the alienated, and restoring the desecrated creation.

Without anger there is no grace; without judgment there is no mercy.

No Jesus, no justice.

No smoke, no fire.

No raging, bloody passion, no real, permanent peace.[10]

Blessing

May you be comforted by the burning
protective strength of your Father's strong and stormy love.
May you be captivated by the focused heat and glow
of your Bridegroom's jealous passion.
May you recline at peace and with veiled face bow.
May you be thrilled and terrified
at the rampaging, irresistible
zeal of this consuming fire who has pledged Himself
to do you good all the days of your life
and who will not hold back even if the good seems bad,
and stings and burns and blisters your skin.
May your heart thrill at the awesome God
who held nothing back that He might hold you close,
who poured on His Son what He never deserved
that you might receive forever
what you would not have desired,
but were created for.
Then may your own heart become an altar
aflame with fiery love and exclusive zeal
to bring Him glory and expand His praise
among all peoples and nations—
among your friends and enemies too.

6

JESUS IS IN THE WAY

The eruption that helped plant the idea for this book took place on the spacious pillared porch in front of my parents' faux antebellum home in west Michigan. It occurred during our bimonthly, extended-family Sunday lunch hosted by the hospitable patriarchs. The circle of fourteen people seated in folding chairs and assorted outdoor seats looked like a poster for a multigenerational therapy session. The ten younger grandchildren were scattered about inside the house and in the backyard.

The topic, again, was *Velvet Elvis*. Its author Rob Bell pastors Mars Hill Church, about twenty minutes from where we had congregated. It's a church in which various family members have worked, served, been on staff, led worship, or forged life-long friendships, and most of the others have attended at one time or another. It has played a significant role, directly or indirectly, in the lives of many of those in our extended clan. So, a book by its pastor was of special interest.

Rob's influence on my son Jonathan goes back to Rob's stint in the nineties-era "punk" band Big Fil. Controversial even then, his aggressive, raw power chords drove Jonathan's teacher from a high school assembly holding her ears in anguish. In subsequent years, though, it was the compelling questions, not the music, that created the intrigue. So much so that Jonathan and his friend Madie, both on staff with Youth with a Mission in Hawaii, of all places, established a regular church service around his teachings.

Around 10:00 a.m., a group of friends would pile into a black Isuzu and make their way to the Starbucks in Kona on the Big Island. They would catch up over lattes and espressos and double-talls with skim milk, no foam, extra hot (seared to 143 degrees), with organic nutmeg and cinnamon sprinkles. They would share life together as they downloaded a podcast of Rob's teachings onto iTunes. But being in ministry with severely restricted incomes (but apparently not enough to put a crimp in the coffee budget), they would avoid Starbucks' wireless charges by sitting as close as possible to the Denny's next door that offered it for free. Piracy complete, they would crowd into the four-wheeler and head out to a small harbor overlooking Honokohau Bay, fifteen minutes north of Kailua-Kona. As they drank in the view of the sailboats and surging surf with their hot caffeine, they would listen to Rob's sermon. And they would return home justified, having been to church, thank you very much, but in a free-flowing, life-enhancing, postmodern kind of a way.

They called it Starbucks Church.

Sounds like fun to me.

So much so that now Jonathan has returned home; I've kind of borrowed the model for the time being. But instead of Starbucks, my three older boys and Christiana, my only daughter, with their friend James gather around a box of donuts on our back deck.

Aaron, who works for that famous coffee emporium, provides the hot caffeine at a significant discount. I call it the Donut Gang. We talk about things that matter, listen to sermons, and pray for each other.

None of us in that multigenerational circle on my parents' porch discussing *Velvet Elvis* had yet read it, but a review had just come out in our local paper. I had read *A New Kind of Christian*, though, almost three times through.[1] It was the book that admittedly laid down the tracks on which many of the theological premises articulated by Rob would speed along. My wife, who has little patience with vagueness and uncertainty in such matters, had pressed some in our group who were on staff for definitive answers. The replies were oblique and diplomatic.

The vocabulary was modulated and equivocal. There seemed to be this hesitancy or unwillingness to make any kind of a clear, categorical statement—about anything.

It was becoming a bit frustrating.

From what we could decipher from the responses, the position of the leadership was that seekers should be encouraged to explore their own spiritual questions and come to answers on their own. The premise seemed to be that it was a really bad idea to tell people what is true and what to believe; that somehow or another it was more respectful and affirming of people's dignity to let them find their own way. The implication was pretty strong: Making definite spiritual truth claims was a throwback to the oppressive-colonial, pith-helmet missionary days.

My second son, Benjamin, who was twenty-two at the time, had been listening intently but quietly as he tends to do in these large-group settings. He takes after his father at that age. The spotlight is generally to be avoided, not pursued. Anyway, at that crucial moment, when civility and moderation were still hanging by a thread, silent-Ben threw restraint to the wind and blurted out, "That's what I hate about postmodern Christianity!"

Quiet dropped like a well-oiled guillotine.

All of us were shocked at the words and at their tone, made all the more surprising by their unexpected source. And Ben didn't stop there.

"What does that kind of Christianity have to say to my generation?" he continued, on a roll now. "They are so confused. They have so many questions. Instead of giving them direction about truth, pointing the way, instead of speaking clearly and with conviction, it just leaves them floundering. What's the good of that? It will leave them worse off than they were at the beginning." There was this passion in his tone I had rarely heard before.

Then he got dangerous. With eyes burning and in a choked voice, he asked, "Who is going to give their life for that?"

I was sitting on my hands at that point to keep from aggravating a suddenly tense moment. But inside I was clapping. I was so proud of my son, who'd had the courage to say something real, honest, and true. And more than that, to speak courageously into the very heart of a pretty complicated discussion.

I admire honesty over diplomacy.

Now to be clear, he hadn't said that he hated postmodern Christianity. He was taking strong exception to certain tendencies within it. He was reacting to some of the fruit of what is becoming a compelling movement. He was essentially wondering:

Who would put their life on the line for such an evasive social, political, or religious platform?

Who would be radicalized or captivated by such vagueness and grayness?

Who ever heard of a revolution led by a diplomat?

I had the same questions.

The reality is, my sons find lots in the Emergent stream that is pretty darn attractive. The thing of it is, so do I. The problem being that I was Emergent before the word had even been coined—in fact, before the word *minivan* had reached the top of the suburban vocabulary list. I was reading liberation theology in the early eighties. As a result I got so conflicted with the conservative church's exclusive focus on souls and unconcern for the poor that I had to leave seminary to get my head back on. That's what threw me headlong into law school. I was trying to get my head straight. Yeah—what *was* I thinking? Down deep I just wanted to live out my Christianity outside the protective walls of the church.

For the life of me, I couldn't make any sense of evangelicalism's strident commitment to the life of the *unborn* fetus and its equally strident support for ending the lives of socialists, communists, and Marxists around the globe, all of whom were quite obviously *born*. And this was before the Iraq conflict. Having been raised in South America and Europe, early in life I was given the opportunity to break free from conservative American nationalism and get a perspective on its narrow and dangerous narcissism. Back in the day, I was all too aware of our national sins of pride, oppression, materialism, and militarism.

It's unclear to me whether I ever did manage to get my head on straight.

Sadly for me, I was Emergent before it was cool.

Now that it's cool, I'm not.

But I've had almost a quarter century to work through its reactionary tendencies. Time has worn the edges off. It's also given some perspective.

» » »

I wish I could say that I knew at that moment, after Ben spoke out, that I would write a book to offer some answers to the questions that were thundering in his mind. But I didn't. Maybe because I was concentrating so hard on keeping this silly grin off my face. Ben's outburst kind of pricked the balloon, though. There was nothing to do but give a polite, restrained assent, and then the older folk began backtracking gracefully. One knows where the family fault lines lie and, unless utter catastrophe is imminent, they are avoided at all cost.

Ben was next to me, so I put my arm around his shoulders, smiled, and nodded. I hoped he knew I was cheering for this sudden stranger whose still waters run deep. Only now as I think back on it do I know it was Ben who moved me off the safe center. At that point all I had was this thirty-four-page outburst in which I poured out my issues with Brian McLaren's *A New Kind of Christian*—and a visceral foreboding.

Strangely enough, it had begun toward the middle of that book and wouldn't let up for over a year. It was kind of like what you feel when you've leaped to head the ball into the net and the other guy drives his shoulder into your solar plexus. Yeah, it is weird, but there it is. After finishing *A New Kind of Christian*, I knew (or thought I knew) two things: I had read a watershed book, and though I loved its critique, the error in it was so subtle but so potent that it would destroy many. It wasn't all false by any means, but there was enough that was, and presented in such a compelling, convincing, and creatively indirect kind of a way that I had this almost physical reaction to its attractive danger. And it was tinged with sadness because I really doubted any malicious intent.

Later, after picking up *Velvet Elvis*, I came across the statement that Jesus was not presenting Himself as *the only way* but *the best possible way.* In his book, Rob tells us that when Jesus declared that He was the way, the truth, and the life, He was not making any claims about His religion being better than all other religions. All that Jesus was doing was telling people that He offered them simply the best possible way to live.[2] I was taken aback for a few moments. It sounded so right yet, oddly, also so wrong. Then it hit me — this is exactly what Jesus was *not* declaring.

He was saying precisely the opposite.

If we are looking at Jesus only as the greatest rabbi, presenting teachings that will allow people to make their way through life in harmony with how things work, it is possible to state that His way *is* the best. Muslims have much to offer when it comes to a disciplined life and sexual restraint between unmarried men and women. Buddhism presents valuable contributions on anger, revenge, and peaceful relations among humans. Hindus show us a way to life in harmony with nature. These are real options if we are thinking on only horizontal terms — how to live on this earth as kindly, respectfully, and compassionately as possible. If we are merely speaking about good, ethical pathways while journeying along on the planet, then — and I would propose *only* then — it may be accurate to say the teachings of Jesus offer the best of the lot.

But this is not how Jesus viewed Himself.

It is not what He taught about Himself. Jesus did not come as rabbi only. He came as King to inaugurate a kingdom, and that is not how kings talk.

Kings have this really bad habit of thinking they are supreme, that everyone should obey and serve and bow to them. They make very lousy diplomats. And though Jesus was many things, a diplomat was not one of them. This should not come as a great shock to us. Jesus made it terribly clear that He was on a mission to establish a royal realm in which He or His Father, or both, would rule. He made such a point of it that when He was nailed to the cross, Pilate put an ironic sign over His head in three languages proclaiming that very thing: *King of the Jews.*

When kings invade your country, you have two very clear choices: submit or die. Typically, they want you to make your mind up pretty quick.

» » »

Several chapters before declaring Himself to be the Way, Jesus is in another tense discussion with the religious teachers who followed rabbis also proclaiming "ways." Since they had misunderstood an earlier metaphor in which He refers to Himself as the watchman guarding the sheep pen, He tries another. Jesus wants to be as plain as possible. He tells them that He is the gate for the sheep, and anyone who had ever come before Him also claiming to be a spiritual gate was actually a thief and a liar. He then states, "I tell you the truth. . . . I am the gate, whoever enters through me will be saved" (John 10:7-9). Furthermore, in the future, many would come declaring that their teaching would lead to life. But in reality they would be murderous thieves on a mission to steal and kill and destroy. Jesus tells the religious leaders in no uncertain terms that He *alone* has come to bring life and life "to the full" (John 10:10).

Jesus has just made a really large categorical and exclusive statement. All those in the past (and anybody in the future) who taught that their way is the path to life are not just mistaken but actually dangerous and wicked frauds. Worse than frauds, they are killers, because no matter how sincere, their path is a rabbit trail that leads to death. Jesus is the only person in all history with the right to declare that true life and true freedom can be found in Him.

So, later when Jesus declares, "I am the Way . . . no one comes to the Father but through me" (John 14:6, NIV), He is not talking as an innovative rabbi only but as Messiah. He is not unpacking His teaching and offering it as the best possible way to navigate life's whitewaters. Jesus is making a definitive statement about salvation, about being reconciled to the Father. He is not offering them a neat, new, safer, more enjoyable ethical map. What He has in mind is something much more profound, much more serious than that.

When Jesus looks at the crowd, He sees that they are all estranged. They are sheep lost and wandering near a deadly precipice. Like the prodigal son, they have turned their backs on home, stormed out of the house with their inheritance in hand, and wasted it. They have grown so disillusioned and become so ashamed that they've lost all hope of ever finding their way back. They are alienated from their Father. They are stumbling about, alone trying desperately to find the road that will bring them safely home. But it's an impossible quest, for they have been wandering in toxic wastelands so long that their eyes and their ears have been cauterized. They are groping about in the dark, stumbling dangerously near the edge of a steep gorge. And most of them are so deluded they are convinced they can see and hear just fine. They have no idea of the danger they are in.

The primary need of the crowd listening to Jesus is not to be taught a better way to a well-adjusted, more fulfilling life or a life more in tune with reality. They need to be rescued, to be found, to be reconnected with their Father, to be grabbed by the hand and dragged away from the cliff. It is in this context that Jesus declares that He is not best but *only*. He is their only hope for ever finding the way back. He is their one and only chance to be reconnected, reconciled with the Father whose heart they have broken.

He is the exclusive path that leads away from peril to safety.

To suggest anything else is simply to get it wrong.

It is also to sneak a quiet little back door through the firewall Jesus designed. It opens an escape hatch for other teachers who trumpet other paths. It allows rival "storytellers" who have much at stake and much pride on the line to save face.

It is precisely what Jesus refused to do.

» » »

He intentionally, very purposefully, forced people into a choice. He never implied that those who opted to go through other gates were making a choice for less than the best. To the contrary. He made it painfully clear that anyone who disagreed with Him and offered an alternative way was not just in error but a liar. And anyone who refused to leave his old ways and enter through Him was in mortal jeopardy.

If we're reading the Epic with both eyes wide open, at some point we have to face up to this Jesus as well. He doesn't fit neatly into either the modern or postmodern box. He's got these sharp edges, these uncomfortable, spiky points, and long scruffy beard. He resembles Che Guevara, or Fidel Castro even, more than a well-educated, well-behaved, and well-bred bureaucrat with a diplomatic brief.

Radicals believe and say some pretty radical things.

That's just the way revolutionaries are.

And, if anything, Jesus was a radical out to ignite a revolution.

Jesus didn't come to accommodate and fit in so much as turn

the world right-side up. He came not to start but to finish a war.

Jesus provoked people. It's what He was supposed to do.

But some disagree. According to these teachers, while Jesus made the way broad and straight and wide open, it was His enemies and then, later on, His confused followers who made Jesus an obstacle and an offense. According to this postmodern spin, it was His tolerance that got Jesus killed, not any harsh, exclusive, categorical, or confrontational teaching.[3]

As Brian McLaren says, "Too often, when we quote the verse about him being the way, it sounds like we're saying he's in the way—as if people are trying to come to God and Jesus is blocking the path, saying, 'Oh no, you don't! You have to get by me first.'"[4]

While this has strong, superficial appeal to those like me who want to distance Jesus from angry, mean-spirited Pharisaism, the truth of it is, this statement, at best, is only partly true.

What infuriated or frustrated most everybody at some time or another—including His best friends—were the categorical, exclusive, inflexible statements Jesus made about Himself and others who disagreed with Him. The favorite term used by Gospel writers for this troublesome trait is *skandalidzo* or "offend," which they use some twenty-five times. At the conclusion of His three-year campaign, His closest companions were so utterly scandalized by Him that they ran away, leaving Him completely at the mercy of His enemies (Matthew 26:31).[5]

Jesus was offensive.

We just have to be honest about that.

Jesus did not let anyone save face, unless it was those who had none to save. This is what He was meant to do.

When Jesus was only eight days old, on His dedication day at the temple, a devout and very grizzled old man named Simeon prophesied that this tiny infant would be destined to cause "the fall and the rising of many in Israel" (Luke 2:34). This prophet is referencing an obscure messianic prophesy:

> For both houses of Israel He will be
> a stone that causes men to stumble
>   and a rock that makes them fall [*skandalon*].
> And for the people of Jerusalem He will be
>   a trap and a snare. (Isaiah 8:14, NIV)

Saint Paul would later explain that the rejection of national Israel was due to their having "stumbled over the stumbling stone [*skandalon*], mentioned in Scripture: 'See how I lay in Zion a stone to stumble over, a rock to trip men up—only those who believe in Him will have no cause for shame'" (Romans 9:32-33). To the Corinthian believers he would explain that the message of a crucified Christ is "an obstacle [*skandalon*] the Jews can't get over." (1 Corinthians 1:23). Isaiah and the apostles are saying that Jesus is the trigger that trips the trap—*skandalon*—and drops the rock on the head of the unwary. That's what the term means.

According to Saint Peter, this offensive stone confronts people with two choices: either believe in Him, finding Him to be precious beyond words, or refuse to believe and thereby stumble over Him and fall on your face (1 Peter 2:7-8). What is important to note is that Peter is simply paraphrasing words Jesus used.

As His crucifixion is approaching, Jesus tells the religious leaders that they also face two options—they can fall on this stone (probably pointing at Himself) and be broken to pieces, or they can let it fall on them and "be crushed" (Matthew 21:44, NIV).

The scandalous quality of this man's life should not have been a surprise. It was loudly foreshadowed by His advance team of one.

John the Baptizer is the herald who sets the stage and establishes the tenor of the coming King's campaign (*campaign* as in battle, not election). He is commissioned to "make the way straight" for the Messiah. His job was to lay out the red carpet. What is so odd is the particular pitch he selects — it is one of conflict and the posture is one of confrontation. Despite what we may earnestly desire and what we may have even heard or read, the tenor of this herald is direct, inflammatory, critical, and intolerant.

Rather than opting for diplomatic indirection, John launches his formal inaugural announcement by getting in the face of his audience. With a rustic's lack of tact and the stridency of the true believer, he bellows at them, "Repent!" (Matthew 3:1).

And how does John describe the one who is soon to come? He has many images to choose from. John does not make it easy, sweet, or comfortable. The coming one is not carrying a shepherd's staff or a medicine bag. He is not bearing a servant's towel or a teacher's scroll. In His hand is a scepter. He is a King coming to inaugurate a kingdom (Matthew 3:2).

And, His instruments of choice are the ax and the winnowing fork.

John warns the crowd that when the Messiah bursts on the scene, He will ruthlessly cut down unproductive trees and beat the grain to separate it from the chaff. He will burn both the dead wood and dry chaff "with unquenchable fire" (Matthew 3:10,12, NIV). The Messiah comes to bless, certainly, but apparently also to burn. What the herald most wants his expectant audience to know is that this royal knight who comes to joust with the powers of darkness is wild and dangerous. He is a valiant warrior who is also a terrifyingly holy King; He is not one to be trifled with. Not only will He burn the chaff, but He will also baptize with the Holy Spirit and with fire (Matthew 3:12).

The message is direct: "Repent! Submit to Him or die!"

In the olden days, we might have said that John was cruisin' for a bruisin', which brings to mind a favorite scene from *Braveheart*. William Wallace has managed to gather the feuding clans to face off against Longshanks, the British king. The armies are assembled. The Celts are resplendent in war paint and ragged, untamed ferocity. They are a wild bunch. But unknown to Wallace, the Scottish lords, succumbing to the lure of gold and real estate, have caved in to their enemies again. When he discovers their duplicity, William impetuously heads out to face down the oppressors. As he gallops away from the line, he is challenged on his motive. Prancing around on his charger, with glorious dreadlocks askew, he tosses back his retort, "I'm goin' out ta pick a faite."

When Jesus takes center stage, He repeats the confrontational message of His herald John. He inaugurates His mission with the same words — "Repent for the kingdom of heaven is close at hand" (Matthew 4:17).

Throughout the next three years, Jesus will underline the hard demands of His message:

Those who are unrighteous or unfruitful or rebellious
will be thrown out and will not be allowed to enter
God's kingdom (Matthew 5:13,20).

While many are on the broad road to destruction,
only a few pass through the narrow gate leading to life
(Matthew 7:13-14).

Whoever claims to follow Him but does not also
follow His way will not be accepted into the kingdom
of heaven. Such persons will be harshly excluded. The

last words they'll hear will be, "Away from Me you evil men!" (Matthew 7:23).

While the doors to the kingdom of heaven will be opened wide for the Gentiles, there will be many Jews who "will be turned out into the dark where there will be weeping and grinding of teeth" (Matthew 8:12).

Those who reject Him as Messiah will be crushed (Matthew 21:44).

The lazy and selfish servants who are self-indulgent and ignore the needy will be cut to pieces and cast out where there will be weeping and gnashing of teeth (Matthew 24:51).

At the end of time there will be a great harvest. It will be marked by inclusion and exclusion. Those "who provoke offenses and all who do evil" will be segregated from the virtuous and the good. The angels will be sent to "throw them into the blazing furnace where there will be weeping and grinding of teeth" (Matthew 13:41-42; 13:47-50).

This is far different from the current spin on Jesus. What many teachers seem to want is an inclusive Christ who can be claimed as a world-class moral instructor: the best possible rabbi — only. Their Jesus is on a mission of mercy, and all He really needs to accomplish His goal is a nice clean trowel. A lot of creative effort is going into figuring out how to talk about this revolutionary abolitionist, this radical insurrectionist, this Holy God who is Holy and wholly man without making anybody mad, hurt, disappointed, or offended.[6]

However, the depiction of Jesus in the Gospels simply will not allow for this one-sided portrayal. It is amazing to look honestly at the textured and complex mosaic painted in the Gospels. When you read all four writers, what leaps out at you is that, as far as Jesus is concerned, He is the only way or no way.

While it may sound accurate to claim Jesus was not in the way, that is exactly how Jesus is described. It is His best friends who depict Him as this scandalous obstruction, an offensive rock that sits in the middle of the road that people avoid only with the greatest difficulty and after much inconvenience. There is also this hint of danger that surrounds Him.

It is also what He says about Himself.

He is very much in the Way.

I realize that that is a very absolutist, hard-line kind of a thing to say. It is categorical and not terribly accommodating. But most would admit that sometimes reality is sharp and hard and pointed. Sometimes—not always, but sometimes—it is either left or right, up or down. It is either "Go ahead" or "Don't move a muscle!" All of us who are parents know that on occasion the categorical imperative, the ruthless, exclusivity of options is the only path to our child's long and fruitful life. When your little boy is clambering up over the porch railing of the tenth-floor hotel room, he needs to know that he is not facing a series of life-affirming options to be discussed over milk and cookies. At that moment, he must decide immediately: obey or die.

In the context of finding the path through life's mysterious and potentially deadly maze toward the loving embrace of your Father, there are not good, better, and best.

The dark wood has only one way out.

According to Jesus—and He was very insistent on this

point—there is only one stairway to heaven. But before it is a way to live, it is a Lord to be loved. The pathway is not just a series of teachings, or even following an exemplary life; it is surrendering to a Person.

The simple, honest, difficult truth is that this one-dimensional, safe, accommodating Jesus who provides options, not commands, does not exist.

He never will.

Kings are a bit more direct than that.

Blessing

So may you glory in nothing but the scandalous cross
and in no one but the mighty and merciful Christ.
May you rejoice in your deliverance
from a cruel death, a deluded slavery;
from a bleak and desperate wandering.
May you be at peace in your Father's house.
And may you who've been chosen by Sovereign Love,
choose to lay your lives down that others may live.
May you take up the weapons of deliverance,
the prayerful instruments of justice and mercy.
May you live out and proclaim the reign of the King.
May you humbly submit to the rule of your faithful Father
and follow the Lamb wherever He goes.
May His grace so fill you
that you overflow with the confident hope and joy
His terrible and glorious death won for you.
And welcome all who hunger and thirst;
who, willing to lose, will gain,
who, willing to die, will truly live.

7

YOU'VE GOT TO LOVE SOMEBODY

Patty and I celebrated our twenty-fifth wedding anniversary in August, 2005. I had wanted to take her on a ten-day (at least) trip to Spain to revisit some of the places I've loved since living there in the seventies. I hoped also to discover some new places to fall in love with.

I had this romantic notion of staying in several Paradores Nacionales, the string of national hotels scattered strategically throughout the country. On any night, you could be staying at a castle, monastery, historic villa, or restored medieval palace for a price that would not cause nonroyals to faint. They are in some of the most picturesque, stunning locations of that most beautiful of Western European countries. I particularly had my eye on a couple in the province of Galicia that sat on top of vertical cliffs and almost hung over rocky bluffs plunging into the Atlantic Ocean.

As it turned out, our traveling money was put to use on two

trips to Guatemala on some orphan-related business, so that delightful celebration had to be put on hold. Patty is, if anything, resilient. She had this sweet idea that what she most wanted anyway was for us to renew our wedding vows. If we couldn't bask in the late-summer Mediterranean sun on the Atlantic Coast, we could at least repeat the promises we made to each other in our early twenties. She was probably figuring that the last ones lasted a quarter century, so these would probably lock in another twenty-five.

So she looped sparkling clear Christmas lights along the railing of our back deck and wound them around the branches of the small trees and tall flowering bushes that border our intimate back gate. She enlisted our children to be witnesses and Ben officiated, since Jon, the oldest, was in Hawaii studying film production. It was evening and lovely music played from the CD player hidden on the porch. Patty had on her wedding veil and Aaron walked her down the "aisle" steps to where I stood next to the tree glowing with starry lights. There we stood side by side with Ben reading the vows and Aaron, Christiana, and Bentu listening in.

I will admit that when Patty first mentioned the renewal ceremony to me, I thought it might be, well, kind of . . . hokey. As it turned out, everybody was taking it quite seriously. There were tears in the eyes of some of the kids. Unexpectedly, I started to choke up too.

Ben gave a very honest and touching little talk, thanking us for remaining married. He told us that our example had been a strong influence in his life and in the lives of his siblings. Our marriage was an encouragement and would be a model for him when he found his wife. He wanted that future relationship to be like ours. Aaron shared his appreciation for our commitment in light of the marriages of many of his friends' parents that had not lasted. I kept swallowing hard and blinking rapidly.

This was far more than I had expected.

When they were done, we repeated the age-old vows that men and women have been saying to each other, at least in the western world, for hundreds of years. We repeated our pledge to remain wedded to each other and live together after God's ordinance in the holy estate of matrimony. To love each other, comfort, honor, and keep each other, for richer or poorer, in sickness and in health, and forsaking all others keep only unto the other as long as we both should live.

Those vows had always given me pause. As a youngster, I would sit on those slick, varnished pews and marvel at the loss of freedom that this guy was volunteering for. I'd shake my head in amazement: *That is an awfully definitive statement he's making. And I can't make out any possible loopholes.* (I was thinking like a lawyer, even back then.) But what especially struck me was not the richer or poorer part. Inevitably, what gave me pause was the promise of "forsaking all others." It was this little lance that burrowed into my skin and pricked me with niggling doubts: *How do you know she's worth giving up all your options for? Isn't it going to be pretty dull being locked in to one person in perpetuity—with no escape hatch? Is it worth it? What if you make a mistake? Does the benefit outweigh the loss? Geez, what a risk!*

I now tend to think these are the very kinds of sobering questions wedding vows ought to trigger in the uninitiated. This is one of the reasons why I wonder at the faddish wisdom of reconstructing (or deconstructing) them on a creative whim. Now, granted, Patty and I also crafted our own, but I was a (semi) trained professional. I had one year of seminary under my belt. I could be trusted with such a burden, or so I thought. Not everyone can.

After I met Patty, I underwent this radical lobotomy in which the bachelor-brain was wiped out and the marriage-brain was mysteriously downloaded. Making a vow of lifelong commitment to one person was the only thing that made sense. What I had experienced was what lovers of all ages, since naked Adam, have discovered: Married love is, at its core, exclusive. A marriage between a man and a woman is established on the essential covenant of exclusivity: "I forsake all others to be devoted to you alone for the rest of my life. I forgo all former or potential lovers, romantic interests, liaisons (actual or imagined) to love you and you only."

The marriage vow is a promise that ruthlessly puts to death every other rival. It places a symbol of mutual ownership on the fingers of two people who now have covenanted to belong to each other, categorically, exclusively. Wedded love is a jealous love, and rightfully so, for the beloved's love is not to be shared. The heart of the beloved is to be captivated exclusively by her lover. This, all of us who have been in love, understand. This is how romantic love works.

This is also how the divine love affair works.

» » »

After Yahweh comes riding in like a gallant knight in shining armor and rescues His fair, beloved Israel from the clutches of evil Pharaoh, He instructs His bride-to-be about her wedding vows. He tells her that, as His royal consort, from that time forward, she would make and repeat promises of fidelity to Him as her Royal Husband, Lover, and King. And He would pledge to her, in perpetuity, His faithful, loyal covenant love in return. The Hebrews called this _hesed_.

He tells her that she alone among all the nations of the earth has been chosen by Him to have and to hold; and unlike human love, this promise is not severable even by death. It is eternal.

> Know then that Yahweh your God is God indeed. The faithful God who is true to his covenant and his graciousness for a thousand generations toward those who love him and keep his commandments. (Deuteronomy 7:9)

Whereas the wedding rings we use today are a symbolic metaphor for the eternality of love, God's love is *actually* eternal. It will never end. Israel, however, is living in a thoroughly pagan, polytheistic culture. There are thousands of gods, of all kinds and shapes, for all purposes. And they are worshipped in a variety of ways. Many of these ways are overtly and explicitly sexual in nature. The pagan gods are manipulated by sexual intercourse between the devotees and their priests and priestesses. It is not surprising that the name Baal, one of the preeminent Near Eastern deities, also means husband.

In light of the multitude of pagan deities that the other nations are devoted to and that Israelites have themselves occasionally worshipped, Yahweh must draw a rigid line. He separates Himself from all the rest. He tells Israel that her wedding vows are being made to the one God, who alone is God. The vow has three parts.

The first part is, "Listen, Israel: Yahweh our God is the one Yahweh" (Deuteronomy 6:4).

The second part describes how she must respond to this One God who is Lord or Husband (*baal*). "You shall love Yahweh your God with all your heart, with all your soul, with all your strength" (6:5).

The third is a warning: "Do not follow other gods, gods of the peoples around you, for Yahweh your God who dwells among you is a jealous God; His anger could blaze out against you and wipe you from the face of the earth." (6:14-15).

In this wedding manual Moses is writing for the nation of Israel, he repeats three times that the God they married at Mt. Horeb is a jealous God. He demands and deserves exclusive love, exclusive loyalty, and exclusive obedience.

We intuitively understand what's going on here. Romantic love that leads to marital love is between one man and one woman. This is ingrained in our genetic structure. This is what Adam found out when he woke up from his little nap and saw that naked knockout looking down at him. Since that time, man and woman have pledged to forsake all others for the sake of the beloved. When we fall in love, we know that being unfaithful to our spouse is a violation of something fundamental to ourselves and to the way things are meant to work in the universe. In fact, the desire for exclusivity is usually one of the first signs that we are in love.

Quite unexpectedly, Patty felt the sharp, tiniest sting of this universal law on our first date. I suppose I could chalk this up to my utterly irresistible charm, but I suspect there is more to the story. In my early twenties when I met her for the first time, I was a conservative, though music-loving, chap. It was December. Sleigh bells were ringing and "White Christmas" was playing on all the radio stations in west Michigan. Actually, it was one of those dreadful, muddy-brown winter spells that afflict us here on occasion. There was no white for miles.

It was the season of Handel's *Messiah*, which has been sung by the Calvin College oratorio in Grand Rapids probably since the score was brought over on the Mayflower. No doubt, back then it was sung in Dutch by an all-blond choir. (I was not a student at the college. At that time, I was attending the rival Baptist seminary in town.) The *Messiah* happens to be my favorite cantata, so I asked Patty to accompany me for our first date.

Considering my level of shocking inexperience in matters of love and romance, we actually had a delightful first date. I recall learning a valuable but untimely dating lesson before arriving at the college chapel. It is not so smart to order French onion soup on your first go-round with a girl you're trying to impress. For most of you this is a no-brainer, as you would immediately recognize the relationship between onion and breath odor. However, as mentioned earlier, on top of my other afflictions, I am olfactorily challenged. So the obvious corollary implications of that menu selection escaped me.

But, the specific difficulty I encountered was dealing with the three-foot-long strands of melted Swiss cheese. What I found out too late was that it is virtually impossible to look cool while you are trying to nonchalantly sip from a spoon that trails yards of cheese behind it. Having been provided with no scissors, I had to use my fingers to pinch off the offending strings. Not the optimum in suave dinner etiquette.

The cantata proved to be a hit, though. I could tell Patty was becoming *interested*. Somehow one knows these things. I detected that my unexpected non-traditionalism was scoring points. Patty demonstrated surprising and impressive knowledge about the performers, commenting that there had been a change in soloists from an earlier performance the night before. At intermission we bumped into one of Patty's girlfriends, who was also there with a first date.

I have some kind of radar that, at times, picks up on odd signals.

It started pinging rapidly in my ear.

We were introduced awkwardly. The girls exchanged the oddest glances, and we moved on. I thought I could detect a blush on Patty's cheeks. But I didn't think much of it, since my concentration was taken up with the crucial final half of the date.

It wasn't till we were engaged that I was told the significance of that chance encounter. Apparently, the day after agreeing to go out with me, Patty had received a call from an old boyfriend. She had earlier decided not to see him again (almost), but when he called, uncertainty overcame reason and she agreed to go out with him — to the *Messiah* — the day before our date. As it happened, her girlfriend was also there on both nights with different young men as well.

The glance I had intercepted was saying, *Shhh! Pretend we haven't seen each other in weeks. I won't say anything if you won't!* That also helped explain Patty's casual comment about the different singers and her sudden stricken expression.

There was no valid reason for Patty to be ashamed about her minor lapse in judgment in going out with two different guys on separate nights. She barely knew me. There were no commitments. Except, as she would tell me later, during this date she had this surprising intuition that this time there was something very different (in a good way) about the young man she was with. The flag of exclusivity and commitment was imperceptibly inching its way up the mast, so she felt this niggling little feeling of guilt.

She did not know it, but she was beginning to fall in love. This mechanism is written into our genes. It is not something we learn. Romantic love is exclusive. Just read Yates or Keats or Browning. Or just read the Great Epic.

» » »

130

Jesus makes it clear to His disciples that He is not offering them a better alternative, a superior plan, or the best option out of the many. He is making a marriage proposal. He is offering to them and requesting from them the loyalty, fidelity, commitment, and devoted love that a bride promises to her groom. At the beginning of his itinerant ministry, John the Baptist makes this clear. He refers to Jesus as the Bridegroom and to himself as the groom's friend who rushes ahead to prepare the wedding banquet (John 3:28-29).

Like a proud Jewish *abba*, Jesus' Father personally selects the bride for His only Son (John 17:6) and negotiates the "dowry" price. In this instance, it was very steep—the lifeblood of His Son. In Jesus' day, after marriage negotiations were successfully concluded, the father would take a cup of wine and offer it to his son. The young man would then offer it hopefully to the maiden and say, "This cup I offer to you." With these words, he was making a formal engagement proposal, for what he meant was "I love you, and I offer you my life as symbolized by the wine. Will you take me as your husband?" If she accepted the cup from his hand and took a drink, she was saying, "I will. I accept your life and I give you mine. I will be your wife."

Jesus takes these well-understood cultural symbols and reinterprets them for His disciples at the Passover hours before His death, transforming their Last Supper into a prewedding banquet. Taking the third of the four cups of the seder meal (the cup of salvation), He offers it to them saying, "Take it, this is my blood ('my life') the blood of the covenant ('marriage oath') which is to be poured out for many" (Mark 14:24).

The disciples must have been shocked.

They understood exactly what Jesus was saying and what He was doing. He was offering them a proposal of marriage. In effect

He was telling them, "I love you as a groom loves his bride. I offer you my life. Will you join yourselves to me?" The disciples all took the cup and drank and by drinking were responding, "Yes, we accept your proposal. We love you too and will be devoted to you for life." This was a direct fulfillment of the prophecy made by Hosea that one day Israel would turn their backs on their foreign lovers and would proclaim their exclusive devotion to God. They would call Him "my husband." At that time, Yahweh would remove the names of His rivals from her lips forever (Hosea 2:17-19).

Before His death, Jesus confides in His Father that He wants the world to know that He loves His bride and wants her to be with Him "where I am so that they may always see the glory you have given me, because you loved me before the foundation of the world" (John 17:24). Just like a Jewish groom would, He tells them that He will be leaving to build a house for His Bride but will come back to take her to their new home (John 14:1-3). In the Epic's final chapter, we see that the Bridegroom kept His promise. The mansion and the Bride are made ready and live happily ever after (Revelation 21:2,9).[1]

God invented marriage to be a metaphor, a living symbol of the relationship of love, loyalty, and faithfulness between God and His people. Metaphors are like bungee cords. They stretch and bounce and are fun. When used off the tops of bridges, they let us cover a lot of territory safely. But when stretched too far, they do tend to snap. Similarly with the metaphor of marriage, while helpful in illustrating the exclusivity of devotion between the Lover and his Beloved, it doesn't help too much when talking about the exclusivity of spiritual options. It may even be misleading. That is why saying that Jesus is the best possible way to live is stretching a metaphor too far.[2] Neither Jesus, the Bridegroom, nor Yahweh, the Jealous Husband, present themselves as the best possible anything; they are the *only* viable, long-term life option. The choice is between Truth and falsehood, Reality and unrealities, Life or death. To speak of "best" can mislead.

In marrying me, Patty may have chosen badly. There may have been better men available had she been more patient. I was certainly not the only fish in the sea, and the best one may, in fact, have gotten away. She will never know. Having made her choice from the selection at hand, she pledged her undying love and forsook all other options.

» » »

All lovers believe that they have found the best of the best. Sometimes they are right, though statistics would indicate that more than half of the time they aren't.

In the spiritual realm, there are no other legitimate options, no selection among valid rivals. "Yahweh, your God is the One Yahweh" (Deuteronomy 6:24). For Israel and every nation, every people and tribe who would choose life in its fullness over life as emptiness and futility, there was only choice: Yawheh, who alone is God among the pantheon of fakes.

Israel needed to be reminded of this constantly. Time and again, the prophets would call her back to exclusive devotion to the only true God. The language they unashamedly use for God's reaction to their wandering eyes and hearts is that of the angry, jealous, jilted lover. This is what is known as anthropopathism—a high-brow word that means applying human emotions to God. This God rages, pleads, forgives, and takes back.

God is playing on our sympathy. He wants us any way He can get us.

What He is after is exclusive devotion, but unlike the human lover who needs the love of his beloved, God is pursuing us unselfishly. He has made us for Himself and He knows that all the other rivals are dead-ends. They are not only losers, they are killers. These others will not only steal affection, but will empty out the soul, leaving an empty shell behind. Every other "baal-husband" is really only a player who wants to take, and after taking will not be husband at all but "baal-master." These suave impostors promise freedom and wind up stealing innocence, joy, youth, and deliver slavery.

God yearns for the wholehearted love of His bride because He knows that this is the only place she will be fully free, fully alive, fully and intensely whole. He wants her love because she is made for His pleasure and to find her pleasure only in Him. Every other love is a fraud that will lead the beloved down a primrose path to disaster.

These frauds not only harm individual people, they also bring spiritual and physical plagues on nations. When these false gods gain mastery over a nation, there is no other recourse. It must all be eradicated. That is why the people of Israel had to place entire Canaanite cities "under the ban." This meant that every single human being living within the boundaries of the radioactivity of these seductive demon-lovers with bedroom eyes and razor teeth had to be destroyed (Deuteronomy 2:32-34; 3:6; 7:12).

These rivals were dangerous; they were rabid and impossibly toxic. So Israel must be reminded to have no other gods before her—ever. Yahweh is not the best possible God. He is the only God.

For her good, not His.

When Jesus comes on the scene, He makes similar categorical claims: Repent! Turn away from all empty and deceptive ways of living, break your engagement with every rival that wants to steal your heart and instead turn to Me. Believe on Me. "Unless you are born from above you can't see the kingdom of God" (John 3:3). "I tell you the truth, whoever listens to my word, and believes in the One who sent Me has eternal life, without being brought to judgment he has passed from death to life" (John 5:24). "Come to Me and take my yoke" (Matthew 11:29). "I am the Bread of Life" (John 6:35). "I am the Light of the world" (John 8:12). "I have told you already: You will die in your sins. Yes, if you do not believe that I am He, you will die in your sins" (John 8:24). "I am the Resurrection. If anyone believes in me, even though he dies he will live" (John 11:25).

Jesus was not making any new or startling claims. He was simply repeating the words His Father had spoken to His people hundreds of years earlier. Exactly like His dad did, He tells them unequivocally that the other possible roads are only a mirage. They appear to be shimmering pathways to paradise, but they are all superhighways to hell.

There is no other God but Yahweh, and Jesus is His only Son.

It is only His blood that provides the antidote for the fatal spiritual AIDS virus that the false lovers on silk sheets have infected His creatures with. As Saint Peter would later put it, speaking about Jesus, and he would get it exactly right, "For of all the names in the world given to men [of all possible paths to salvation] this is the only One by which we can be saved" (Acts 4:12). Saint James gives us the flip side of this truth when he writes about the intensity of God's exclusive love for us: "Surely you don't think Scripture is wrong when it says: the Spirit which He sent to live in us wants us for Himself alone?" (4:5).

» » »

In my last year of college, before I met Patty, I fell in love, but it was not with a girl. Strange as it may sound, I become infatuated with a theological perspective about God. I was taken over by the beauty, the symmetry, the cadence, and the majesty of Reformed theology.

I became a Calvinist.

Back in the day, there was this big debate between Arminians and Calvinists: Is man radically free in his decision to come to Jesus (Arminianism) or does God sovereignly and ultimately control that choice, yet without violating man's freedom (Calvinism). My college was Arminian, though my philosophy professor wasn't. Being a rebel, a tad elitist, and of a philosophic bent, I opted for door number two.

I may have had some invalid reasons as a youth, but I tend to think door two is still by far the most solid and biblically honest and gives the most complete answer to a most complex and vexing question. I like what C. S. Lewis says somewhere: If you are raising questions about a reality that is messy and complicated, it stands to reason the answers will be too. Today, the argument is surfacing again, but it's now called Open Theism: for man to be truly free, the argument runs, God cannot know in advance what these moral agents will choose to do. This frees Him from being responsible for the bad things that occur in the world.[3]

It also makes Him massively ignorant.

I'm not convinced by this new slant on covering for God. I do not think that we solve the paradox of God and man by making God less so we can make man more. If we are reading the Epic with both eyes wide open and are able to see and hear in stereo, we know that any answer that gives God a lobotomy or cuts off His right arm to ensure man can still claim "freedom" just quite won't do.

In my twenties I became a Reformed Baptist and began reading lots of books published by Banner of Truth Trust, a publishing house specializing in Puritan reprints. And I began reading their flagship newspaper. It was called the *Sword and Trowel*. Its name was taken from the book of Nehemiah, where the Jewish remnant are rebuilding the wall around Jerusalem after returning from exile. Their enemies begin threatening to attack, so Nehemiah has the workers strap on a sword even while going about the task of cementing the stone blocks in place. The threat is so intense that some even have a sword in one hand while carrying their tool of choice in the other (4:17-18).

Sword and Trowel was a good paper. It featured many quotes from Jonathan Edwards, one of my heroes. But I stopped reading it during my first year of seminary when I decided I had to exit stage right. It wasn't the theology exactly that turned me away, nor the not-so-subtle tendency to legalism, though that might have done it eventually after the eighty-minute sermons started to get old.

What did it for me was a conversation I overheard in a bathroom.

It was Bible conference week. An old, godly, and much-loved pastor was speaking. He was highly respected in Baptist circles, not only for his ability to teach the Bible but for His character and humility. I should be such a nice person. It was lunch break, and I was washing my hands in the bathroom. With me were two other men, perhaps just a bit older than I. They were talking loudly to each other, so I could hear easily. They apparently did not care.

They were discussing the message they had just heard and were not hiding their scorn. The smug superiority in their tone made me feel queasy. I wanted to slap the one standing near me and tell him to show a little respect.

By the jargon and insider language, I could tell immediately they were a part of my camp.

"Guess what?" the one said, a little sneer in his voice. "How many theological errors do you think I counted in the pastor's sermon?"

"How many?" asked his hand-washing brother.

"Thirty-six!" was the triumphant retort.

"Really?" responded the other rather dryly, as if asking, *What else would you would expect from a stupid Arminian?*

Apparently, I was listening in on the conversation of the self-appointed Puritan Reformed Purity Police.

I left the men's room feeling not so much angry as sick. Neither did I feel like pointing the finger at those two self-righteous, avowed neo-Puritans. I was embarrassed for *me*—and just a little ill. I had just overheard others saying out loud what I had, on other occasions, only thought. What almost floored me was the realization that I had just gotten a little preview of coming unattractions should I keep heading in the same direction.

I didn't so much change my theology as my theological context.

» » »

Though that Reformed Baptist paper may have had flaws, its title was exactly right. The editors understood that reality is not flat or simple. They were refusing to accept either the modern or the postmodern dichotomies: Jesus is either tolerant and inclusive, or intolerant and exclusive; Jesus either came making peace or making war; Jesus wants His followers to embrace the good of creation and culture or be antagonistic to it.[4]

Either He carried a sword *or* a trowel.

The editors of that paper understood what Nehemiah did. We live in this world where there is danger and beauty all around. There is evil and goodness everywhere you look. In the most unexpected places, there can be beauty — occasionally even captured by correspondents in stark black-and-white photographs of war's aftermath. Our paradoxical reality is such that in the middle of war there can be peace and light and heroism — and in the peace, there can be unimaginable ugliness, depravity, and brutal selfishness. Christians don't have the luxury of choosing whether to carry a sword or a shovel. They have to have both very near at hand. That is why the Jesus presented to us in the Gospels cuts and heals, tears down and builds up, screams out and dances in joy.

This is not schizophrenia.

Jesus is reflecting true reality.

He knows that He is in hostile territory taken over and desecrated by His enemy, Satan. All creation is under a death curse. Humans have been hacked off the tree of life and expelled from the Garden. They have been tossed out from the center of reality, the core of existence where they were meant to be at home and are wandering aimlessly in empty and monotonous cycles of meaninglessness. Mankind has sided with the usurper who has declared war on the rightful king. Those who support the perverted power structure are under the delusion that they are protecting their own freedoms. Like the slaves who fought for the South, they are fighting to save their own way of life, not knowing that what they really are dying for is to ensure their continued and permanent bondage.

Jesus shows up in the middle of a war zone.

He has not entered a political convention or spiritual retreat or self-help seminar. He is in a free-fire zone. He has come to destroy His enemy. He is a realist; He has no illusions. He knows that the battle will cost Him His life. But He also knows that this terrible, inconceivably brilliant strategy will be the means of routing His foe and liberating millions of captives.

Jesus came as a Spartacus, proclaiming freedom for the slaves. He came to resist the slave culture, to expose its deceptive claims, and to lead a massive insurrection that would bring true freedom. Unlike the mythological figure, He will be astonishingly successful.

So He comes with a sword.

He also came to build a massive underground railroad on which the released captives can make good their escape from their wicked masters. It would have to be long and costly and durable; it had to last thousands of years.

So He also carries a shovel—as well as a pick, and a sledgehammer, and had they been invented, he would be driving one of those front-end loaders with thirty-foot wheels.

And all of these would have been in the shape of a cross.

There will only be one Freedom Road, but the Enemy is devious. He is a master of deception and has built many alternative routes. Like the British OSS constructing false armies to confuse the Germans about the Allied invasion, he has built a host of bogus trails. His intention is not only to deceive but to kill.

He's very good at what he does—all these counterfeits look amazingly authentic. However, they all lead inevitably back to captivity.

That is why Jesus sometimes speaks in such severe, definitive, and even harsh tones. He is on a rescue mission, not a political campaign, and the lives of multitudes are on the line.

At the heart, what it basically comes down to is rivalry. There is the passionate, faithful Bridegroom and then there is the father of murder and lies. One is the Creator and the other is a finite creature. It is the finite who is in competition with the infinite. So this is not ultimately about opposing ways or systems or ideas. The conflict is not so much over propositions to be believed as it is over the questions, who will we love and who will we serve?

There is a person who demands, deserves, and elicits love. He is a winsome, wooing warrior who fights for His bride with His last ounce of blood. He is a royal husband pledging His undying, ferocious covenant love. And He is a persistent lover who yearns for the exclusive devotion of His beloved.

We were designed for One Lover. We can only serve (or love) God or money (Matthew 6:24). And here is where Bob Dylan hits it out of the park in his song, "You've Got to Serve Somebody." In hoarse tones he says that we've either got to serve the Devil or the Lord. It's going to be one or the other, for the truth of it is, we've got to serve somebody. Bob knows best. There are lots of masters and substitutes, but they are all impostors. Jesus is the one and only true and real thing—only He is the lover of our souls. Only He is the Lord. Those are His words.

He—is the Way.

He—is Truth.

He—is our One True Love.

Blessing

May you find Him whom to know is to love.
May He kiss you with the kisses of His mouth
and may you find His love sweeter than wine.
May you hear Him say,
"How beautiful you are, my Beloved, and how delightful!"
May you enter the holy and joyful wedding chamber
and say, "My Beloved is mine and I am His."

May you see what He sees (in you)
and listen to what He declares (over you):
"You ravish my heart, my sister, my promised bride.
You ravish my heart with a single one of your glances."
So may you open the gate of your secret garden and welcome
Him in.
May you set Him like a seal on your heart,
a sign of exclusive devotion and undying commitment.
For His love is strong as death,
and His jealousy is as relentless as Sheol.
The heat of it is like a flame of Yahweh Himself.
May you rest in the arms of your faithful Lover
And forsaking all other untruthful rivals
May you keep only unto Him forever and forever.

8

WARRIOR FOR JUSTICE AND RIGHTEOUSNESS

I grew up with this amazing, towering orange canvas tent in my backyard. It was the official Barnum & Bailey Circus-approved size. Its middle post was easily thirty-feet high and nine-inches in diameter, weighing as much as a small elephant. It required the help of a pickup truck to pull erect, while six brave men would wrap their arms around the bottom to keep it in place as a long rope attached to the bumper lifted the pole over their heads. It was a most impressive sight for a six-year-old. I was never allowed to lend a hand.

Two other lesser posts, perhaps twenty-feet high, held up the opposite ends of the tent. There must have been at least forty six-foot posts around the circumference that I could assist with. Ropes the width of my index finger would be looped over the metal shaft at the ends of the posts that protruded from large grommets in the edges of the canvas. The rope's end would be staked to the ground. Two stakes per post. I could hold the ropes to keep them taut. What I really wanted to do was swing the small sledgehammer.

The tent was not up all year-round. It came out only to dry and air out at the beginning of the evangelistic meeting season. My father was part of a traveling band of missionaries who roamed the length and height of Chile in the early sixties. One of the men played a variety of musical instruments, including trombone, electric accordion, and guitar. Another played a mean trumpet. All of them sang. It was the era of the male quartet, and my dad was the tenor.

In South America, televisions were only within the reach of the upper 2 percent. The evangelists had little trouble gathering a crowd. The season for tent meetings lasted much of the year. My dad was gone a lot.

Each campaign would last for a week at a time. The band traveled as far south as Tierra del Fuego, which is about as far as you can go without dropping off into the Straits of Magellan and hitting your head on Antarctica. They would also travel north till they ran into the Atacama Desert, the hottest desert in the world. Or so I was told. Chile is a very long country.

My mother remembers that during one twelve-month season, my father was home only five weekends. It was also the era in which missionaries were instructed to burn out for Jesus. My father did not, but my mother—perfectionist, overachiever, rookie missionary, learning to speak Spanish, with four little boys at home—nearly did.

The priority of life was simple and straightforward. If missionary efforts had slogans like presidential campaigns, theirs would have been, "It's About Souls, Stupid!" The emphasis was on salvation because people were lost and were in jeopardy of a Christless eternity.

The imperative was clear. Jesus had sent my dad and mom on a mission, like Jesus, to seek and save the lost.

Around forty years later, I do not have great cause to criticize or critique. I honor the commitment, compassion, and single-mindedness. I wish I felt a little more of that urgency and dedication to verbally share about Jesus. I don't believe I have any basis to point a mocking, supercilious finger at their evangelistic zeal. I happen to think that Jesus Himself was pretty insistent and had what might be called a rather fundamentalist conversional agenda. After all, He did start out of the blocks on His own three-year campaign challenging all his hearers to repent. He came trumpeting the inauguration of the Kingdom of God and calling for everyone to throw aside old loyalties and be "born again," "believe in Me," "take up the cross and follow Me," and become loyal subjects of the True King. So I do not feel any compulsion to ridicule or deprecate.

Still, I believe the evangelical missionary band of brothers missed, not the boat necessarily, but a big point.

Baptist missionaries did not ignore the physical needs of the poor—completely. When the massive earthquake hit southern Chile in 1960, my dad and his friends rushed in to help. It was devastating. It reached an 8.5 on the Richter scale. The plates shifted so dramatically that my father recalls seeing houses whose door handles had slid down to street level. For a while, a storeroom at our missionary compound was filled with hundred-pound white paper bags filled with dried milk and burlap bags filled with corn meal. These were to be distributed among the thousands who'd lost everything.

Word began filtering out through the missionary grapevine that Bill Stoner was getting involved with the social gospel. There was also this nagging concern that free food would turn impoverished Chileans into what were known as "rice Christians": commitments to Jesus as merely verbalized ploys to obtain more food. How much worse, I now wonder, is that motivation than making a decision just to get out of hell, or debt—get prosperous so I can afford that new Beemer? I suppose we could call these "hell Christians" or "prosperity Christians." How about hell and wealth Christians?

Baptist missions in the sixties and seventies had very little room, time, or energy for issues of justice and mercy. At least the ones I knew of. Those were the hot buttons liberals were fulminating over, and then later what anti-establishment (rebellious and long-haired), marijuana-smoking hippies were railing on about. While I avoided the grass, my brothers and I did succumb to the long hair, which caused my parents no end of misery from the fundamentalist brethren. My father and mother somehow had the sagacity to recognize that simply because our hair hung well over our ears, we were not thereby condemned to burn in the nether regions. So they opted to let sleeping dogs lie.

It did, however, become an issue one furlough. My younger brother was forced to go to the barber so his ears could be properly exposed before being allowed entrance at the summer Bible camp.

That still rankles a bit.

You just don't mess with people's hair.

Everybody knows that.

When we moved to Spain in 1969, the year after dictator-for-life Francisco Franco opened the doors to non-Catholic missionaries, there was another reason to resist the biblical imperative of justice. We were in an aggressively adversarial relationship with the Catholic Church. Spain was one of the most devoted Roman Catholic countries on the globe. Mariolatry, medieval superstitions, and a touch of fanaticism were rampant. After all, the Inquisition was born, incubated, and flourished in that lovely land. It got its jumpstart with Torquemada in 1478 and terrorized the Catholic and non-Catholic worlds into the nineteenth century.

Old habits die hard.

The landscape was dotted with sites purporting to hold magical splinters and nails of the cross, miraculous dolls and bones from the bodies of multitudes of saints. The land teemed with religious fervor and mysticism. It also was devoted to the pre-Reformation doctrine of salvation by good works. The majority opinion among Spaniards was that entrance into heaven was only assured if, on the divine scales, the good you did outweighed the bad. So you did good stuff hoping against hope that it would cover up the bad stuff. But you never knew for sure—until it was too late. Guilt and fear were ubiquitous.

"Good works" was a filthy, rotten phrase because it obliterated faith in the work of Jesus.

And speaking of dirty words, there was another one: *Protestant*. My dad and his hardy band transplanted themselves to the Basque country in northern Spain; they often set up book-and-tract tables at the local flea markets. It was a (highly) religiously conservative area. When the curious asked who they were, the standard response, before they knew better, was "Protestants." There was an instantaneous recoil. Shock would fill the lined faces of the rugged men in black berets, and they would turn away shaking their heads, muttering to each other, "Protestants! That's some kind of criminal, isn't it?"

The local security police, the feared Guardia Civil, whom Hemingway made infamous in *For Whom the Bell Tolls*, got into the act. (They wore the strangest polished-black-hats-with upturned brims one can imagine. Because of their headgear, I had a hard time taking them seriously. The submachine guns they held in their arms like lovers were a different matter.) Informers had leaked the presence of a cabal of Baptists and so they were hauled in for questioning at the police station. Phone calls were made, and when it was clear there were no longer any legal grounds to hold them, they were grudgingly released to continue peddling nefarious Protestant propaganda. But the black-hatted goons still kept hostile (and very obvious) eye on the intruders.

The intensity of the conflict was brought home to me when, a few years later, I was told about Carmelita. We were now living in the quaint white-washed and red-clay roofed town of Garrapinillos on the outskirts of Zaragoza, a city on the northeast diagonal between Madrid and Barcelona. There was a small group of Protestants who had begun to gather in our garage. Our two-story white stucco house, a converted livery, was near the central plaza dominated by the imposing Catholic church. The priest had gotten his fill of the American heretics and their proclamation of salvation by faith alone, their lack of reverence for the Virgin Mary, their denial of the Immaculate Conception (Mary was sinless), and their disregard for the saints. He began preaching rather vehemently against my parents and the religious and moral turpitude they represented.

One of the families who were members of our small Baptist church had several children who also attended the local Catholic school. When the priest found out that some of his pupils were being swayed by the Americans, he became incensed. He threatened the children with expulsion. When the parents declined the demand to immediately cease and desist fraternizing with the heretics, the priest decided to make an example of their oldest. She was told to go into the sanctuary and atone for her sins by licking a cross in the dirty floor of the church. On her hands and knees, Carmelita was forced to comply.

So I grew up with little respect for Catholic hierarchy and their doctrines—particularly their teaching about good works. As far as I was concerned, this was nothing more than a blatant rejection of the perfect work of Jesus in favor of imperfect human efforts to gain salvation.

» » »

After attending a good Baptist university, I went to a solid, approved Baptist seminary. Somehow, I got my hands on *Sojourners* magazine (published by leftist Christians caring for the poor in Washington, DC), which led me down the slippery slope of liberation theology. I began reading books written by highly articulate and angry Central and South American priests and ex-priests that were way outside the required seminary book list. My eyes were opened to an economic, social, and biblical critique of western-colonial, conservative Christianity.

And I was appalled.

I had lived in South America, one of the hotbeds of this movement. What I thought I knew was being brought into question. We left Chile right before this awful Communist named Allende made a run for the presidency. He was elected in 1970 on a platform to redistribute the wealth and nationalize the copper industry. At that time, 2 percent of the population owned 46 percent of the wealth. I had been told by my betters that redistributing money was an awful thing to do. Investors and owners and businessmen—nice, law-abiding capitalists—would lose lots of capital. All I knew was that three years later, because of the chaotic economy (proof that Communists wreck efficient capitalist economies), the Chilean military launched a coup. On September 11, 1973, Salvador Allende, to avoid capture, took his own life in the presidential palace.

Years later, as I looked back on all that, I was not so sure that what I had been told was anywhere near the truth. As I read a little more broadly, what I had been fed was no longer adding up. What it came down to is that I had to come to grips with the fact that I, and many others, too, had been lied to. As I read about my country's interventions in smaller countries south of the border during my happy and innocent childhood years in Chile, I came face to face with undeniable evidence of our complicity with some pretty horrific regimes. And just the opposite of what I had been raised to believe, the impetus behind most of these "limited military excursions" was not national security, but *economic* security. Captain America was not so much about truth and justice after all, but good, stable returns on investment.

Greed, not righteousness, seemed to be the compelling motive.

My cocoon of blissful ignorance was pierced. The shroud of national righteousness was shredded. The United States was in the business of propping up, bringing down, and manipulating governments and would-be governments for the sake of our economic well-being and the stockholders of multinationals who controlled economies to the south.[1]

Later I came to see that there are nuances and it is not a purely black-and-white issue. While I regained some respect, I did permanently stop swearing allegiance to the flag. (I decided to follow the example of the early Christians who refused, even on pain of death, to swear loyalty to any leader or nation other than Lord Jesus.)[2] There are plenty of demons to go around, but the essential point about our national economic selfishness —

our obsessive self-interest — stands.

Liberation theology opened my eyes and ears to the cry from the margins. I began to hear the screams of the weak and the oppressed, and I began to rethink what the Bible had to say about good works. I had to reconsider my prejudice against matters of justice and the social gospel. This forced me to take another look at Jesus.

I reread the Gospels, but this time with an eye attuned to those on the lower rungs of society's ladder. I began to recognize that Jesus was not Savior only, but also a revolutionary. Since I was also tracking with Mennonite-pacifist scholar John Howard Yoder and others critiquing our will to power, I was kept from falling into the hands of the radical Marxist, gun-wielding, grenade-tossing crowd.[3] It seemed obvious to me that the biblical option for the poor did not include killing the oppressor in the name of Jesus. But neither did it mean blessing or sanctioning or enabling the oppressor and his oppression. It also could not mean pretending it is of no consequence simply because the injustice is occurring far from my safe suburban neighborhood and I can't hear the screams over the lawnmower or the football game on TV.

It's not like I changed all of a sudden and went out to the backyard to burn my draft card (there was no longer a draft, and I was too old anyway), plant an organic garden, or stop eating steak. I didn't even switch political parties. Not that I wasn't tempted on many an occasion. (It's difficult — one side sees beauty in fifty-six baggies of multicolored urine and a mural of Mother Mary with shellacked elephant dung,[4] while the other sees it in burning mosques. While one favors killing the unborn, the other favors doing in the born. I guess, at present, I have to side with the most obviously innocent and defenseless. I know this is all a gross over-simplification, but how else can one make a choice between evils?

It's very possible that Jesus wouldn't vote at all. He advocated paying taxes—that seems to be about the extent of His commitment to good citizenship.)

More than anything, I probably disconnected from emotional investment in our nation (as in its politics and propaganda) and began to align myself more consciously with the kingdom of God.[5] We sponsored a child through Compassion International, and my wife and I started a "mustard seed conspiracy": we began a little neighborhood Christmas outreach.[6]

For many in our church, it became the highlight of the year.

Due to my administratively brilliant wife, this event grew into a delightful, finely tuned, efficient, joyful extravaganza that provided Christmas gifts to more than fifty of the poorest families in our town. At its height, there were more than two hundred children receiving presents. We would take large bags that were coded for specific houses, filled with age and gender-specific gifts, personally labeled. These would be distributed among the excited youngsters in the group. Gathering in a clump outside the front door, we would sing carols until shy heads began popping out from windows and doors. After handing out the gifts, we exited singing "We Wish You a Merry Christmas" to single parents restraining their children from tearing open their unexpected bounty.

The hundred volunteers would gather back at church for hot chocolate and cookies. It didn't radically change the world, but it did bless a lot of little children and a whole passel of middle-class white folks who got to reach out beyond their homogenous circle of safety and comfort.

Nine years later in 2000 at a new church, we were ready to be pushed off the continent with a self-contained band of intrepids to help rebuild a flooded orphanage and hang out with a bunch of

African children. That is where *orphan* became more than a word. That is where we met Bentu, who would become our son eighteen months later. And that is where I discovered that the pain of abandonment runs very deep and can afflict us profoundly, despite having an intact nuclear family.

That is what drove me to look at the Jewish Scriptures with eyes trained on issues of justice. Because of our exposure to the orphan crisis, I wanted to prepare an essay focusing on the issue of the fatherless. I visited every biblical text on the issue and titled it "A Cry for Justice." It wound up becoming an extended meditation on the Bible's emphatic challenge to the church to administer justice by caring for orphans in their distress.[7]

Not too long thereafter, God also turned it around on me and used it to call my bluff. It became evident that I had to do more than merely adopt or help others adopt. I needed to become more concretely involved in obeying the imperative to care for orphans in their distress.

As I mentioned in chapter 5, I visited Guatemala in 2005 with the intent to investigate the possibility of establishing relationships to facilitate adoptions at a greatly reduced rate. Very quickly we were made aware of the pervasive corruption of the adoption enterprise. After coffee, babies are Guatemala's second largest export, after coffee. The clever and unscrupulous have developed a virtual infant monopoly. Baby brokers scour the country, seeking poor women who are willing to sell their babies for a year's salary. The entire system is geared to the high-end baby market. The end result is that if you are an orphan over two or three years old, you probably have no chance of finding a home.

We visited five orphanages and found them filled with older orphans chronologically shut out of the adoption stream. The door of hope was barred to them. One of our visits was to Casa

Ayau, a marvelous Greek Orthodox orphanage in the center of the capital. Sister Ivone, a gracious nun in gray tunic and distinctive ancient black headgear, led us to two large, brightly painted baby rooms filled with cribs. They were all empty. When asked why, she told us that because they had refused to pay bribes for the infants, Casa Ayau had been shut out of the infant supply chain. We left seething.

This gross injustice and abuse drove us to do something more. That's why two of my friends and I felt obliged to form an advocacy organization called Orphan Justice Mission.[8] It became an official 501(c)(3) in early 2006.

What was wrong with the evangelistic model I grew up in was not, of course, that it cared about souls. The problem was that it acted as though souls were not encased in bodies. It misunderstood or misconstrued the message of Jesus to say that He came seeking to save the inside of man and ensure that the interior soul was eternally safe. It closed its eyes to the physical component of Jesus' ministry, reinterpreting it as merely a device to grab the attention of those attending His evangelistic crusades.

Salvation was about the invisible not the visible. It was about the immaterial spirit of man, not the material creation of God.

The priority was life in the great by-and-by, not life here and now.

For me, growing up Baptist, missions was about righteousness not justice.

To be fair, it wasn't that those fundamentalist preachers I grew up listening to disagreed with the need to show compassion to the fatherless. Many orphanages and hospitals had, in fact, been set up by their missionaries. It just did not fit very well into their theological system. It was mostly blocked out by their assumptions about Christian ethics and the mission of Jesus. When they read the Bible, they could not see what was right there in front of them.

Such is the danger of assumptions, presuppositions, and controlling points of view, especially when they are religious.

Such is the power of paradigm. This is the frightening unconscious effect of believing you know. I went to a Baptist university and seminary. I have read the Bible straight through from cover to cover at least fifteen times, in a variety of versions. I'm sure I've heard more than five thousand sermons from pulpits on several continents. Yet I was absolutely convinced Jesus wanted us to win souls, not ease the orphan's distress. I believed that Jesus handed over to His friends a spiritual, not a social, gospel.

My paradigm put blinders on me. Whereas I was pretty clear on the one passage admonishing the wife to submit to her husband, I somehow missed all forty-five references addressing the mandate for orphan justice.

We all need to watch out for those glasses that block not only the glare but the sun itself.

» » »

I decided to reread what the Bible had to say about good works. For an anti-Catholic-biased Baptist boy, that is a dangerous thing to do. I began to read with new eyes the words of the prophets expressing God's repugnance for their religious acts of devotion devoid of mercy. What I had read around and over was now suddenly right in my face. Jesus was not impressed by religious activity, tithing, ritual, or religious rule keeping. What He cared much more about ("the weightier matters of the law") were matters of "justice and mercy and good faith" (Matthew 23:23). Having consistent "personal devotions" didn't even make the list.

Then I had to confront the unavoidable: Jesus' description of the End Times judgment. Jesus is telling us *sola fide* (faith alone) types, and everyone else who cares to listen in, that at the end of the day there is going to be an entrance exam. But kind Rabbi that He is, He is giving us the question and the acceptable answer ahead of time. What I had to face up to was that this examination will not be like a religious MENSA exam, evaluating my spiritual IQ or a doctrinal exam to test my theological competence. It will be about one thing: works. "Did you give Me —hidden among the poor, the hungry, the orphan— a cup of water, a plate of spaghetti, a pair of new pants or one of your designer coats? Did you welcome her in and give her not only a warm place to sleep but a safe place to belong?" (Matthew 25:31-46).

The ultimate separation (and there is that awkward issue of division again) is based on what we did or did not do. Reward or punishment is levied based on whether (in prophetic language) we walked with humility before our God by displaying justice and mercy (Micah 6:8) or (in apostolic language) on whether we demonstrated authentic religion by taking care of orphans and widows in their distress (James 1:27). Insofar as we neglected to do this, we consign ourselves to eternal punishment (Matthew 25:46).

Apparently, for Jesus—no works, no heaven. These are categorical and very inflexible statements, but they are the words of the Messiah and His friends, not mine. I grant you, this is not such an easy thing for someone like me to swallow.

The final question is, "Did you demonstrate your love and loyalty to me by doing the things I did and commanded you to do?" Not, "Did you believe in my deity or in the inerrancy of the original documents?" If our final answer is, "I believed what I learned in Catechism, that there is one God," according to James, the brother of Jesus, that will trigger a second, more intrusive question, "How can that type of faith by itself possibly save you?

What good was your faith to anyone?" (James 2:16). The final conclusion will then be, since good works did not go along with your faith, it is worthless and dead. The demons believe what you believe, and they at least have the good sense to tremble. For clearly, "a person is justified by what he does and not by faith alone" (2:19,24, NIV).

Where I and some of my early mentors had it wrong was in believing that Jesus came with a catechism to memorize and a text to be studied rather than a costly, sacrificial, compassionate way of life to emulate. We got it wrong; we were convinced that the entrance exam was filled with complicated true-false questions testing our knowledge base, not a simple essay inquiring about our actions of love and obedience born out of heartfelt gratitude.

But here a qualifier is required. In their overreaction to the evangelical dismissal of works and its imbalanced fixation on sexual sin, some are dangerously close to concluding that the only thing that really matters is justice. They are proposing another false antithesis. It is not about cognitive and moral rightness at all, it would seem, but about deeds. It's not what you have in your head or heart, necessarily, but what you do with your hands. This is understandable, but it is also wrong.[9]

James grew up with Jesus and had his ears carefully tuned to the Jewish drumbeat on social righteousness. He brings both ends of the poles together: "Pure, unspoiled religion, in the eyes of God our Father is this: coming to the help of orphans and widows when they need it [justice], and keeping oneself uncontaminated by the world [righteousness]" (1:27). James does not believe that the one must choose between these two supposedly mutually exclusive options.

Jesus was the Water of Life. He came to satisfy the thirst of the parched and the desperately dry. He also came to fill up His followers with this water. It was His intent that they become like Him, life-giving streams burbling up and pouring out and giving cold cups of living water to the needy (John 7:37-38).

Sadly, most opt to remain large, placid reservoirs.

James understood something crucially important about works. When it comes to being a person whose life is a percolating artesian spring flowing with humble obedience and compassionate service to the needy, inner contamination can pollute the life-giving water and completely clog the channel through which it is meant to flow. Unrighteousness dams up the river, turning it inward into a fetid pool centered on the self and its needs and desires. Righteousness is meant to unclog the heart and open the sluice gates, letting the pure waters of justice and mercy flow. Which is why he ties together orphan care and inner pollution.

"But let justice flow like water *and* integrity like an unfailing stream" (Amos 5:24) is one of the best known and strongest prophetic slogans for social activism. What many today don't see is that it works equally well as a slogan for moral activism.[10] Amos thunders that judgment is coming on Israel because she denies justice to the poor and because father and son frequent strip clubs together (Amos 2:7). Apparently, God cares about the boardroom and the bedroom.

The world (inside or outside the church) can contaminate with the message that it is ultimately about me, satisfying my needs, or saving my butt. That will stop the flow of justice dead in its tracks. But there is an even more subtle way in which pollution works hand in glove with narcissism: Guilt over our sin twists the channel into a labyrinth of self-loathing or condemnation or excessive introspection.

Shame stops the flow too.

Both righteousness and justice, we are told, are the stable

foundations of His throne (Psalm 89:14). And both are absolutely required to climb the mountain of Yahweh, to enter into the mystery of God Himself. The psalmist asks who can climb and stand in His holy place. The answer: "He whose hands are clean [free from passive and active injustice] and whose heart is pure [committed to a righteous life]" (24:3-4). Loving God with our whole heart has to do with personal *and* social righteousness. It has to do with the internal and the external. Jesus is so committed to this that when He returns, He has this fiery sword and this thunderously stunning new name. This rider on the white horse is called "Faithful and True, A Judge with Integrity (righteousness) a Warrior for Justice" (Revelation 19:11).

God cares about both.

Which is why I have to repent a lot about what I do and what I don't do.

Which is also why I am involved in an orphan justice organization — not due to compassion only, but for the sake of my soul.

Blessing

May you find your life in losing it.
May you live your life by dying, daily.
May you give it all and keep nothing for yourself.
May your treasure chest be filled to overflowing
with the priceless crowns of sacrificial devotion.
May you give yourself away
in a joyful and risky abandon.
May you follow the Lamb,
even if He takes you up a hill and onto a brutal cross.
Especially if He takes you there.

*May you turn your back on safety and comfort and
predictable and soft
and pour yourself out like a drink offering of love
on the least of these, on the most of these,
for the death and the life of these.
May you spend what you cannot keep
to gain what you can never lose.
May you awake to live His dream,
not yours or your country's, nor your family's.
And may you rejoice to hear the applause,
which is a weight of eternal glory
too heavy to bear.*

9

SERVANTS OF THE GLORY, PART ONE

My early years did not provide the most fertile environment for nurturing a would-be writer. After all, I was raised in one of evangelicalism's most conservative separatist tributaries. And I was reared by missionary parents devoted to planting Baptist churches in Catholic countries.

Some of you may know what it is like to grow up knowing that there is really only one way to justify your existence. In our family's paradigm, devoting your life to "overseas" missionary work was the only justifiable vocational option. Nothing else would make the cut, not by a mile. Along with sips of *yerba maté* (drunk out of a round gourd with a metal straw, or *bombilla*), we imbibed the unspoken message that every other road that diverged in the yellow wood was a path away from true north, a cop-out, a bit of a failure. If you wanted to truly serve God, there was only one thing you could do.

I don't want to give the wrong impression. My parents weren't the stereotypical fifties fundamentalist missionaries—a fact for which I heartily and frequently give thanks to God out loud. It matters not if it's at the grocery store, at Barnes and Noble, or waiting to receive my speeding ticket from the officer, who is just doing his job. I am a very appreciative man. So I have no real anger issues. No inner hostilities. No compulsions to mock colleges with dress codes and music codes and hair codes and movie codes and poker codes and code codes. I am sane and quite happy and not bitter.

I most emphatically do not feel compelled to stock my refrigerator with twelve-packs of Pabst Blue Ribbon and smoke Marlboros just to make a point. So graciously, room was made by my parents (with just that microscopic inflection of regret) for other career options. On the scale of vocational choices, art scored around a 2.5 with 100 being at the spiritual summit. If I recall, repossessing vehicles from trailer trash was just below artist. And below that was acting, which was right above the bottom dweller of all careers—producing "Hollywood movies." That my oldest child, Jonathan, wants to do that very thing is just an absolute, utterly insane coincidence. It may also be incontrovertible evidence that the Maker of the Universe likes the occasional inside joke.

It would be only fair, at this point, to own up to my influence in this career choice, though it was no doubt only subliminal. Movies and me go back a long way. It is due to movies that my shelf-life may have been significantly shortened. It has to do with the effects of dread drawn out and heightened to an impossibly high pitch. Like a Spanish butcher's blade slicing off a slab of premium ham, this shaved off a good year or two.

My father was helping a missionary lady who was living alone in the Chilean backwaters of Maipu. She was trying to start a church. Do not ask me why this single female missionary was "church-planting" on her own in the heart of Chile, in light of the denomination's emphatic prohibition against women preaching or pastoring. This is one of life's great mysteries.

My brother David was ten and I was nine. At that age our patience was shorter than our hair. We grew disinterested very quickly with the interminable conversations after the Sunday meal. As quickly as we possibly could, we would skip out to go mix it up with the locals. It was a dusty town that would have made a perfect backdrop for a Clint Eastwood spaghetti western. It had its bars and something better: a movie theater.

We were raised to believe that beer-drinking, smoking, and what occurred inside a bordello (though we had no clue what it might be) were on the same level as setting foot inside a theater. Murder and movie attendance were sinful kissing cousins. Hollywood was a very brief way-station on the path to hell.

Our friends at school took undisguised pleasure in regaling us with what they'd seen. It sounded like the most incredible fun and greatest excitement one could possibly conceive.

We were helplessly, hopelessly intrigued.

We had to take a bite of that luscious, heart-pounding red fruit.

Even at the peril of our mortal souls.

So as my parents engaged in long, meandering missionary conversations in the cool interior of the kind lady's house, David and I slipped into the quiet confines of another cool interior altogether. We saw a number of shows and never paid a thin centavo. Our method was quite simple and relied exclusively on the kindness of a stranger. It worked like a charm.

The dirty street urchins and two little gringos would sit on the curb facing the theater's entrance, which was plastered with garish, melodramatic posters. We stared pathetically across the unpaved street, our eyes limpid pools of misery. Inevitably, after the movie had been playing for several minutes, the proprietor would take pity on the wretched lot of us and invite us in. We would rush in quietly, lest we disturb the paying customers and find our seats along the sides.

Marco Polo was playing. It was perhaps our sixth or seventh movie. The only other movie that sticks in my memory is *The Man with the X-ray Eyes*. I still see this image of a group of partygoers. Everyone is dancing and the protagonist is using his X-ray vision to scope them out. I vividly recall naked necks and shoulders and calves. It was strangely stirring.

But *Marco Polo* left a different imprint entirely. It was the scene where Marco has been captured by someone looking like Genghis Khan. He is on his knees and a heavy wooden yoke is around his neck. Marco is receiving the most terrible verbal abuse. I recall bulging oriental eyes and necks. That is what remains frozen in my mind's eye. I have no idea what happened to the intrepid explorer, for the next thing I recall is the jiggling light of the usher making his way in our direction.

It was like the bursting of an aneurism.

In a flash of blinding insight I knew that David and I were dead.

We had been found out.

The usher was looking for the only two American boys in the entire town. To be sure, the only two Yanks inside the theater. Finding us required no advanced degree in forensics. He told us what we already knew: *"Tus padres están aquí."* Your parents are here to get you—*and wipe you off the face of the earth!*

The death sentence.

They had decided to leave early.

My dirty sneakers dragged on the burgundy-carpeted aisle. The inclined walk to the foyer took a lifetime. My throat was tight and parched. It was as though I had swallowed a mouthful of baking soda.

Our parents were outside waiting. They had not even entered the forbidden establishment. There was this taut, angry whiteness on their faces and along the sides of their mouths. Their eyes burned through us. They could barely articulate the depth of their disappointment, humiliation, and anger. My mother grabbed me by the arm and led me out to the Ford pickup with its covered cab. As dust swirled up around my terrified feet, she told us in a tight voice shaking with indignation that we would discuss this thoroughly when we got home.

It was the longest two-hour drive of my entire life. My heart hammered a drummer's cadence and my pulse raced madly as I awaited my doom. The apprehension as we bounced on the wooden benches in the back just about gave me a coronary. It is simply not possible to live through such an experience unscathed. I'm certain that it sliced precious years off the tail end of my life.

The odd and awful and glorious thing was our disobedience and debauchery had so utterly traumatized our parents that when we got home we were sent to our rooms—and nothing more was said of the matter. All I can make of it is that we must have blown out some parental circuitry. Maybe our misconduct did some shaving of its own.

So I suppose I should not have been surprised to be told by Jonathan, my eldest, that he was heading off to study film production. And as if to prove that good can in fact come from great evil, it was my son's passion for movies that broke the grip of my three-decades-long artistic amnesia.

In my childhood, I had wanted to be a writer. As I grew up,

the dream was flattened under the logical and spiritual weight of making my life "count" for God. I did have this momentary psychological "freedom-break" in the early nineties which led to writing my fantasy novel, *The Paladins*. As I mention in chapter four, due to a series of unfortunate events, it died a slow and unremarkable death. But I still have this letter from a young girl in Chicago. She was on her sixth reading. My novel had changed her life, she told me. I think that's a good thing. There's also that school in the inner city of Atlanta named Paladin Academy in honor of the book's theme of honor and sacrifice and its call to destiny. While less than I hoped, it was on a few levels much more than I had envisioned.

Several years later, while Jonathan was in Hawaii studying filmmaking at Youth with a Mission's School of the Nations, he connived to get me on the speaking schedule for the Author's School. He'd gotten permission for the Film School students and staff to listen in. I had, after all, written that novel nine years earlier. My amnesia had kicked back in with a vengeance, such that I almost had to be reminded that such a book actually existed. With a show of reluctance, I accepted the offer to speak on the Big Island at a school perched on the sloping edge of stunning Kailua-Kona Bay on one of the most beautiful islands in the entire Pacific Ocean. Having given my assent, I had to come to terms with the challenge: what could I possibly say that would make an impact on these concentrationally challenged artists?

I have to confess that when I speak, my goal is never to be "interesting" or "very clever" or "really insightful." What I aim for is radical transformation. Yes, I do have agenda issues. More likely than not, what I suffer from is projection issues. Since I feel like I've been bound up, like I have not fully tapped into who I am and have not lived out of my true heart, I assume (or project) that most others haven't either. I assume that what they need are electrical paddles on both sides of the heart.

I also have this theological notion that as a result of the Fall, we have very real spiritual enemies who exist to crush hope, kill dreams, flatten out fullness of life and joy wherever it raises its fragile head. So I believe that all of us, at some level, at varying times in our life, need to have our shackles shattered and our hopes rekindled. And I believe that all of us, whether we know it or not, at least once in our life need to hear William Wallace scream at the top his lungs, "FREEDOM!" We all are bound up in a myriad of ways and need to be called out into the light and into the joy where we were meant to exist. That's my working premise. Thus, I prepared not for a talk but to jumpstart a modest revolution.

My aim tends to exceed my skill set.

The title I settled on for my talk was, "Forty-Five Degrees, An Acute Slant on the Artist's Vocation." It was skewed—or slanted, as the case may be—toward Christians in the arts, but a lot of it covers territory on both sides of the religious fence. Art is art and truth is truth, after all, no matter where it is and where it comes from or to whom it is aimed. All truth *is indeed* God's truth. I decided to blow a wad and bring along our two youngest kids with us to the Big Island. I had arranged to speak at the beginning of our vacation week. I am inflexibly committed to the policy of putting the hardest thing first. This was the first talk to artists about art that I would ever give, so I wanted relief from the gnawing anxiety as quickly as possible.

I wanted to snorkel in peace.

» » »

There were about twenty-three people in the classroom. Fortunately, my back was to the window that looked out on the idyllic bay, so I wasn't distracted by the view. Believing the indirect approach is always best, I asked the students, "How can you possibly justify wasting your lives on the arts instead of devoting your talents to cross-cultural missions?"

They sat up in their chairs. I met my son's eyes and smiled imperceptibly. He wasn't smiling—he was mopping the sweat that sprang suddenly from his forehead. That's not really true. He knows me well, so he simply sat back and waited.

As the students looked at me warily, I proposed a definition that I suggested might be of benefit in helping them evaluate their artistic calling, as well as critiquing and measuring their own work and that of others. I then proceeded to put their suspicions to rest. The tension dissipated when I divulged my conviction that the aesthetic is perhaps the best missiological "cover" for the Christian today. Rather than being antithetical to mission, art is intrinsic to mission at the highest level and has the capacity to impact the globe to the broadest, most profound extent. So regardless of what messages they may have picked up from authority figures, I let them know that in my opinion, their artistic drive is truly a missional calling. The artist receives a "call" just like those missionaries did decades and centuries ago, except that the artist's call is more subtle, more complex, and more confusing than theirs was. This is a call not to avoid, or flee from, or demean the arts, but to embrace it.

This I believe: The calling of the artist is to be in the world and *for the world* but not of the world.

No easy task, that.

The artist is plunged into a world of symbol, paradox, mystery, and indirection. It is communication not only with words, but also images. The significance of the symbols is rarely self-evident or obvious. Meaning is in the eye of the beholder, so what is being communicated is visceral, not necessarily logical. This is the land of parable, metaphor, and ambiguity. It is happy and harrowing and heady.

It is a land that can also eat you alive.

Art is God's good gift, but as Rabbi Jesus tells us, the artist is still in enemy territory. Like Master, so His students. Jesus the Artist was on a mission: He came to reveal the Father, bring Him honor and praise, and rescue a people who would love Him forever. His agenda was to look for the poor, the desperate, the sick, and the demonized—those who were so needy they would freely admit they were not only physical but spiritual wrecks—that they needed healing not only for their bodies but also their souls. These were the humble who willingly acknowledged that they were also plagued with an internal disorder that made them love themselves above everything else in the universe. They were not only slaves of Rome, or poverty, or some disease, but they were also diminished by and enslaved to the worship of self.

But Jesus had a secret. He came with a hidden agenda. It was a revolutionary plan: to expose and subvert the power of the powers that be by His death. He came to lay down His life as a sacrifice. But in order to "defeat death by death," He had to shine a light so brightly and so offensively that He would ultimately drive the "world" to deicide.[1] The darkness in all of us (what the Bible also refers to as "death") loathes the light. Darkness despises exposure. The life and message of Jesus brings a beam that exposes every secret, darkened crevice. It lays bare not only acts but intentions, not just behavior but motives.[2]

Jesus was not killed for being tolerant, as we hear so frequently today.[3] He was murdered for exposing humanity's sin, for pulling up out of the cellar not paintings of Elvis but icons to self. And all the people got in on the act because they had all been forced into the light.

And they were mad as hell. Literally.

It can be excruciating. No philanthropist wants the world to know that at the end of the day, at the deep core, for him or her, it's really about fame and reputation and honor. No politician wants it made public that it comes down to the sexual favors. No professor or deacon or elder wants it publicized that it comes down to a raw need for power. And no pastor wants it paraded about that "ministry" reduces to receiving accolades; it's about the respectful glances and special little public privileges. He would rather it not be known that when all is stripped away, it's really about the delightful intoxication of being "reverend." Or that it's about being known as somebody, building an empire and finally getting the approval of Daddy. Or when it's pared to the bone, it's about compensating for secret, dark, inner demons.

This is why the Rabbi tells His disciples that He was sending them out as lambs among wolves; there is going to be real hostility to the Jesus message (Matthew 10:16). And their modus operandi was to be this: be as wise as serpents and as harmless as doves, for where the enemy lurks there lies ambush and trip-wires and landmines. This caution would not preclude them from also dancing joyfully; they just needed to watch where they put their feet.

When you are behind enemy lines, you need to tread carefully.

C. S. Lewis (novelist, poet, philosopher, theologian, and literary and social critic of the first order) found that good fiction "can strip truth from its stained-glass and Sunday School associations" and "thus steal past those watchful dragons."[4] He was referring to those invisible cultural "watchers" who stand ready to pounce on any truth that poses a threat to their monopoly. He had in mind those mighty dragons of materialism, hedonism, narcissism, pragmatism, and even mysticism. No doubt he would place on his list our current dragon of "whatever," that cynical, ironic guardian that turns anything of real substance, pathos, and weight into an *SNL* skit.[5]

In writing his novels, Lewis was camouflaging those offensive but vitally necessary truths that would otherwise cause his readers to close the covers or take potshots at it on network television. Fiction for him—and were he to be writing today, I am sure he would include movies as well—was a means to surreptitiously slide crucial truth into the minds of his audience. For Lewis, a Christian artist has an agenda: smuggling in those life-changing, life-promoting, hope-enhancing but culture-offending realities that define the essence of the Jesus follower.[6]

In the same way that we don't conclude that a person who makes his living critiquing films hates films, so it is a mistake to argue that a cultural critic like Lewis or any other Christian who writes in critical tones necessarily hates culture. Recognizing that there are dangerous and rabid "wolves" in the woods doesn't mean you hate the forest. Defining an artist as a cultural secret agent does not imply that she despises or rejects everything in the culture. She may love it and appreciate the good in it better than most because she is able to evaluate it with clear eyes; she doesn't idolize it but values it appropriately, sanely, objectively.

C. S. Lewis scholar Peter Kreeft makes this point:

There are two possible reasons why indirect communication sometimes works better than direct. Both reasons are features of the audience. First, the audience may be bored, jaded, skeptical, sleepy and suspicious, i.e., the audience may be modern. . . . Second, the content of the message may be deeply threatening to the presuppositions, prejudices, or worldview of the audience [i.e. the audience may be postmodern]. . . . So the Christian writer must be a spy today. . . . Now a spy needs cover. The Christian spy's best cover is literary, or aesthetic.[7]

Lewis and Kreeft agree with Jesus that the Christian artist is undercover and works much like an agent dropped behind enemy lines. He poses as one thing while in reality he is something else. On the surface, he may look like, sound like, and probably smell like an American, but he is really a loyal citizen of another race, another kingdom. He swears allegiance not to a flag or a country but to a Messiah who is King and Lord of all. Whatever your profession, artist or otherwise, if you follow Jesus, what few know about you is that you are really a *provocateur*, a subversive agent intent on planting the flag of a kingdom that is not of this world.

That is how I tried to view my own work as a lawyer. My senses were attuned to pain. What I found was that suffering and genuine compassion opens doors that might stay closed forever. As a lawyer dealing with planning for and passing on decedents' estates, I heard many stories and got involved with a lot of broken relationships, fractured families, and broken hearts. Frequently, my only response was simply to ask if I could pray. On many occasions, when I was done my clients would be wiping tears from their cheeks. As they stood to leave, they would clasp my hand and whisper, "Thank you! Thank you so much." Before leaving the office they usually would look at me with this dazed, grateful expression that said, "That was weird! I thought I was coming to see a lawyer. How'd I wind up with a priest?" A few times I was asked if I was part of some Catholic order. I took that as a compliment.

The undercover agent looks like one of "us" while in reality he is one of "them." As Rob Bell writes, "I am learning that the church is at its best when it is underground, subversive, and countercultural. It is the quiet, humble, stealth acts that change things."[8] While Clark Kent has to take off his disguise to save the planet, Christians keep theirs on.

Now I realize that in writing this, I run the risk of offending current sensitivities. I also am disagreeing with teachers I respect, those who say we shouldn't build relationships with people in order to convert them into followers of Christ. Where there is an agenda, the argument runs, it really isn't love.[9]

For many, the evangelistic or conversional paradigm is no longer valid. We are to enjoy each others' valuable and valid stories without some lurking conversional intent. In the postmodern world, we are not to talk in exclusive, ethical categories of right and wrong, saved and unsaved, heaven or hell—because they are offensive and contradict Jesus' law of love. However, since that is precisely how Jesus, the apostles, and the early church fathers talked, I do not find this suggestion very persuasive. Jesus spoke in these inflammatory terms and did so with such frequency that He, at one time or other, offended everybody who hung around Him. That is what an honest, thorough read of the four Gospels will make really obvious.[10]

The wild thing about this "secret agent" thing is that some of God's best agents don't even realize who they are. At least, they did not know that when they started out. Some know they're sleepers. Others find out later—those are the agents who've been turned. Some are doubles—they work for both sides, though they also don't know it.

After all, who would believe that Bono, an Irish mega-rock-star with crazy sunglasses and a potty-mouth, would turn out to be a sleeper prophet calling the world and the church to love mercy and act justly and walk humbly with their God? What's even crazier are those agents who claim to be loyal to the other side but whose art winds up serving God anyway.

You are shocked and surprised when it happens. I think that they are a bit taken aback themselves.

Like the death scene in *Magnolia*, where Tom Cruise's foul-mouthed, perverse, sex-addict character falls on his dying father's chest and pours out this paean of love. It rocks you in *Good Will Hunting* when another vulgar, violent character breaks down and, for the first time, accepts the healing possibility that his father's abuse was not deserved. God's hatred for the absurdity and futility and horror of war shatters you in the last frame of *Platoon*, and its selfish brutality is exposed at the end of *The Mission*. The mindlessness and cruelty of human oppression was even driven home in an old black-and-white movie of *The Hunchback of Notre Dame*. I can still feel the impact of Quasimodo's innocent, childlike question all the way down to his death: "Whhhhyyy?" *Blood Diamond* depicts the power of the Father's persistent, reclaiming, and renaming love that restores sonship. To my knowledge, none of these directors overtly claim to be a follower of Jesus.

But through their art, they have served Him nonetheless.

»»»

The artist who follows Jesus explicitly resides in the world and participates in culture in a truly unique way. She helps others pay attention to, take notice of, and celebrate the goodness of the good creation. She does not shy away from the dark and the broken, the sorrow and terror—but crafts it in such a way as to point toward hope. It is revealing a pathway out of despair and chaotic meaninglessness. Her work is a candle that flickers and flares.

Her art is for the good of the world.

She does it for the blessing of the world.

She is intent not on reinforcing the curse but breaking it. She has and is a gift. She is sent, like Jesus, to open the eyes of the blind, open the ears of the deaf, or give words to the mute. She is sent on a mission of freedom. Her mission mirrors that of her Savior. She is sent to break chains of despair, set at liberty those tied up with cords of emptiness, futility, and death, and bring sight to those who have lost the capacity to see.[11] She is sent to give us the forgotten vision of the glory that peeks out behind the bush and branch and sea and life as it was meant to be. She sings and shrieks and falls to rise again, to give voice to what we've forgotten or refuse to hear.

She pours out her blood that a world may be saved.

She serves not always willingly or well but in her best moments, when she has forgotten herself, she serves.

Still, her loyalty is not here. She loves, but is not *in love* with the world. She has had her idolatrous attachment broken. She is free to be *in* but not *of*. She is not slavishly loyal to the patterns, the values, the demands, and commands of a world in love with itself. Her eyes look up even as she looks out, and in looking around she sees through. She is not bewitched by appearances nor overly and permanently distraught. She has seen a city whose builder and maker is God, and she pines for the day when it will come here so there will be light forever.

And the light will be the love and the joy of her life.

She has this secret. Her heart has been captured by a lover who is out of this world. But He is coming back. She wants to make herself ready and her friends and even her enemies too. So she does her work as best she can and prays that it is good, that it will shine so brightly as to bring glory not to her but to Him.

So as I told those twenty-three students,

> *Be an artist (and a saint)*
> *and change the world,*
> *for God's sake.*

10

SERVANTS OF THE GLORY, PART TWO

I was eager to finish my talk to the would-be authors and film-makers and staff. When you are not accustomed to being the center of attention and are looked upon as the proverbial fount of wisdom and insight, it is a daunting and exhausting experience. I suppose one gets used to it. I am told you can get used to anything. Even start to like it. I had not yet reached that point. I figured the crowd had heard enough of me. Plus, I was ready to hit the emerald green Hawaiian water.

I'd seen the pictures of the tropical fish festooned with flamboyant, hilarious color. I had watched them from behind thick glass in large tanks at the Shedd Aquarium in Chicago. But I wanted to swim with them. I think it has to do with something C. S. Lewis refers to in my favorite essay about wanting to be inside beauty, not merely observe it from a distance. I think he was right. There is this sometimes painful, sometimes insistent yearning to enter into the beautiful. Lewis called it "our inconsolable secret."[1] But when we reach out to hold it, or drink deeply of it, she shyly lifts her skirt over her shoes as she runs away. "Beauty has smiled, but not to welcome us; her face was turned in our direction, but not to see us. We have not been accepted, welcomed, or taken into the dance."[2] As Lewis observes, we are then left standing outside again, not having been given the access we craved. The door is closed to us, for now. But as he also reminds us, it will not always be so. The door on which we have been knocking all our lives will open at last.[3]

At the beginning of my lecture in Hawaii on the vocation of art, I had challenged the students to justify their artistic existence. I asked them how they could justify devoting their lives to something that appeals more to the senses than the mind, that is focused more on pleasure than conversion, that tends more towards self-indulgence than transformation.

To help point them toward a possible answer, I proposed another question: What is your magnificent obsession? What will drive you and consume you and give your work purpose and meaning? These are questions all of us who want to live from our real selves need to ask. How we answer them can change the whole trajectory of our lives.

While preparing for the lecture, something had struck me that was so simple I was a little embarrassed it wasn't the first thing that had come to mind. It came to me in a sublime flash of the glaringly obvious: God our Father is an artist! He is the supreme artist—the Creator of art, artists, and beauty, for pity's sake. Why not look at Him for some pointers?

I just might learn a thing or two.

So I mused: What is God's artistic motivation? What is His magnificent obsession?

This is what came to me:

When God sets out to paint a picture, He flings billions of stars into deep blue canvas of space.

When God sets out to write, He inspires and collects sixty-six manuscripts into a cohesive narrative of story, poetry, history, and instruction.

When God decides to sculpt, He brings man out of the dust.

When God sets out to direct a movie, He takes man and woman, fills the earth with His image bearers, allows them the freedom to disobey Him and wreck the planet, and then sends His Son as a perfect, obedient man to give His life away to save those who will submit their lives to Him.

And what drives everything God does is one preeminent motive: to glorify Himself. Every act of divine creativity, is intended to reveal and display His existence, character, and attributes. He is intent on showing off His majesty—His glory. As odd as it may strike our jaded contemporary ears, God's magnificent obsession is Himself.

This is why King David writes that the stunning, jeweled splendor of the starry, starry night is all about God: "The heavens declare the glory of God, the vault of heaven proclaims His handiwork; day discourses of it to day, night to night hands on the knowledge" (Psalm 19:1-2). The carpet of stars in the broad expanse of the black skies trumpets out the existence of their Creator. They "pour forth speech" (19:2, NIV).

What is this speech? It is a wordless communication centered on the power, beauty, wisdom, goodness, and extravagant joy of Yahweh, the Almighty God, the Creator of the heavens and the earth. Therefore, we can say without sacrilege that the stars and the sunsets are all about making God look good (that is what it means to "glorify"). When God was done with His creative labor and declared that the creation was good, He was approving not only the quality of His workmanship but also its effectiveness in displaying some facet of His infinite and beautiful being.

When judging the work of an artist, you turn to his masterpieces. How could one possibly critique Da Vinci without looking at *Mona Lisa*? How could you critique Michelangelo and ignore the Sistine Chapel? How could you critique Handel and not listen to the *Messiah*? So when we discuss God's artistry, we are required to evaluate the epitome of His artistic endeavors: Man.

We are told that Adam and Eve were created in the image and likeness of God. They were created to reflect God. They were little image bearers who were to walk about on God's good earth showing God off for all the creation. On a creaturely, finite level, they were to display God's infinite attributes of mercy, goodness, knowledge, leadership, creativity, intelligence, and love (no doubt, humor as well).

While the first Adam failed, the second succeeded. Jesus, the incarnate God, the divine image bearer, came to bring His Father glory, and this He fully accomplished (John 17:4). His great joy and driving passion was to glorify His Father. His mission was to put His Father on display and, good Son that He was, He reflected or mirrored His Father perfectly (John 17:1). Thus, He said, "If you've seen me you've seen the Father" (John 14:9). Even the work of salvation was driven by this conscious primary motive—to display the Father and in displaying Him draw men to know and love Him. This is why, at the end of His life, Jesus prayed, "This is eternal life that they may know you the only true God" (John 17:3).

So as creatures crafted in the image and likeness of God, redeemed by the perfectly obedient Son, devoted to lovingly imitate Him in the world, it would seem only right that we at least consider the possibility that perhaps our magnificent obsession should be the same as His.

» » »

My follow-up question for the twenty-some artists looking over my shoulder at Kailua-Kona Bay and those artists in less hospitable climates is this: As image bearers who have declared exclusive devotion to Jesus, are we not obligated to do our art for the glory of God — to somehow, in some small but concrete, conscious way show that God *is* and who He is? Are we and our art not supposed to be some kind of mirror — some kind of a reflector that makes our God look good? C. S. Lewis, writing about the Christian as an artist, says that our destiny lies in becoming "clean mirrors filled with the image of a face that is not ours."[4]

The apostle Paul says it this way: "So whether you eat or drink or whatever you do, do it all for the glory of God" (1 Corinthians 10:31, NIV). Admittedly, this is one of the big mantras in fundamentalist-evangelical circles. It is language every faithful Sunday school student can recite by memory and is used to cover an awful lot of unexplored and unexplained territory. It manages to squeeze its way into the vast majority of public prayers. It was part and parcel of that mindless Christian jargon that by my college years had begun to make me nauseous. I remember gritting my teeth after the obligatory public prayer and wondering for the thousandth time whether anybody within a twenty-five-kilometer radius had the slightest real clue what it meant to do that particular activity to God's glory. What did it mean when we were telling God we wanted to give an algebra lecture or perform the music that had been polished to absolute perfection or sing the song that should never have been sung or soundly thrash your opponent in soccer or act like a drunk in the play or have a conversation with your date whom you are lusting after — to the glory of God?

I have to admit I used the lingo too. It was inescapable. It was as ubiquitous as the words *conversation* and *story*. You try not using those words for a week.

The word Paul uses is *doxa*. It is an exceedingly deep word. It is so deep you could drown in it. In the Hebrew Bible, the writers use the word *kavod*, which means to have weight, substance. One might even say it connotes gravitas. Cheech and Chong, the seventies stoner poster children, were on to something. When in a drug-induced euphoria (which was their normal condition), they would express profound appreciation by remarking in awed lethargy, "That's really heavy man. Heavy!" If they had instead been Jewish stoners, they would be looking dully at each other saying, "Kavod, dude. Kavod."[5]

We hear traces of this when we say that "this person carries a lot of weight."

Certain things have glory, others not so much.[6]

When brought into the New Testament period, the word adds connotations of honor, splendor, outward impressiveness, luminance, and most remarkably for me, even a layer that touches upon approval, reputation, and appreciation. The "everlasting weight of glory [beyond all measure, excessively surpassing all comparisons and all calculations]" that our temporary trials are achieving for us (2 Corinthians 4:17, AMP) is, unbelievably, about becoming famous in heaven — being honored by Jesus in front of the angels and the Father.[7]

What we were *trying* to say and what Paul is saying has to do with "godness" and with goodness. Our goal is to reflect the godness of God by doing our work, whatever it may be, in such a way that God is made to look good. When wholeheartedly seeking the defeat of my opponent in a soccer match, I compete in ways that honor and give dignity to my opponent. I act like God does when I am fouled; I do not kick the hooligan in the shins when the ref is not looking. I extend mercy. When I head the ball into the back of the net, I do not run up and down the sidelines, pounding my chest, and go through contortions, proclaiming, "It's all about me!" Winning or losing, I manifest grace. Whether playing or performing or producing, I take seriously my obligation to enhance God's reputation. I'm His kid, after all, so what I do reflects on Him, either for good or for bad.

If we are artists rather than soccer players, we ask:

Does our work build up or tear down?

Does it provide hope or steal it?

Does it point to joy or to despair?

Does it reflect the world merely as it is or as it is intended?

Does it contain life or death? (And even when depicting darkness and evil, does it, unafraid, give it weight and honesty with perhaps just the merest chuckle, knowing that God uses even the wrath of man to praise Him?)[8]

Does it evoke a desire for God or a world-weary disillusionment?

Does it sing, or is it simply banal and monochromatic?

Does it call forth a desire for the good?

And this is very big: At heart, is it sacramental?

For those like myself who grew up sacramentally challenged (a terrible malady that can destroy the capacity for good art), a sacrament is something physical that points away from itself to Something and Someone who stands above and beyond the thing itself. It is a real thing that turns our heads and hearts toward the Real Thing.

Art was devised by the Artist to be a sacrament. As the Greek Orthodox priest Bishop Timothy Kallistos Ware says:

An abstract composition by Kandinsky or Van Gogh's landscape of the cornfield with the birds . . . is a real instance of divine transfiguration, in which we see matter rendered spiritual and entering into the "glorious liberty of the children of God." This remains true, even when the artist does not personally believe in God. Provided he is an artist of integrity, he is a genuine servant of the glory [*doxa*] which he does not recognize, and unknown to himself there is "something divine" about his work.[9]

Whether he knows it or not, an artist who is being faithful and is producing art that points up is a servant—"a servant of the glory," we might say. It's what we hear in that music that leaps out at us, grabs us by the throat, and takes our breath away. What we see in that painting or movie that transfixes us, speaks to the best in us, calling us to sacrifice, love, forgive, risk, and soar, that arouses hope and kindles joy is—*doxa*. We are resonating with the glory that the artist, though resistant or oblivious, has faithfully served. He has caught a glimpse of the transcendent and has transmitted it to us. He has smelled the fragrance of eternal beauty, and we are breathing it in with him. Not surprisingly, the servant of the *doxa* is an instrument designed to provoke doxology—ecstatic worship of the uncreated God.[10]

This then is what we must ask: Does the material, the quality, the intention of our art contain and point toward the transcendent: to truth, reality, beauty, to the One who inhabits eternity? Does it indicate, if ever so slightly, the way to true north? Does it evoke longing for our "home"? Does it reveal some facet of what is substantial, true, beautiful, noble, enriching, and holy? Does it have *kavod*, does it exert a gravitational pull upward—does it *glorify* God?

» » »

The artist, when in her right mind, recognizes that she is not master but servant. But a servant that carries a deep wound. All of creation, every creature but none more poignantly than the artist, hungers to (re)connect with the beautiful—to be possessed by it. We could call it being wounded by transcendence. It is the guilty secret mankind desperately, through a thousand tricks, tries to deny, hide, and muzzle. It is that sweet, painful desire "for our own far off country" that nothing can fulfill. The psalmist refers to it as "having eternity in their hearts." It is that nagging suspicion, that dreaded voice that whispers in the dark, "You were meant for more than this. There is more to life than satisfying your appetites. This is not ultimate reality. You are an eternal being created for something bigger, someone greater. You were meant to love and be loved, eternally, perfectly. There is a Lover who is also King, and there really is a palace and it is prepared for you."

This is what is so notoriously absent in much art today, whether Christian or not. There is a large, empty chasm, an aching transcendent void. Few indeed are those who address that hidden wound, that "inconsolable secret." There is a flatness, a shallow emptiness, a bland repetitiveness in so much contemporary art. There is an almost unbearable vacuous lightness where there should be a weight of glory. There is no transcendent standard or focus or purpose to the lyric, screenplay, or painting. Contemporary art, as with much preaching and writing, is flat, two-dimensional. It is almost exclusively horizontal.

We image bearers (using Lewis's metaphor) are holding our mirrors at right angles to the world. As a result, our art is merely reflecting the world we see and the world everyone knows. It is nonsacramental. It is art without a heart or soul. It points nowhere because it has no point.

When we talk with our friends about the latest movie we've seen, we generally critique it using purely horizontal, nontranscendent standards. These are the types of questions we ask: Is it authentic? Is it creative? Is it honest? Is it courageous? Is it technically meritorious? Is it entertaining? Is it original?

If we're being honest, these are the basic standards used by Christian and non-Christian alike. These are flat-world criteria devoid of a transcendent reference point.

The Christian artist, if she is trying to be faithful to her commitment as a follower of Jesus, must break from such exclusively horizontal categories: the need to be original, authentic, or creative.

Referencing 2 Corinthians 3:18, "we with unveiled faces reflecting like mirrors the brightness of the Lord." Lewis states:

> In the New Testament the art of life itself is an art of imitation: can we, believing this, believe that literature, [art] which must derive from real life, is to aim at being "creative," "original," and "spontaneous." "Originality" in the New Testament is quite plainly the prerogative of God alone. If I have read the New Testament aright, it leaves no room for "creativeness" even in a modified or metaphorical sense. Our whole destiny seems to lie in the opposite direction, in being as little as possible ourselves, in acquiring a fragrance that is not our own but borrowed, in becoming clean mirrors filled with the image of a face that is not ours.[11]

He goes on to say, "And always of every idea and of every method, he will ask not, Is it mine? but, Is it good?"[12]

Art is meant to remind us of what most of us suspect but

prefer to ignore. In her deep heart, the artist knows that we were meant to live in a garden of perfect beauty, that something went terribly wrong, that we've been estranged from our real home and our real Father, that we are lost in a dark wood. All is not what it appears. There is meaning behind the meaninglessness. When doing her art well, she is stirring up longing.

So the definition I proposed to those students on Kona Bay was this:

> The artist is a servant of the glory who is wounded by transcendence and afflicts this wound on others.

To be obedient to our calling, what we may most need is to change the angle of our mirrors so we do not reflect what is apparent only to the natural eye but those more real eyes that see behind the veil.

Our art will then reflect not only our face, or that of our fragmented world, but the reflection of a face not our own but resplendent with beauty and a raging, irrepressible, compelling love.

Blessing

As faithful image bearers (artists but saints first),
may you reflect not only the creation
but its beautiful and good Creator.
May you embrace your true calling
to humbly serve the glorious One who promises you glory.
May you accept and acknowledge
the wound your faithful friend has inflicted,
and may you in friendship and loyalty inflict it on others.

May your art be worship.
May your worship be art.
May you afflict the comfortable with jolts of inconsolable joy.
May you call forth the good, the beautiful, the eternal hope of
your true city.
And when people step back from your painting,
put down your novel,
or leave the theater,
may they leave having been fatally stabbed,
inconsolably wrecked with a longing for home.
And may you reflect faithfully the face of your Father
who strides through the galaxies with brush in hand.

11

DANCING IN THE DARK

I remember only her last name. She was my seventh-grade English teacher. She was tall with graying hair worn in a long braid. She looked like the classic spinster. Though she was hardly hip, I liked her a lot. She made me feel like I was special somehow, like I had promise. It was the first time I recall ever feeling that way.

The assignment from Ms. Anderson was simple: Write a short story that describes a strong emotion. What I decided to attempt was horror. It managed, at best, to rise to the level of dismay. I was aiming for a gothic romantic tale that would end unexpectedly in terrible heartbreak. It was about a brother and sister orphaned at an early age. They live in a bleak and spirit-numbing orphanage where they are each other's only link to hope and sanity. Being precocious youngsters, they manage to escape. They go into hiding in a cemetery, which provides safety but at a cost. At night they are almost driven mad with fear. The authorities discover them, and they are cruelly separated. The girl, who is six years old, winds up being adopted, and her brother, three years older, never sees her again. The boy, in his late twenties, after a failed marriage, contracts some terrible illness and is nursed back to health by a gentle and patient nurse who slowly manages to break through his shell of a heart. She is hauntingly beautiful. Against his will, he falls desperately in love and asks her to marry him. It is only then that he allows himself to tell her his story. As he talks, she weeps. Soon she is sobbing. Through racking sobs, she tells him hers, and the young man's heart is shattered when he finds out that he has fallen in love with his long-lost sister.

As I think over this storyline, I feel suddenly as though I must have been an awfully sad youngster. Kind of like Richard Dreyfus's preadolescent son in *What About Bob*, who wore black, quoted Sartre, and was fixated on his own mortality. The reality is, I was a relatively balanced, though somewhat lonely and probably a bit introspective, missionary kid who happened to stutter a lot. And who read quite a bit more than the national average.

I didn't know it at the time, nor did my mother (whom I almost drove to drink—alcohol, that is—in her laborious but unsuccessful attempts to teach me the piano), that I was also a bit dyslexic. I just had an odd imagination, that's all.

Later that same year, driven by a fit of precocity, I found myself with another project in the library of the American Air Force middle school I was attending in Zaragoza, Spain. My missionary parents had migrated to Europe in the late sixties. It was at the height of the hippy movement, which sadly I was too young to participate in. It wasn't the free love; it was the incredible bead work on the bandanas and the leather-fringed Davy Crockett jackets you got to wear as you railed against "the man," whoever the heck he was. The tokin' looked cool too but was kind of scary. I knew it could lead to degradations I was not quite up on but knew enough to be leery about.

Kahlil Gibran was the author of choice for the high school

kids. *The Catcher in the Rye* was also big, as was *A Clockwork Orange* and George Orwell's *1984*. Then of course, there was all that incredible music. I still get goose bumps listening to Crosby, Stills, Nash & Young, The Who, Grand Funk Railroad, The Moody Blues, or a group not many seem to recall: Blood, Sweat & Tears. Of an independent slant, even at that age, I also loved Frank Sinatra. I still do.

What can I say? I was eclectic.

When it came to literature, I had a classical bent, so I was drawn to really old writers. I liked them even better if they were English. I was told by Ms. Anderson to spend that semester's English class working on an independent research project. I had never done one before. I don't recall being given an awful lot of direction. She had these great expectations about my prowess.

Don't ask me how or why, but of all the authors available to me, I narrowed it down to a dead Russian, Fyodor Dostoevsky. Fortunately, I did not opt to do a study of *The Brothers Karamazov*. At thirteen years old, I might have been done in by that one. Instead I selected to do an analysis of *Crime and Punishment*.

A few years later, when I was about fifteen, I read a book that affected me oddly. It was a biographical novel about Michelangelo written by Irving Stone, *The Agony and the Ecstasy*. I did not so much read it as drink it in. I don't know if I actually trembled as I read, but in my memory I feel this quivering excitement somewhere in my chest and stomach. From that time forward, I knew exactly what people meant by visceral reaction. I didn't know why I loved this story; why it affected me at such a deep level. But whatever it was, I was reading something that was calling me and moving me profoundly.

It was awakening something dormant.

After finishing it, I never looked at it again.

I promptly forgot that I had been moved, that I had been shaken.

It took about twenty-five years before it began making sense. It took an epiphany. It came to me in a rush, and I knew immediately what had been happening in the viscera of that young teenager with a romantic bent, who as he read felt his pulse racing and had to keep pushing strands of long brown hair out of his eyes.

It came as a shock.

I had been resonating with that creative energy that compels artistic expression regardless of its form. Pulsing in my veins and chest and stomach, as I read the life story of this artistic genius, driven to rob graves in his obsessive quest to study the musculature of human bodies so he could get his sculptures exactly right, was a reciprocated hunger for expression. Something in the story was speaking to my true self and reminding me who I really was. No, not Michelangelo, but an artist—though on a much more modest plane, to be sure; a craftsman not with paint but words.

In my late teens, I was encouraged to gravitate toward the logical and analytical and received affirmation and enjoyed scholastic success in those pursuits. I was encouraged to pursue a left-brain career track. In college, I studied theology and philosophy and history, all of which I loved. And I forgot I was an artist—a writer, to be exact.

And I began to believe something about myself.

Somewhere during those years, I bought into a very simple, very deliberate message. It would pulsate in and out of my brain at moments when inspiration sputtered. It would spring out of the dark and effectively asphyxiate the brief glimmer of light. The message was dry and cold and calculated. It came in this steely-hard, deathly calm, precise tone. It was the voice of an infinitely patient teacher who has mastered his emotions but is not unwilling to let on that he's restraining his natural tendency to bite your stupid head off. In those moments, the phrase would drop down like an icy shroud: "You are not a creative person. You are not a creative person."

On occasion, when the daydream was about a more analytic form of expression, the message would alter just a bit: "You have nothing of value to say. You have nothing worth saying. You have nothing . . ."

There were no exclamation marks.

There was no hurry or anxiety, just an insistent quelling and crushing repetitiveness.

It performed its job with admirable efficiency.

It robbed me of hope.

It numbed and smothered me.

It shut me down and sucked me dry.

And it lied.[1]

I was a writer before I became a lawyer. But between there and here, I forgot I could fly. I forgot I could paint with these colorful, malleable, amazingly complex, and infinitely simple words. I forgot I could get so high and look down at the stars and invent worlds. Or maybe I never really believed it was me or that I could do it on purpose or that it was worthwhile, worth devoting my best energy and life force to. I took on the persona, expectations, and career path of the objective, logical, deductive type. I took up the law.

Then I had that epiphany.

I met my wife while studying theology at a Baptist seminary in 1980. I left seminary two years later and went on to graduate from law school in 1987. We produced our first three children in rapid-fire fashion. As they grew older, I enjoyed reading to my three little boys. (Christiana, our only daughter, had come a bit later; she was only two years old at the time. She wasn't yet interested in the classics.) I was working for the Michigan Court of Appeals as a research attorney. It was 1990 and I found myself desperate for another book for us to read. I'd read through *The Chronicles of Narnia* and the Peretti kids' adventure series, and the remaining options were frankly—how should I put this?—not terribly impressive.

Having grown up on Christian radio for children as the dubious source of family entertainment, I couldn't bear to read to them any ham-fisted morality plays dressed up in the garb of children's fiction. So as I grieved the absence of authors like C. S. Lewis or Tolkien, I had a word flash through my mind.

It was a Sunday afternoon. We were at my folks' house for the bimonthly family, after-church dinner. I was in my dad's office; the television was turned off since the Detroit Lions were simply too unbearable to watch. That's where it hit. It was the title of a book. It was called *The Paladins*. There were four protagonists, each based on one of my children, three boys and a girl, and it would be a spiritual warfare thriller. So I set out to find someone who could write it. A year later, having failed in my quest to pass the buck, I began writing under the decided and clear conviction that I was embarking on a ludicrous and impossible path.

Over the years, I had occasionally toyed with the idea of writing. Inevitably, it would be a historical treatise or a biblical critique of modern culture based on Reformed, Calvinistic theology. Never had it occurred to me to write fiction and most decidedly not fantasy. The reality was I wasn't really a fantasy kind of a guy. I'd read *The Chronicles of Narnia* and that was about the extent of it. It was a genre that really did not interest me too much. As I sat down in front of my monitor and began to sketch out the story, each time I began I had to fight off the assaults of that insistent phrase that battered and dogged me with each key stroke: "You are not a creative person; you have nothing to say; you are not a creative person; you have nothing creative to write."

About five years later, it was finished and it was published in 1997. The process of writing was an arduous but delightful, at times intoxicating, adventure. Collaborating with my highly visual and creative wife was an unexpected bonus.

But it was battle.

I had to repeatedly wrestle down and pin to the mat that relentless, hypnotic heavy-caped assailant who kept speaking in my head. Maybe that's being too nice. Perhaps the more real truth is that I had to face him out back and try to shoot him. What I came to realize was that in this private little war, there was no place for mercy. You have to shoot to kill. But I've always been a terrible shot, so I kept hitting him in the legs and arms. He was able to keep talking at me just fine. Though my aim was off, eventually, after a few years of dueling in front of my monitor, I finally managed to get him in the head.

So as I wrote, I was also being liberated. I was being set free of deceptive shackles and leg irons and metal collars and leather head coverings like Hannibal Lecter's in *Silence of the Lambs*. As I wrote of the four Paladins breaking prisoners out of these terrible and imposing strongholds, I was breaking out too.

It was a spiritual warfare allegory influenced by C. S. Lewis first and then Peretti. It was a story about anger, pride, forgiveness, and heroism. It was about looking for and finding Father and about restoration and hope. But most of all, it was about glory and destiny. It ends with this Great Dance, of course. (Once Lewis gets a good hold on you, he does not let go easily.)

But despite the high hopes and the energy bled out over its pages, my book never had a chance to fly. For a brief period, it became one of the best-sellers in the local Christian stores, then the marketing arm of the fledgling publishing house went belly-up and my book fizzled. Its legs had been cut off before it could make a real run for it.

The struggle had been exhilarating but exhausting. It had also been a little scary getting lost in this other reality and taking on this new and unaccustomed identity. As sales plummeted, I decided the effort outweighed the benefit. Pouring yourself out on paper, while somewhat therapeutic, was insufficiently productive (financially, that is—I did have seven people to support after all). My day job was calling. So I settled back into the comfortably familiar confines of the safe, well-known padded coffin.

And again, promptly forgot who I really was.

But I still couldn't shake this irrepressible compulsion. Like a cocaine addict with an insatiable craving, I would type feverishly on my keyboard and quietly, behind closed doors, keep adding to my already distended assortment of (mostly) theological essays.

Then this odd thing happened. One by one, the three oldest boys turned their faces away from the traditional college path and began gravitating to the arts. Jonathan headed into film production. Benjamin got a degree in cosmetology and began pouring himself into his guitar, writing songs and experimenting with acrylics and abstract art. Aaron had begun to master the drums and so he and Benjamin formed the nucleus of a band. Their goal was to perform music that would provide glimmers of hope in settings far from the church. They wanted to help point their peers, adrift in a sea of meaninglessness, to purpose and to a love that was big enough to hold their heads above water.

I was forced to face the question of art and creativity—its place and its value and its function. I needed to be able to understand the calling of an artist (for my sons' sake) as a means of gaining a livelihood. Subconsciously, I see now I also had to do it for myself, to come to terms with a passion that would apparently not be remunerated. Just beginning to get in touch with the depth of my own frustrations, I wanted to find some sort of wisdom for my sons' futures. Could I make any sense of the jarring dissonance formed by a creative drive that forces you to concede that, at the core, this is who I am, and of the mundane but inescapable obligation to provide for your family by doing what does not flow out of that center?

The question, on the surface, was quite practical: How can I help give my artistic sons a sense of perspective about their hunger if they were not part of the 1 percent that is signed by a label?

As I began digging around inside, I had to ask, Why have these maddening impulses been inflicted if you are deprived of a platform for communicating the vision that has been offered? If the driving force behind art is not self-expression but communication,[2] what's the point of yearning to create and being utterly unable to get any kind of an audience for the creative offspring?

Must artists view themselves as failures if they are not published, marketed, televised, signed, or booked? Can you only lay claim to the identity if you make money at it? If you just do your art in the studio, or den, or bedroom, have you flunked your AEEs (Artist Entrance Exams)? Success (some measure of fame and financial reward) thus becomes the hallmark of artistic authenticity.

When I finally allowed myself to think honestly about it, I have to admit, I believed I had pretty much failed at being who I truly was meant to be.

I had washed out at fulfilling my calling and had to settle for being a fraud, living behind a stifling façade the remainder of my life.

I decided to stop fencing and parrying away these questions and allowed myself to look them straight in the eye without flinching. It did not take too long. What came was a picture: a little shepherd boy alone on a hill. He is the baby of the family and gets no respect from his seven older brothers, who secretly despise him. This youngster's name was David, and he was an artist before he was anything else. He wrote poetry and sang songs by himself on the Bethlehem hills long before he was lauded as Israel's poet laureate and premier warrior king.

In the still of the night, with no one applauding or fawning or flattering, he pours out his heart. He plays on his lyre and sings to the skies until his voice breaks or gives out. He then lays down his wooden instrument and lifts his arms above his head as he stands to his feet.

And he begins to dance in the dark.

And there is this wild, happy, crazy gleam in his eye as he looks up at the whirling stars.

If you read his life story carefully, you will be struck by something unusual. He seems to be singularly unimpressed with himself or his status. He strips off his royal robes and dances ecstatically in full view of all the populace. He is so shameless he embarrasses his blueblood wife with her highly cultivated sense of propriety. Michal despises him in her heart (2 Samuel 6:16). She mocks him for being a crass, uncouth rustic, a "buffoon" (6:20). David will not be deterred. He does not allow her to shame him. He responds that he will keep dancing before Yahweh and will demean himself even further. "You thought *that* was bad? Check *this* out!"

Later, we read that he is absolutely staggered by the enormity of the promises God is making to him and his bloodline. He does not feel the slightest bit deserving. He even refers to himself as God's own little "dog" (7:21).

Toward the end of his reign, as he is fleeing for his life, he is cursed and assaulted with stones by an enraged Shimei, a descendant of the former king Saul. David does not retaliate. He does not automatically conclude that he is blameless. He seems to assume the opposite. *Maybe Shimei is an instrument of God's discipline*, he muses. And even if Shimei is acting on his own, God can set the record straight (2 Samuel 16:5-12).

What is the reason for the meekness?

David knows who he really is.

He has no grand illusions about himself. When the robes are removed and the pomp and circumstance quieted, when the royal veneer and the position and titles are taken away, he knows that at heart he is just a humble singer. He's a simple, abandoned worshipper who delights in God's presence more than anything in the whole wide world.

If you've lived deeply and truly alone in God's presence and grown still and safe there, doing your best work for Him first, it doesn't make a whole lot of difference anymore if you happen to find yourself seated on a throne, a crown resting on your head, with servants at your beck and call, or signing your name to a million-dollar advance.

They may call you king and flock to your concerts, but you know you are just a shepherd writing lyrics and singing till your heart breaks.

Your secret identity remains intact: you are a worshipper.

» » »

I was raised a Baptist. There is much that I am deeply grateful for in that heritage. It is a tribe that specializes in building solid foundations. It does, however, have some serious deficits when addressing issues that pertain to windows and doors and quiet decks out back. While I learned to know and honor the Word of God—very well—I did not learn to enjoy the God of the Word—much. I recall being taught that congregational singing was merely a device that served to transition the order of service into the sermon, the part that really mattered. In the churches where I grew up, there was no theology of worship. I never understood the purpose of music or its unique power.

In the late eighties, God began opening up my heart, and I experienced for the first time the palpable, delicious sweetness of His presence. "*Taste* and see that the LORD is good," no longer were mere words (Psalm 34:8, NIV). He made Himself real to my emotions. The disconnect between my head and my heart began to be healed. Suddenly, my formal intellectual knowledge was set ablaze, and I began to actually sense and enjoy His favor. Like Eric Liddell in *Chariots of Fire*, I could "feel His pleasure," not when I ran, but when I sang.

I feel it now when I write.

I began falling in love with Him.

I discovered an insatiable hunger not only for His words, but also for His tangible presence. And the expansive panorama of worship opened itself up to me. I discovered that I was created to worship.

I found that my truest home, my most real me, my deepest heart was the heart of a worshipper. And I realized that I needed to break free from the restrictive shackles of tradition that looked down on demonstrative physical expression.

I was not told I had to.

No one made me.

I was simply compelled to raise my hands in abandonment, in surrender, in wholehearted adoration: "You are Lord!" I was the only one in the entire Baptist congregation. I admit feeling really stupid and awkward and conspicuous. Hard eyes were turned pointedly in my direction. But I could not restrain myself. If I stood staid and true and still, I would burst.

I recall going to my first large-scale Christian concert. It was sponsored by the Gaithers, old-school gospel recording artists. It wasn't the musical style I much liked, but they had invited this crazy solo trumpeter, Phil Driscoll. When he sang, he sounded and acted like Joe Cocker (he made famous the song "With a Little Help from My Friends"). He was out of control, and I loved him. He led the whole gathering in a closing worship anthem. We were all standing. I had come with a group from our church. They were all very conservative. We had dutifully complied with the instructions from the stage and were holding hands. Toward the conclusion of the song, I gave in to the irresistible impulse and raised my arms. I forgot that my hands were clasping others, but it was too late. By the time I came to my senses, the entire row had this chain of arms in the air. The hot waves of embarrassment and discomfort were almost stifling.

I did not lower my arms.

On another occasion, I was alone in our house. We were renting an old dairy on nineteen acres. It was a wonderful place to raise four wild hooligans. It was really old, though. I had finished eating a sandwich and was singing to music blaring from our speakers. I love the feeling of the percussion pounding against my chest. I had been overwhelmed with this feeling of awe, so I was lying on my face. Somehow I fell asleep in that position. I was jolted awake by an unusual tickling against my fingertips. I knew immediately what was happening. Before I could stop myself, I did three things simultaneously: I screamed, jerked my hands off the carpet, and hopped up on my knees. The mouse that had been nibbling on my fingertips almost died of shock but still managed to throw himself down the air vent.

I did not stop worshipping, but I did not lie on the carpet for a good long while.

This fundamental discovery about myself provided a way through the dense forest of frustrated artistic passions. I realize that all of us, regardless of our wiring, are created to worship. Jesus told the Samaritan woman that what His Father was looking for were worshippers who would worship Him in spirit and in truth (John 4:23). The last chapter in the Epic shows us not surprisingly that He is successful in His quest. When time reaches its limit, surrounding God's throne there will be a numberless host: "Everything that lives in the air and on the ground, and under the ground, and in the sea, crying, 'To the One who is sitting on the throne and to the Lamb, be all praise, honor, glory and power, for ever and ever'" (Revelation 5:13).

Ecstatic worship will be the musical score of eternity. We are told the worship gets so intense that the leaders keep falling on their faces (Revelation 4:10; 5:14; 7:11; 19:4). In some circles, this is known as carpet time.

Whether or not they are consciously aware of it, every creature was created to find its center in God. No matter the level of our artistic capacities, no matter how humble or distinguished, skilled or unskilled, whether the quality of our gift compels attention or not, we were made to find our truest joy and our highest delight in God. At the end of the day, whatever gift has been given, whatever hunger has been granted, it is about God, not us.

Not applause but adoration.

We may rightfully ask, why is my gift so paltry, so deficient? In comparison to my desire and vision, compared to the talent of the other person, why is so much given there and such a miserly deposit here?

Salieri in *Amadeus* was driven mad by such jealousy. How could God lavish such an exquisite, otherworldly musical gift on Mozart, a perverse and profane "little monkey," while denying it to someone whose sole passion was to glorify Christ with his art? His anger drove him to the conclusion that God did not exist. After all, how could there be a God in light of such a gross affront to logic and fairness and simple decency?

Salieri was broken on the rocks of envy. He was shattered by the always-paradoxical reality of God's exuberant, extravagant freedom to scatter His gifts widely upon whomever He wants. God gives whatever He wants to whomever He wants, and all He requires is that it be used fully and gratefully. It is to be enjoyed, to bring happiness and pleasure, to even be delighted in, but ultimately, it is to become a means to delight in Him.

When we recognize that the gift is not primarily for us, but Him, we can accept what has been placed in our hands and gladly play our little tune and sing out our simple song as we sit gazing up at the dark night skies. If our identity and our joy and our creative passion is for Him first and for Him last, then we can do it with all our heart even in utter solitude and anonymity and be happy.

But why the frustration? Why the desire that seems to always exceed its reach? Why is what we tend to hear and see more beautiful, more luscious and poignant than what we can possibly express? Why does our reach always exceed our grasp?

Could it be that these stabs of unrequited, unmet, unattained artistic yearning are really brilliant shards of eternity sent to pierce us and make us bleed? Maybe they are intended to turn our eyes up and away to where beauty dwells in light inaccessible, hid from our eyes. Maybe they function like sacraments that are meant to point through and beyond the physical world to One who is real, substantial, and eternal.

Beauty finds its source, its strength, and its satisfaction in Him. For of Him and through Him and to Him are all things.

Your passion is a reminder that you come from a different reality altogether, your suspicions were right: you really are from another planet. You are an eternal being, and your home is an eternal and infinite and exquisitely beautiful place where everything and everyone is complete and whole and in harmony. It is musical and magical, and it is where we all were meant to be. It is where the dance begins and never ends. It is where you fly because all the weights and the waits have been removed. All the nos and the can'ts and the shouldn'ts, all the stops and flops and failures, all the bads and wrongs and wickeds and brokens, and all those long, needling, crushing, killing regrets are erased.

For good.

It is where you shine.

And (as a much finer and wiser writer than I said) you will then be so resplendent that if we could see you now we would take you for a god or a goddess. We would be tempted to fall down and worship.[3] The glory will be just that intense. That's what that ache is about. That's what's calling you.

You create and express yourself for your Daddy first, and He is always so pleased and so proud and He will cry with you because He knows what's in your heart. What you really need to know is that what you most yearn for, what is driving you at the core is not human approval or recognition or applause. For you were created for His praise.[4] To bring glory and—unimaginable as it sounds—to receive His glory, to receive His praise, to be "approved of" by your Father who created you and formed you for His own.[5]

It really isn't about fame after all—it's about Father.

It's about standing and hearing, "Well done, my dear child,

receive your blessing: take for your heritage the kingdom prepared for you since the foundation of the world" (Matthew 25:34).[6]

Blessing

May you take up the bittersweet cup
and drink it dry.
May you become dizzy with hope,
drunk with joy.
May it make you sway in a slow dance
and fall down in love.
May you bear your wound gladly.
May you do good work for Him.
May you do your best work for Him.
May you sing your song,
soar and fly,
and paint and write and create
at peace, content,
with your eyes lifted up.
Then may you drop your brush to join your good and happy Father
as He rejoices over you with singing.
In the solitude and in the dark,
may you dance
with Him and for Him.

12

GOOD SEX AND BAD SEX

I have to admit that I was really pathetic about telling my boys about, well, you know . . . the birds and the bees . . . the "talk." I was kind of traumatized by the awkward discomfort of the whole thing. Not my own as much as that of my parents'.

Now I know a lot of you are automatically writing me off as weak and pathetic for dumping on my parents instead of taking it on the jaw like a man.

But I am not blame-shifting. Not really. I can take it as well as the next guy. But my memory of our "sex talk" is one tense, foggy blur of awkwardness and, yeah, embarrassment—theirs and mine and my other brothers', too.

So in a wonderfully adept passive-aggressive dance, I managed to put it off with my boys until I was shamed into it by my faithful wife. In fact, now that I think about it, she was the one who had the initial talks. In retrospect, I'm sure I didn't totally drop the ball. My passivity does have its limits, so I know for certain it was mentioned in an oblique fashion when my kids were approaching college age or thereabouts. In any event, they knew all about it when I managed to bring it up, so I could take a breath and relax.

I recall emphasizing the correlation between self-control and pleasure. At some point, I stressed the enhancement of pleasure that results from restraint and the mutuality of erotic satisfaction. Okay, I didn't use that particular phrasing, but the whole topic is, you know, kind of uncomfortable for someone my age. Euphemisms and verbal codes still provide that indispensable veneer of safety.

I am trying to get over it.

They understood what I was saying, though. It's not like they were born yesterday. Let's be real, they drank in subtle sexuality as they munched on Sugar Pops while watching Saturday morning television. And when we caught on and censored certain shows, we were outflanked by the commercials or the movies or what not. Then, even if denied that venue, their friends at school would fill them in on what they'd missed.

My boys heard me loud and clear.

Looking back, I know I blew it. I didn't want my awkwardness to spoil what should be holy and precious. Still, I should have gotten over my stupid prudery and been real with them in some age-appropriate way. But I admit it. I chickened out.

I wish I would have done it better.

I wish I would have been clearer, more forthright, more European or Jewish or Irish about the whole thing. When I re-create the conversation in my mind, I'm at an outdoor cafe, on a sunny sidewalk on the coast of Spain. The chairs and table are a dark, rich, sturdy oak. My son takes off his sunglasses as I adjust my beret. I accept a sangria from the camarero and twirl my glass slowly as the chunks of peach, orange, and melon—and a slice of lime—swirl lazily in the red wine. Because he is of age and it is perfectly acceptable by European standards, I order one for this young man seated with me. We talk about the World Cup and about Beckham and his wonderful, looping, curling, slicing, oh-so-elegant goals. Then smoothly and naturally I segue into a conversation about sex. World-class athletes and sex, get it? I lay it all out for him in an earthy, honest, comfortable, humorous, whimsical, solemn, and very wise way. I sound like Marlon Brando in *The Godfather*, without the mumbling. I am so cool. We leave arm in arm. It is Europe after all. And ten years later he gets married in my impossibly lovely, though appropriately modest, villa in Tuscany.

He is a virgin, and so is his wife.

» » »

Although that conversation on the Mediterranean coast is one I did not have, somehow or another our children have embraced virginity as a high value. This, I take little credit for. I'm sure it was my wife and her talks that were real and honest and sweet and, apparently, convincing. So now I get to make up for my sins of omission. This is me undoing the silence.

So we're at that cool European bar (atmosphere is important) and then I'd start. First of all, based on the standard Jesus set, I would have to acknowledge being an adulterer. After all, "if a man looks at a woman lustfully, he has already committed adultery with her in his heart" (Matthew 5:28). I have had more than a couple wayward thoughts and looks. By His yardstick, which is way different from what we commonly use, I have sinned against myself and my wife and my God, who was present when I made some very specific, demanding, and exclusive vows of lifelong fidelity (of thought as well as deed). Before I was married, I had plenty of those thoughts too. Though I remained a virgin, I did, on a few occasions, exceed what is chaste sexual behavior. I was able to remain well back of the line of intercourse by the mercy and restraint of a power not my own. My wife and I were virgins when we married, but I readily admit that I get no credit for heroism. Had I had the wrong temptation at the wrong moment combined with the right opportunity, there were times I could have fallen.

God protects when we are without a clue and without defense. Lots of times, though not always, He steps in as our shield when we are unaware of the gravity of the danger. Maybe that's what happens when we pray for others. God hears, then holds His hand up, and what could have or should have happened didn't. I don't know. Prayer is another one of those Big Mysteries.

So I've been guilty of immorality, as most all of us have been at some level. So what I say doesn't come down from Mount Olympus or wherever ethical heroes dwell. I've needed Jesus in this area as much as I've needed Him with my temper. As He tends to do, God has used marriage to significantly rewire me, for much of the old wiring was not sound. He is still at work, but there has been a rewiring nonetheless. As Francis Schaeffer (an old, really smart and wise long-haired white guy who was very secure, since he frequently wore knickers) would have said it: The healing has been substantial, though not complete.

Over these past twenty-five-plus years of marriage to one woman, God has revealed to me the beauty and glory of sex—and its perplexing frustrations as well. Like most young men, I viewed or anticipated it as a means of release, fulfillment, and personal pleasure. The more personal and the more pleasurable the better. Early on in our marriage, I figured it out: Selfish sex is bad sex. And that is where my euphemistic comments to my sons about mutual eroticism came from.

Unlike the negative medieval gloss, pleasure is not sinful, nor is sex just about having children (that is one of the few places that Saint Augustine got it wrong). However, the rejoinder is not that sex is all about pleasure either. In general, I believe, sex *is* about pleasure so that there *will be* children. If it weren't so pleasurable, there would be fewer of them. And it would seem that God wants more not less. After all, one of the first positive commands to humanity right out of the gate, so to speak, was "have lots of kids and fill the earth" (Genesis 1:28, author's paraphrase). It's like God was thinking, *Once they figure out what a pain children can be, and how expensive they are to feed, they won't make any more. So I'll make the process virtually irresistible.*

God is way ahead of the game.

Pleasure is big. It is way big. It is huge. Pleasure is very good. God gave us sex so we could enjoy it—a lot. He is very good after all. Joy was something He invented. No, actually, it is something that is intrinsic to who He is. It's how He is wired, we might say.

Because He is able to ultimately bring about everything He ultimately desires.

God does not worry.

He does not risk, not really, despite what Open Theists assert.

How could the God of the prophets (who I would wager knew God better than most of our current teachers) possibly be said to take a chance, to wring His hands in worry: *Maybe it will work out; maybe it won't?*

This is what Daniel prays after God gave him not just the interpretation of the dream of the most powerful king in the whole world, but revealed the actual dream itself:

> May the name of God
> be blessed for ever and ever,
> since wisdom and power are His alone.
> His, to control the procession of times and season,
> to make or unmake kings,
> to confer wisdom on the wise,
> and knowledge on those with wit to discern;
> His, to uncover depths and mysteries,
> to know what lies in darkness;
> and light dwells with Him. (Daniel 2:20-22)

That He may choose to bow down over our cribs and use baby talk so we are able to emotionally relate and trust this massive Reality, this King of the Universe does not change who He is in His essence. Because He paints down to our level and draws stick figures of Himself with arms and legs and big, big hands, doesn't mean God has a body or that He really fears or worries or wonders. (This is what Open Theism's wooden literalism so wrongly suggests.)[1]

The Creator of the heavens and the earth who rides on the heavens to our rescue and on the clouds in His majesty is exceedingly—and joyfully—secure. He actively and confidently works in and around, behind and underneath everything for the good of His children. He is so confident that He allows evil and Satan's devious schemes, because He knows that even what He hates He will turn around ultimately to make work out perfectly for the final glory of His name and the good of those who love Him. Who wouldn't be happy?

How does this all happen?

I don't have a clue.

It is, however, what He says, so I just happily believe it. As those who have read the last chapter know, this Great Epic turns out very well in the end—for those who lay down their weapons and throw up their hands, that is. Joy, not only in tantalizing glimmers but long, drenching, exhilarating cascades is what is in store. But God allows us tastes of it here. Sex is one of them.

The joy that comes from physical intimacy is a reminder of the glory that is to be ours forever. It is an ecstatic celebration of the wondrous beauty of loyal, committed, permanent love in its full trinitarian wholeness: physically, emotionally, and spiritually.

Thus, without any exaggeration I can tell my five children that it is a mystery, a sacrament: two image-bearers in an ecstasy of mutual love symbolizing and reflecting and enjoying the holy beauty, the joyful symmetry, and loving perfections of God's pleasure in Himself.

That is another reason why sex is so powerful—because it is one of those darts of heaven ("pangs of joy") that are meant to pierce us and remind us of where we are headed and where we belong. Unhappily, only few feel in its surge and rush and excitement the joy of a good and Holy Father who laughs and plays and dances; the intimate delights and mutual satisfaction of this perfectly loving and supremely happy Divine Threesome who is One. Idolaters that we are, we tend to take the symbol and make it a god. That is where sex is no longer good. That is where life becomes death.

Sex at its core is not about bodies and pleasure but God.

I did not always recognize it to be so. It took me a while to understand that when sex goes bad, when the icon is mocked and torn out of its holy frame, it is an unconscionable debasing.

It is a rape and a robbery, and it is a form of murder.

That is what I wish I would have said to my children, so I say it to you instead.

When we twist and pervert sex into a means for personal, private, secret (and guilty) pleasure (whether in our minds or in our bodies), we are defacing a masterpiece. It is like walking the corridors of the Louvre with brush in hand and splashing obscenities on the paintings of Van Gogh, Cézanne, Velazquez, and Rembrandt. It is a debasing and a cheapening of what is incredibly precious and holy. It is a violation of a wondrous sacrament meant to give us a window into eternity—like taking the host, throwing it to the ground, and trampling on it with muddy feet.

It is also to defraud. For it is a bodily promise of something the spirit has not made or will not keep. Sex outside of marriage is fraud. This is actually the term Paul uses in a little verse that is mostly overlooked. We are not to lead each other on ("take advantage"), he advises us (1 Thessalonians 4:6).[2] What is probably in view is stimulating each other sexually when we know we have no moral and divine sanction to consummate the relationship. That is fraud, for with your body you are saying, "I am yours and you are mine, exclusively, permanently, and ineradicably" (even though you have not entered into a binding covenant to establish the validity of those fundamental vows).

You are lying or at least misleading, intentionally or not, because you have no basis on which to make those promises and assert such guarantees.

And that is where the deep hurts come.

If you are a decently informed product of our permissive culture, you may well raise the question, What about the casual "friends with benefits"? What about when promises have purposefully *not* been made and both people understand there are "no strings attached"? Isn't that harmless since both parties agree to the ground rules?

I might concede the point if we were essentially machines or mammals or merely a combination of complex chemicals. The reality is that we are primarily, in our essence, spiritual. Thus, what our mouths say and what our spirits are communicating are radically opposed.

Your body is saying, "No commitments, baby," while your spirit is saying, "I am one with you."

And that is where the deepest cuts are inflicted.

That is why bad sex is also a theft, for it takes away pieces of the other's soul.

Whether we believe it or not, sex is about spiritual bonding. It is such a profound, mystical cementing of souls that when the affair ends and the bodies separate, it removes not bits of skin but spirit. The result is inner hemorrhaging. With time, the wound becomes scarred over and desensitized.

It hardens, until the heart begins losing all real feeling, then dies. It works kind of like a psychic form of leprosy. Just ask those who've given themselves over to indiscriminate sexual indulgence. Ultimately, there is barely a hint of pleasure left at all. That is where bad sex leads to really bad sex and then to terrible, even deadly, sex.

Here is where we get a graphic glimpse of the awful cruelty of Satan's end game: promises of increasing delights tied to slowly decreasing fulfillment; bigger lies bleeding into diminishing enjoyments. He seduces with free and full pleasure then enslaves you to bleak pleasure, sad pleasure, empty pleasure, death-dealing pleasure. This is why I would tell my sons and daughter that bad sex is a twisted form of murder. It perverts a joyful, life-affirming, life-celebrating, and life-producing gift and mutates it into an instrument of death. Yes, even though it may feel so good at the moment.

Here is perfectly illustrated how little we can trust our

feelings. (As millions have asked, or sung, "If it feels so good, how can it be wrong?") Sure, it feels good; that's how God made it. Glazed apple fritters and chocolate éclairs taste good too, but that doesn't mean they're *always* good. There are boundaries and limits and restraints. Uncontrolled sexual appetite, like physical appetite, can kill. And it may feel good all the way to the emergency room or the morgue.

What do I mean that it is murder?

Simply this: It kills some precious, important, and very necessary virtues. Sex, when it is out of bounds, kills what is ultimately at the heart of the best sex imaginable: trust. Complete, utter, unqualified trust is the single-most important erotic component to world-class sex: sex that is joyful, happy, guilt-free, shameless, explosively delightful, sacred, and holy. That is the element it puts to death. It also kills integrity, honor, and loyalty. And it is also a death blow to purity and chastity, both of which are actually elevated and honored in the healthy sexual union of a husband and wife. And when it twists out of shape, it is an avenue to the extinction of all possibility of producing life. This is most obvious in homosexual sex.

I would also go on to explain that there is another aspect to equating bad sex with killing. It is what is going on when we indulge in pornography. It kills by reducing a living person, a holy being, into an unholy object. Like a death-wielding dagger, it takes a living person and turns them into a corpse-like mechanism for private and personal pleasure. What it is doing in essence is stripping human beings of their unique dignity; taking away from them their holiness and value as image bearers of God, and with their life force drained, shrinks them down into cold, lifeless, sexual pleasure things. That is a form of spiritual murder. Even where the lust is two-way, all that has been accomplished is doubling the crime by reducing two creatures to selfish, sensual, enjoyment-objects.

And here is the great sadness. Here we enter into a real but unflinching grief: bad sex is also a great and profound loss. The body, once it is given away, cannot ever be fully reclaimed. That is why Paul rings the changes on the theme of sex as bonding with another, even the ritual prostitute (1 Corinthians 6:15-17). Serious matters are in play, and the more serious, the greater the consequence. When we give our body away to a friend, acquaintance, companion, or one-night stand, we have given it away.

There is no option of getting it back.

You are a virgin or you are not. It is just that inflexibly stark and true.

There is only one first time.

Sexual innocence is yours or it is not.

By surrendering this precious treasure to another, no matter what the intent or hope or expectation, you cannot present yourself to your bride or groom as a pure, unsullied, unopened, mysterious treasure that they alone can unpack. Certainly, there is forgiveness, healing, and cleansing in the mighty death and resurrection of Jesus. That is what the blood of Jesus guarantees, absolutely. But there are certain intractable, unavoidable laws woven into the very fabric of reality. One of them is that every action has its corresponding reaction. In the spiritual world, that means sin has its inevitable consequences: Virginity once given away cannot be reclaimed.

Those are the harsh and brutal facts of life.

If we surrender our virtue we come to our spousal bed unable to reclaim what has been lost and unable to provide what our spouse deserves and we so desire: our bodies pure and innocent and untouched; an unsullied offering reserved exclusively for our beloved. We also undermine our ability to enter into intimacy with psychological exclusivity. We bring the memories and experiences embedded in our heads and imprinted on our souls into our bed. And what few will admit, they surface at the worst possible moment. Sex is beautiful and virgin sex is a marvel and a mystery, a surprise, and a very costly gift.

So I say to my four boys and beautiful daughter, hold it fast, hold it close, guard it well. Honor your bodies, your virtue, and that of the spouse you have yet to meet but whom even now I pray is doing the same.

» » »

Though the above is unmistakably true, though innocence and purity given away cannot truly be restored in this life, there is still a good and strong and lasting hope. Our God who is indeed a righteous and holy Judge is also gracious and merciful, slow to anger, and abounding in love. This pardoning God takes great joy in restoring what has been stolen from us.

He can give us beauty for the ashes of misspent passion.

He can fill us with the healing oil of gladness where there was once despair.

He can remove the mourner's cloak and drape us with a mantle of praise.

Though you may have fallen, (and who hasn't—somehow, somewhere, someplace?), He can still make of you a strong and sturdy tree: an oak of righteousness for a display of His splendor (Isaiah 61:3, NIV).

And while it is rare that He completely erases every earthly consequence of sexual sin, He does promise a full and complete restoration on the day that really matters. The last chapter of this

Epic of all epics ends with this stunning reversal and restoration: All of us are gathered, the bride of Christ united, from every corner of the globe and every epoch in history, and we are so happy for we are celebrating together a Wedding Day.

And on this day that never ends, purity has been fully and forever restored. Each of us has been made ready for our Glorious Groom, our dirty and shameful rags removed once and for all, our bodies covered with fine linen, white and clean. And we are singing in a thunderous chorus: "Alleluia! The reign of the Lord our God Almighty has begun, let us be glad and joyful and give praise to God, because it is time for the marriage of the Lamb. His bride is ready." (Revelation 19:6-7).

And we will hear these words: "Here God lives among men. He will make His home among them. They shall be His people, and He will be their God; His name is God-with-them. He will wipe away all tears from their eyes. There will be no more death, and no more mourning or sadness. The world of the past [with all its shame and regrets] has gone" (Revelation 21:3-4).

And so it will be, and so will it forever be.

All this is what I would have said to my children in my secret fantasy, and though I did not, I am grateful that they picked up on enough that matters. And though I did not do so at that time, this is what I pray for them and for you now:

Blessing

May He who created the birds to soar
and the bees to skip and dance
give you the desires of your true heart.
May He bless you with a life-long love.
May He fill you with an abundant joy in loving and in being loved.

May the holy Father keep you holy.
May the gracious Father forgive your failures
and give you fresh starts.
May the merciful Savior wash you clean again and again.
May He give you more than you ask for and more than you even
hope.
May you maintain your bodies in holy love, devotion, and purity.
And if you fall and if you fail,
May the eternal good Shepherd of your souls
pick you up and wipe you off and dress you with holy robes
and a sturdy confidence,
and say to you, "You are forgiven, go sin no more."
And may you delight in and be enjoyed by the spouse of your youth
all the days of your life.
(Or if not,) in the Lover of your Soul
whose love is like a blazing fire
that many waters could never quench.

13

DAVID'S DANCE

Coming from such conservative Midwestern Baptist roots, my fashion-conscious son demonstrated an unexpected artistic flair. After graduating from high school, Ben had an irrepressible urge to create, paint, and write music, which led to an interest in hair design. So he got a degree in cosmetology. That opened further avenues of creativity.

Eventually, Ben discovered a flair for designing clothes and accepted an offer to show off his creations at a local fashion show. It was a place and an environment where my wife and I never expected to find ourselves, but life has its little surprises. It proved to be an interesting evening.

Anticipating the hors d'oeuvres to follow, I concluded with a father's professional detachment that Ben's stylings and unique point of view did stand up well if I did say so myself. The young man (I'll call him Luke) who'd offered Ben the opportunity was distinct among his male peers in that he was heterosexual. Like

Ben, he had also had a solid, conservative evangelical upbringing. These similarities created a lot of contact points between them. Soon thereafter, Luke moved to New York to pursue a career in the fashion industry. While completing his studies, Luke was selected for internships in Milan and London and since then has garnered national and international attention.

Some months after Luke moved, Ben and I were together in our car. We weren't talking very much as I recall. I was distracted. I will admit what my wife would readily betray if she were writing this—that, at times, I have the ability to drive amazing distances in utter silence when plunged in thought. I will also concede that my wife is not terribly appreciative of that particular trait. In any event, it was quiet in the car and had been for a while. My son glanced at me with certain intention in his eyes. I noticed that his face was drawn and paler than normal. I also detected a troubled sadness in his eyes. He looked out at the Michigan foliage, which was just beginning to burn red and brilliant ocre. I could tell he wasn't really seeing it.

Before I could ask him if he was all right, still looking out the windshield, he asked, "Dad, is it true what they say, that homosexuality is genetic? That it is a condition you are born with and can't change?"

I know for sure that my hands didn't wobble on the steering wheel; only the knuckles changed hue a little. My mouth went suddenly dry. As I said, life has its unexpected, sometimes shattering, surprises. I feared that this would be one of those. To my credit, nothing else in my appearance betrayed the radical spike in my blood pressure. Though my son's question had blown through me like a cyclone, my expression remained inscrutable.

With steady voice, I commented that, as far as I knew, the studies purporting to establish a genetic connection were blatantly biased and not scientifically convincing. I told him that even if a genetic connection could be made, all it would prove is that violating God's laws can rewire our circuitry or that of our children. It would be the same as a gene for alcoholism or some other type of addictive behavior. The genetics would only serve to establish our particular predisposition, our proneness to a particular type of misbehavior inherited from our imperfect ancestors. Genes don't absolve us from responsibility.

I believe the Bible teaches the depravity of man: We are broken in all our parts, intellectual, moral, and spiritual. I also believe that, thankfully, we are not so thoroughly broken as to lose our likeness to God. We can still reason and love and create beautiful things and perform acts that are beneficial for humanity, though none of them perfectly. But all of us left to ourselves, love ourselves, love our sin, love what leads to death not life. That is the reality of the human condition.

Saint Paul describes this sad state of affairs by saying that because of Adam's sin "death [or sin] reigned" over mankind (Romans 5:14) and as a result we are "slaves of sin" (Romans 6:17). This is why Jesus tells Nicodemus that the final verdict is that men love darkness *instead of* the light (John 3:19, emphasis added). Men are free to choose and what they choose is sin, because sin is what they love. Sin is the master and we are its servants.[1] Thus, our propensity to sin or our orientation toward a specific sinful pattern does not pose an insurmountable moral problem.

My grandfather on my father's side was a sexual predator—probably a sex addict, in modern parlance. Ben knew, but I reminded him anyway, that as far as I knew, his dad and his uncles had all had their battles in varying degrees with pornography. I explained that if at some future date a brain scan were developed that could detect that twisted little gene it would not thereby exonerate any of us from our choices. Scientific proof, if it were attainable, that I am genetically wired toward child abuse or wife beating, or murder would not provide me with a get-out-of-jail-free card. The gene would only help identify the arena of battle.

After offering this explanation with a studied calm but with fingerprints now embedded in the steering wheel, I asked, "So, Ben, why do you ask?"

"Oh," he said, "I just got an email from Luke, and he told me he was coming out of the closet." There was a sadness in my son's face.

My blood pressure dropped to almost normal, and my knuckles returned to their familiar color.

I took my first normal breath in several minutes.

Ben continued. "He told me that he'd battled it since he was a kid and now that he's in New York City, he decided to let his friends and family know."

My relief was tempered by the realization of the agony and self-blame his parents must have been struggling with at that moment.

"It's so hard to know how to talk to him, Dad," he said. "I don't know what to say. I don't want to come across like a judgmental fundamentalist. I want him to know that we're still friends and that his choice doesn't change that. I still really like him."

He was looking at me hopefully as if I could untangle this massive ethical knot for him with a wave of my hand. Yes, my sons have been trained to believe I do have all the answers. Jonathan, the oldest, is past the quarter-century mark and is beginning to have some glimmering doubts, but the others still seem pretty confident in my Solomonic wisdom.

I didn't want to let him down, but I couldn't think of anything to say.

Since I didn't come through for him right away, Ben went on. "I don't agree with what he's doing, but I also don't want to cut him off or have him feel like I'm just another religious bigot. I know several of my friends who are gay have been hurt really badly by Christians, and that's the last thing I want.[2] How do you remain committed to what is right and not alienate people? How can I still be their friend but keep from appearing as though I'm supporting their wrong choices?"

Now there's a series of questions worthy of Solomon, I thought.

My mind was a blank. Then the memory of my friend David hit me like Newton's apple. I exhaled and began to tell my son the bittersweet story that had happened several years earlier when he was only eight.

After working for almost three years as a bilingual attorney for Michigan Migrant Legal Services (a federally funded program that was kind of a watchdog between migrants and their farm employers), I needed a job that could actually support my family of five. It was the fall of 1999 when I joined the Prehearing Division of the Michigan Court of Appeals. In short order, I discovered a hidden talent for taking a box of transcripts and summarizing them into a coherent and logical flow. The position required researching the legal arguments on both sides of the appeal and recommending a verdict for the appellate panel, for or against the moving party—the appellant. Each file was assigned a projected time limit. The game, for those of us who liked that sort of thing, was to see how far under the limit we could come. I've always been a sucker for competition. Somehow or other, I became the specialist in parental termination cases. These are appeals of a lower court's decision to take away the parental rights of a purportedly abusive parent. The arguments were so redundant and uncomplicated, nobody else wanted to have their brains numbed by them. I used the goal of beating the deadline as a means of maintaining focus.

David joined the division at the same time I did. He was six foot two, dark haired, charming, and quite good-looking. He looked and moved like the dancer he was. He had spent a few years dancing professionally before going to law school. He was just a little bit younger than I. We had a lot in common. He had lived in Spain, spoke Spanish, and loved fine cuisine. But unlike me, he was gay. Very much so. Due to his charm, brilliant wit, and razor-sharp intellect, he quickly became a leading figure in the homosexual community. Despite our obvious differences, we became friends.

Not infrequently, I would see him looking sideways at me and could tell he was trying to figure me out. He knew I'd attended a conservative Baptist seminary for three years, studying for my masters of divinity. Yet from our conversations, he knew that I appreciated liberation theology's Marxist/Christian critique of the oppressive third-world regimes my Baptist brethren supported. He was also confused that I did not side reflexively with the hostile and militant element of the Right to Life crowd.

To be honest, I enjoyed upending his stereotypes. I still sort of looked the part of the conservative seminarian, but I was really a Che Guevara radical at heart. I just hadn't yet had the benefit of culture-sensitive teens to teach me some fashion sense. It worked out, though, since my polyesters provided excellent cover for the occasional conversational ambush. David would be convinced he had me figured out, then I'd come down on the side of the disenfranchised minorities or side with the Democrat Party and his head would start to spin. It was great fun.

David had an acerbic wit. I liked that too, though it could easily draw blood. Surprisingly enough, he would tend to censor himself around me. Occasionally he would apologize for his salacious comments. He also had an infallible radar system. Here and now, I will admit to having a "conversional agenda" — I wanted him to encounter the love and grace of Jesus. I wanted him to discover the kind of life Jesus offers all who come to Him: abundant and lived to the full and free.

I was quite clear on one thing: What David most needed was Jesus, not self-esteem or validation. The best possible thing I could do for my friend was help him find cleansing and reconciliation and freedom. I took the admonition of Saint James seriously: "If any of you strays away from the truth, and another brings him back to it, he may be sure that anyone who can bring back a sinner from the wrong way that he has taken will be saving a soul from death and covering up a great number of sins" (5:19-20).

Although we enjoyed a lot of topics, David studiously avoided waters that were more than ankle deep. His ability to sense the subtlest conversational shifts was maddening. He could smell it when it was still incubating in my head. His head would jerk up, aquiline nose wrinkled, and he would toss out a dismissive, "Stoner, I know where you're going, and I'm not going there."

It was so frustrating because the more I grew to love David, and I did, the more obvious it was that his heart was lead and his spirit was dust-dry. His eyes told me a hundred tales of a long sadness and a hunger that would never be satisfied. I could sense that he wanted to tell me about it, but the walls were too high, the protective buffer too thick. But he knew that I was his friend and that I loved him. The reason I know that is because he told me — in so many words — the day he dropped into my office with a bombshell.

We'd been working together for almost two years. He got bored, I think, and wanted to be a real lawyer, so he took a job at the Defender's Office. Before leaving, he came to see me. He shut the door behind him. I knew immediately that something was terribly wrong. His abnormally excellent posture was gone. He sagged like a punctured air mattress. He sat down heavily in the chair across from my desk and tried to tell me. It was difficult since he'd always been so careful to maintain safe, surface-level communication between us. Now that he needed to break through the superficiality, it was a struggle.

"Can we talk?" he asked, his face drawn and tight.

"Sure," I said, my heart already beginning to race. "What's up?"

He took a deep breath then took a second to compose himself. His dark eyes were pools of anguish. "I went to the doctor and found out that I tested HIV-positive."

My mouth went immediately dry, and my heart sank to my stomach. I had never known anyone with HIV. All I knew was that, at that time, infected people generally died.

"David," I croaked out, "I'm so sorry."

His eyes had become red, and mine got wet, and I couldn't say a whole lot more. I felt this terrible dread come over me, and I wanted to put my arm around his shoulders, hug him, and cry with him but knew that wouldn't be right.

"I haven't told anyone else in the office," he said. "There was no one I felt I could trust. But I knew I could talk to you."

The lump in my throat got bigger.

"I'm going to be leaving soon," he went on, "but I just somehow felt like I needed to talk to you before I went. That you would understand. I knew I could trust you."

There it was again.

I shook my head sadly, tried to swallow, and pushed the terrible sadness down.

I looked him in the eyes. "David, can I pray for you?" I asked.

He did not know that I never really wanted to preach at him. I just wanted him to know that Jesus knew him by name, that He loved him and had given up His life to rescue him just like He had me from a meaningless, self-destructive existence. All I had ever wanted him to know was that homosexuality was not the Big Issue—that the real problems were the self-absorbed, God-repelling, prideful patterns that had alienated him (and all of us) from the Father. And that, yes, Jesus would in fact free him from his tyrannical bondage that was eating him alive, and he would be washed clean and made new.

David just nodded. And in his eyes I could see gratitude and relief and humiliation, and I just wanted to bawl. At that moment, I felt so honored, so blessed to be invited in and yet so angry. I was angry because his eyes were telling me about the shame and fear he'd had to break through to talk to me; the shame of countless sly jabs and self-righteous judgments; the fear that now, at this crucial, most vulnerable moment of his whole life when all was unraveling around him, I would decisively and finally raise my religious hackles, wag my finger accusingly in his face, and tell him God was cursing him for his sexual perversion. The relief in the room felt light and warm like rays from a morning sun.

I prayed as best I knew how. I told God how sad I was and how worried David was. I thanked Him that He knew everything in David's heart and that He loved him. I poured out my desire that He would perform a miracle and bring about a supernatural blood transfusion. I told Him that I trusted that He knew what was right and good and best, but that I still desired for my friend to be healed. I claimed the scriptural promise that we don't have because we don't ask, and so I asked boldly. I then asked that Jesus would reveal to my friend how deep His love is for him. I had to keep choking back the tears, but I managed to make it through.

Soon thereafter, David took his new job, and I quickly lost track of him. The Defender's Office is a pretty tight-knit, insular little circle, and the gay contingent is even smaller and tighter. I did not see David again for over a year. Slowly, these irrepressible urges to find out how my friend was doing began nagging at me. We hadn't talked since he left the Court of Appeals. It would be awkward. He had his new friends. He wouldn't want me calling like a voice out of the past and bringing back old memories. I stalled and argued and then one morning as I stared out over the Grand Rapids skyline from my fourth-floor office, I knew I had to make the call.

Someone at the Defender's Office told me David was on leave. That's all they would say. I knew they were covering. I called up a friend who worked there and when I told her that we had been good friends, she divulged the truth. David was very ill and had been in the hospital for several weeks. The HIV virus had become full-blown AIDS, and he was not doing well at all. I was overwhelmed with guilt. I had secretly feared that this is exactly what I would find and wanted to avoid being sucked into the mess of it all.

Face it. You were just scared, I had to admit to myself. AIDS was an awful, wretched disease that I knew nothing about, and I've always been kind of squeamish. Ashamed of myself, I had to face the reality that I was pathetic and selfish and cowardly.

David's coworker gave me the number for the hospital room. When I called, David answered almost immediately. His voice was no longer strong. It was the voice of a tired and not-so-young man. I could hear people speaking in the background, and he didn't sound terribly happy to hear from me. The knife twisted in my gut.

"I've been thinking a lot about you and wondered if I could come over and see you sometime," I told him.

"I'm doing fine," he said. "I have a wonderful group of friends. They are very strong and supportive. I don't really need anyone else to come by right now. Thanks, though."

I could hear the steel doors of the gay-lesbian-hospice-protectiveness community being slammed in my face. The knife twisted some more. I had waited too long.

"Well, I'd love to see you again sometime," I offered. "Give me a call when you get out."

He said he would and hung up.

If I'd only responded to those nudges sooner, maybe I would have been allowed in. Now, as it was, the homosexual guard had circled the wagons around my friend, and I had been pointedly excluded.

I felt sick.

» » »

A few days later, I received a call in my office. I was stunned. It was David's voice on the line. He sounded much happier and hopeful. He was calling from home.

"The doctors let me leave," he said. "They felt I'd made so much progress that I could return to my house. They think I'm really improving."

He was upbeat, and his tone was much more like the David I had known. My hopes rose.

"Tim," he continued, "while in the hospital, I felt like I really needed to reconnect with my faith. I didn't know who else would understand, but I knew you would, so I called you."

The fog of shame and recrimination began to evaporate.

"Could you come over and talk with me about it sometime?" he asked.

I tried to keep the relief and excitement out of my voice. I didn't want to sound too anxious, but I knew I needed to see him—immediately. I didn't want to give him time to change his mind or have it changed.

"How about tonight?" I said.

With the briefest hesitation, he responded, "Sure."

David was staying at his father's house. When I was let in, David was standing in the hallway outside the door to his bedroom. A shock ran through me. Only in movies of World War II concentration camps have I seen bodies *that* emaciated. He must have dropped forty pounds and probably now weighed only 150 pounds. He did not speak immediately. I wonder if even then he was gauging and measuring me. There was still just the hint of the dancer's straight back, but there was also a weariness to him now. He was in pajamas, and he was no longer wearing contacts. His glasses were thick. They were the kind he would have enjoyed mocking a few years earlier.

His voice was soft and raspy when he welcomed me.

There was no sarcasm, no oblique mockery; he was worn down.

I went up to him, and he held out his hand. It was like shaking hands with an eighty-year-old. The skin was like parchment, and I could feel the bones beneath. I could have wept for him. What I felt next was a wave of anger. I think I was feeling just a hint of the wrath God feels at the ruination of His creation. As I followed David into his bedroom, hatred for the merciless cruelty of sin rushed over me. I raged in silence. I was seeing with my eyes what is usually only apparent in the spiritual: Satan, like a vampire, pierces us and drains away life, hope, and joy in languorous gulps till we are left empty, hollow shells. The husks of dead souls are what he leaves behind.

Dead men walking. I was following behind one.

I prayed desperately, *"Lord, have mercy! Have mercy! Reveal your love to David. Please!"* It comforted me to know that Patty was at home praying too.

He lay down, and I helped cover him up. It was clear he was exhausted with the effort, but his voice, though soft, was strong.

He smiled from behind his large spectacles. "Thanks for coming to see me."

"I'm so glad you asked me over, David," I replied. "I've been wanting to see you again for a long time."

He nodded, and then his eyes grew distant. He told me something I had not expected. "While I was in the hospital, I felt like God was in the room. I don't know how, but I began to feel like I wanted to get back to my faith. Something began changing inside me."

He stopped, his cheeks reddening. "I can't explain it, Tim, but all the stuff in my past became" — he was searching for the right word — "repulsive."

He pointed shyly toward a brown paper bag in the corner of the room. "I knew I had to get rid of all the stuff I had. I filled up that grocery bag with pornographic magazines and videos. I don't know what to do with it."

"Don't worry about it, David," I said. "I'll get rid of it for you."

I'd never had a serious spiritual conversation with a homosexual before, much less one who was afflicted with AIDS. I didn't want to sound preachy and "religious." And I didn't want to say something stupid and offensive that would slam those steel doors down between us. I was afraid to open my mouth but terrified not to. My throat was so dry that I wished I'd brought a glass of water in with me. Slowly, it just came to me. I had this inexplicable deep knowing about what I needed to say.

I decided if I didn't plunge in, I might lose my nerve.

"David," I began, "can I share with you what I think God's been trying to say to you?"

He nodded somberly. There was this little glimmer of hope in the back of his eyes. He was listening intently.

"What He's been trying to communicate is how deep is His love for you." An odd confidence had swept away my awkwardness and confusion. "You were made to love and worship and be ravished by the God who created you. And your whole life you've been madly trying to fill up this hole in your heart that only He can fill."

I quoted one of my favorite passages from Saint Augustine: "Lord, you have made us for yourselves and our hearts are restless till they find their rest in thee." His eyes, through the thick lenses, were as big and as dark as an owl's.

I was gaining momentum. "You've rushed from one relationship to another hoping to satisfy your hunger for God and nothing ever satisfied. They all left you empty and dry and desperate. But what God is telling you, David, is that He is the one who you've been looking for your whole life but never knew it. You've been running from Him your whole life. He wants you to stop and turn to Him."

I then explained that we were all created for a relationship of intimate love with our Father, but our sins had built this impenetrable wall between us. I told him of the astonishing love of this God who, wanting to make a way for His rebel creation to be restored back to Him, sent His best and only Son on a mission to tear this wall down at the cost of His bloody death.

As David's eyes grew more luminous, and as I could see the Word penetrating, I began having a hard time talking over the lump in my throat.

"You can be reconciled to Him right now," I sort of croaked. "If you confess your sins to Him and ask Him to forgive and cleanse you, He will."

He had barely moved as I talked.

"Do you want to give Him your life?" I asked.

His eyes were shining. "Yes," he whispered.

He prayed simply, and I prayed too. On the basis of the clear words of Scripture, I declared to him that his sins, every one of them, were absolved, forgiven, washed away—he was totally clean. He was a brand new creature, a child of God. He could enjoy eternal life now, and he could enjoy it forever.

"Thank you," he whispered as I hugged him. I knew he wanted to cry but couldn't or wouldn't. I think he was probably too embarrassed.

I decided to leave him with my new red leather Bible. I wrote a dedication in the flyleaf:

To David, who like King David of old, is also a worshipper. The Lord has redeemed you and is going to free you to dance, no longer for men, but—out of a pure and undiluted gratitude and love—for your heavenly Father. And like David, you will dance with abandon, filled with an overflowing joy.

Your brother, Tim

Later that night, Patty and I hugged and hugged as I told her the happy story. I was so excited to share this journey with my friend and now my brother. The impact his life would have among the gay community in our city was beyond calculation. I couldn't wait to help him take his first steps on this brand-new path.

My first thoughts as I woke that next day were, I wonder how David is doing? How must he be feeling this first morning—totally free and totally clean?

When I got to my office, I rushed to pick up the phone. I was so excited to talk with him that my fingers slipped on the numbers. I called his home and got no response. I called the Defender's Office.

"Do you know where David is?" I asked.

A brief pause and an intake of breath. "Didn't you hear?"

My heart skipped a beat.

"He died last night."

I felt as if the floor had dropped out from underneath me.

"He began hemorrhaging, and they rushed him to hospital, but they couldn't stop the bleeding."

I was making inarticulate sounds.

"I'm sorry—you didn't know?" It was more a question than a statement.

I mumbled something and hung up. I could hardly breathe or speak. My thoughts were in this crazy, confused whirl. I was so sad and so disappointed. Mostly, I felt bad for me.

I had this whole scenario planned, this whole cool story line. David and I were going to be such good friends. Now we could have honest conversations about stuff that really mattered. We would be soul mates. He could teach me how to cook his phenomenal eggplant parmigiana. Together we could make serious inroads into this suspicious and resistant community. The tears were running down my face, and then suddenly I was jolted. It was as if I'd gotten zapped by a bolt of electricity. The words I'd written in his Bible only hours earlier came back to me.

My God! It had been a prophecy!

"The Lord will free you to dance."

David was dancing! He was lost in an ecstasy of pure, abandoned love and gratitude. How could I possibly be sad? He was finally free and whole and in love—forever. He had finally found what his heart had been yearning for.

» » »

I turned to look at Ben sitting next to me in the car. He had this big smile on his face, and it was happy and at peace as he stared at the glowing russett and amber leaves zipping past our car window. He nodded his head as if I'd solved a complicated puzzle for him, more than just telling him a simple story out of my life.

There was a calm that had come over him. "Thanks. Yeah, that's what I want for Luke too, Dad," he said.

Deep down, it's what we all want.

We all hunger to be embraced, absolved, and restored.

We were all meant to receive and to live out of our Father's favor and forgiveness.

We were all meant to walk out of the dark closet into His glorious light.

Blessing

May the compassionate, unyielding love of your perfect Father
draw you in and draw you out.
May you receive and extend
the unqualified, unmerited mercy you have yourself been given.
May you hear Him say to you,
"Come forth!
Come out of the dark, hand-crafted closet-coffin
of shame, humiliation, resentment, and unsatisfying passion."

Face your weakness and fall into His strength.
Admit your abject failures
and accept His ample triumph,
for where you lost, He won,
where you rebelled, He obeyed—perfectly.
So bow to embrace His victory as yours.
May you kneel down and bathe in His pure and cleansing stream.
May He replace your dirty rags with regal robes
and taking you by the hand,
make you stand drenched in pure, transforming light.
And then may you lift your arms,
pick up your feet, and join the dance.

14

WAITING TILL FATHER RETURNS

Remember the elite private school reserved for the children of America's top 2 percent in *Dead Poets Society*? The buildings were crafted from blocks of granite, and ancient ivy clung thickly with the tenacity of many years on the craggy walls. The fields where competitive games among gentlemen were played had the look of carpet, lush and green and flat. The teachers were strict but imminently and inflexibly fair. Potential was meant to be achieved not squandered.

That was my privileged environment during fourth and fifth grades.

The school's name was The Grange Preparatory School (TGPS). It was in the manicured suburbs of Santiago, the capital of Chile. Its emblem was the griffin (also spelled gryphon), which for the mythologically challenged is a legendary creature with the lower body of a lion and the head of an eagle. It was a fearsome animal. Since the lion was the king of the jungle and the eagle was considered the king of the air, it was regarded as an amazingly powerful creature. It was the *capo di tutti capi* of the animal world. So I went to school under the insignia of a creature who ruled the earth *and* the skies.

Interesting.

I believe Nietzsche would have approved.

It was a British boarding school for the coddled offspring of the elite—international business owners and political and corporate leaders—of Chile and its environs. I was no doubt swimming in the same educational tank alongside the children of some of the prominent fascists in South America. I probably studied with Pinochet's brood, come to think of it.

It probably goes without saying that my older brother David and I were not admitted based on lineage or power or connections. We got in the traditional American way—we bought our way in. Though our parents were simple missionaries with zero political clout and subsisted on ministry wages, they were paid in greenbacks, and back in 1966 and 1967 Washington and Lincoln's portrait carried serious weight and stretched a mighty long way. They managed to reach up to, and then through, the wrought-iron gates bolted into the granite wall barring entrance to the majestic educational facility within. Though many students boarded there, we did not. We walked home every afternoon.

My mother, who is no pushover, discovered at the beginning of our tenure who was in control. It was not she. When it was explained to her that gray shorts were to be worn all year round, she immediately resisted. She boldly petitioned for a special dispensation on behalf of her two little American youngsters. Would we please be allowed to wear long pants in winter? In Santiago it never snowed, but sometimes winds would blow and rains would fall with a vengeance. The buxom matron in charge looked at my mother over the tops of spectacles that would do postmoderns proud, and in a voice dripping with English disdain responded, "My de-ah madam" — here she paused to lend emphasis to her disgust — "we have yet to lose a student at The Grange Preparatory School because he was wearing short pants." We wore the gray wool shorts year-round.

The Brits understand the importance of dressing for success. Our ensemble was rounded out by gray shirts with striped woolen ties, striped, knee-length socks to match, and patent leather shoes. The outfit was completed with a blue blazer with brass buttons and our fearsome emblem on the left breast pocket. We also wore a gray short-brimmed cap with our mythical emblem proudly affixed on a blue seal. When we went out for recess, we changed into white tennis shoes and put on our gray coveralls to avoid soiling our dashing outfit.

There came a year when I began "acting out," as they say. The strange thing is, I have no recall as to what I did to get into so much trouble. Perhaps there were national issues and prejudices involved that I can no longer remember. It is possible the teachers may have been on special alert for the smart-aleck Yank who retained a bit of a rebel streak.

I have this memory of sitting at my wooden desk in English class (English! I spoke it as well as the teacher — almost). I was being educated in the proper pronunciation of certain words, like *Peter* and *water*. My teacher adamantly insisted that I say "Peetah" and "wahtah." I have a slice of mental videotape in which I see this stubborn little colonial whose hackles are up, refusing to give the teacher satisfaction. The cheeky little chap is insisting on using the Midwestern inflection his forefathers have used for generations, while the teacher slowly becomes unglued. The strange truth of it was, I thought their accent was cool and still do. But I was not about to be forced into it by some smarmy know-it-all.

I would be horse-whipped first. In effect, I eventually was.

I left an indelible mark at good old TGPS that may still be standing to this day. That year, which shall be known as The Year of Acting Badly, I set the all-time record for number of detentions. Now detention was no joke. At the end of the school day, the recalcitrant students who had breached protocol and offended honor would be marched into the gym. We were lined up in rows. We would then be instructed to stand with our hands behind our heads like small prisoners of war.

We were to stand in formation for an hour.

No talking.

No moving.

And most definitely no peeing until time was up.

Though unpleasant and boring, it was not painful. One did not dread detention. The same could not be said for being called to the headmaster's office. The lord of the school was a thin, bony man. He had a blunt Hitler moustache, though probably this is a defect of memory. He also had a long, very supple switch. It was kind of like the instrument lion tamers use, minus the leather thong at the end. That appendage was superfluous. Over the course of his career, the headmaster had refined the skill of "caning" to an exquisite science.

The frightened miscreant is brought trembling to stand in front of the heavy desk that dominates the oak-paneled room. Shelves of books line all the walls, with the occasional hunting print and faces of famous Brits in ornate frames breaking the monotony. The headmaster reads the charges lodged against you, but there is no opportunity of a defense. Sentence has already been issued. The rap-sheet is laid lovingly on the burgundy blotter on the polished wood surface. In clipped, disapproving tones, you are ordered to bend over. Though the tone is dry, you think you can detect the barest gleam of repressed excitement in those cold, lifeless eyes.

At that point, time begins to slow as you dutifully comply and place both hands against the flat edge of the desk in front of you. This is when time stands still as you await the inevitable. Your heart pounds in your ears as you remain motionless.

All other sounds die out.

The delay is carefully calculated.

It is perhaps the worst part.

You cannot see, but you can almost hear the switch being bent back and forth as if being calibrated for maximum effectiveness.

Apparently, justice must be served, but it took its bloody time.

Your knees begin to tremble just the slightest bit.

It is then that you finally, awfully, hear the slapping sound made by a sinuous cane hitting cloth covering a skinny bottom. Only after hearing that smack do you feel the impossibly painful sting of the cane that has masterfully just barely grazed your buttocks with infinite precision. It is the towel sting of all stings, delivered by a Picasso of pain. And though you have sworn on a stack of King James Bibles that you will not cry, the tears jump to your eyes anyway. But if you are very good at what you're about, you make no sound. That is your small but precious victory.

I made that particular trek probably three times. I cannot be quite sure. I know it was more than once—that's about all I can say with any certainty. Pain does something to the memory circuits.

» » »

The year that my dubious discipline record was set, the administration had no other recourse. Detentions were clearly not making an impression. Spankings were not working. The only consequence remaining was to take away from me the event we all lived for. It was the brass ring and crown jewel of the school year, the highlight of our combined existence: The Final Year-End All-School Steeplechase.

All hundred-plus students would dress completely in white, which included our Keds or Converse tennis shoes. We ran around a course that traversed the six soccer and rugby fields and included rope climbing, clambering through tunnels made of barrels and over, through, or under barriers and bars and walls. We would leap over small pools and make our way around an amazing obstacle course that ended on a small hill that led up to a fifteen-foot-wide wall of thick brush. The sweaty and begrimed competitors would be funneled up to a barrier of bushes that we could not see through or over. To end the race, we had to crash through this final obstacle. It was a metaphor for all those restraints that would someday seek to impede our accomplishments.

It was all about mastering your fear.

It was about conquest and confidence and supremacy.

It's what drove mighty Britannia to rule the waves for centuries.

For the initiated, it was a challenge. For the novice, it was terrifying.

But for all, it was inexplicably intoxicating.

What awaited the daring and the brave, the few, the bold, the champions, about six feet below the hedge, was a deep pit filled with cold, muddy water. The brown brackish water was slimy and filthy and came up to your armpits. It was somehow intensely frightening and impossibly exciting at the same moment. When your sweaty body overcame the sudden shock of frigid water and began clambering over the muddy top, you felt like you had conquered the world, or that you easily could.

The Brits may not know cooking, but they do understand male psychology. My hat's off to them.

But at the end of that ignominious year, I had frustrated and disobeyed too many authority figures and garnered too many red deportment scores to be allowed to enjoy the mythical challenges of that obstacle course. I was forbidden by the authorities from participating. I was so mad that I could have torn the hinges off the front gate, chewed them up into little wads, and spit them out like bullets.

My father was on an evangelistic campaign. My mother understood how much this meant to me, but she believed it imperative that I learn that sin has its consequences. I deserved this punishment. She assured me that I would never learn if it didn't hurt. And then she uttered those dreaded words:

"But wait till your father returns."

I had the remaining weeks of school to look forward to being excluded from the race and perhaps banished from the human race. The severity of the punishment broke me, almost.

The rebel in me went underground.

» » »

Jesus talked a lot about punishment. He referred to hell and judgment so much that it's a wonder He didn't lose His entire audience. In the course of His three-year ministry, He mentioned those offensive and unpalatable subjects, directly or indirectly, over seventy times. Some of those references are repeats where the Gospel writers are describing the same events, but most aren't. In any event, these writers are making a definite point as well.

Even when He doesn't sound menacing, He is. When He is gathering His band of brothers, He tells them that He is going to make them "fishers of men" (Mark 1:17). This is a technique called *remez* in which the Rabbi quotes only a small portion of Scripture, leaving His disciples to fill in the blanks. What He is doing is not promising them an idyllic and peaceful expedition along a human trout stream. He is selecting a phrase from ominous prophetic passages warning Israel of impending divine judgment (Jeremiah 16:16; Ezekiel 29:4; 38:4; Habakkuk 1:14-17). Commentator William L. Lane says, "The summons to be fishers of men is a call to the eschatological task of gathering men in view of the forthcoming judgment of God. It extends the demand for repentance in Jesus' preaching."[1] In other words, He is telling His hand-picked students, "The ax of God's justice is about to fall. I will show you how to save people from this inevitable divine calamity."

It's kind of surprising that Jesus is still seen as this essentially kind, gentle, nonconfrontational, tolerant, peace-loving guy. It just goes to show how incredibly appealing this man was. He could say the most offensive, intolerant, even brutal things, and people would keep following Him. It was evident to them that He spoke out of love, not hatred. It was obvious to all that He had no cruel private ax to grind. He did not relish the prospect of punishment. Though He occasionally became furious with His enemies, He did not despise them. The crowd could overlook and forgive His harsh and critical words because this amazing compassion poured out of Him like an overturned vat of perfumed oil.

They tolerated it for almost thirty-six months.

Then it wore thin. They eventually sided with the religious elites and had him murdered.

The fact that they failed to take His warning seriously does not mean that He wasn't serious. Nor does our ignoring or avoiding or evading that warning change much either. According to Jesus, judgment and Judgment Day are inevitable. Punishment is certain and definite, and it is to be avoided at all cost. Though He explains that His three-year ministry was not one of judgment but of salvation (John 12:47), He adds this caveat: The Father has "entrusted all judgment to the Son and appointed Him Supreme Judge" (John 5:22,27). Later He goes on to state that "it is for judgment that I have come into this world" (John 9:39). The word He uses is the legal term for issuing legal verdicts and imposing the sentence. He is saying that He is (or will be) both Judge and Jury.

The point He appears to be making is that the first time He made His appearance His work was not that of condemning and sentencing. He was not here to punish but to save and deliver. Judgment was not so much deleted as saved for later. Those who refuse to turn their lives around and submit to Him are the ones who will face the terrible consequences of their rebellion — they will perish, be destroyed, cut off, burned in eternal, unquenchable fire, and cursed when He returns the second time. He uses these different metaphors more than ten times. If nothing else, He was very creative in His imprecatory descriptions.

According to Revelation, Jesus will, in fact, return. But this time, He will come in a different persona. This time He bursts in on the scene looking like William Wallace with his war paint on. He will not be so much splattered as "soaked with blood." He will be known as the Righteous Judge and the Warrior of Justice. We are told He will tread the wine of Almighty God's fierce anger and on His cloak and on His thigh there will be a name written: The King of kings and the Lord of lords (Revelation 19:11-16).

The wait is over — justice must be served.

He is coming to punish and to rule and to marry His beloved.

He is coming to fulfill the Messianic promises of ruling the nations with "an iron scepter" (Psalm 2:9; Revelation 12:5, NIV). This is a time when the bad news of the Good News is to be carried out. The proclamation is bellowed out with the force of seven thunderclaps by a powerful angel whose shout is as loud as a lion's roar: "The time of waiting is over!" The time has finally come for "God's secret intention to be fulfilled, just as He announced in the Good News told to His servants the prophets" (Revelation 10:7).

It is not only fifth-graders who must learn that sins have consequences, and some more intense than others. It was Jesus who declared that "anyone who refuses to believe in the Son will never see life: the anger of God stays on him" (John 3:36). The Gospel writers report eighteen instances where Jesus warns His Jewish listeners about the coming judgment. He paints these awful and graphic pictures of hell even more times than that.

In the very familiar passage where Jesus the Judge at the end of time is dividing the sheep from the goats, He says to those who have lived selfishly and unjustly and all for themselves: "Go away from Me, with your curse upon you, to the eternal fire prepared for the devil and his angels" (Matthew 25:41). This is no metaphorical temporal, earthly punishment, though we may wish it were.

But that punishment is not yet here. Not in its final, severe, irreversible, and permanent form. There are earthly, temporal effects of sin, but this is not what Jesus is referring to. This is punishment that has been prepared and reserved with Satan and his emissaries in mind.

According to Jesus, this is the gracious period, that interlude of mercy in which judgment is on hold. It waits while most shut their eyes and close their ears and play.

But it waits.

God is patient.

According to King David, God is merciful, tenderhearted, slow to anger, very loving, and universally kind; Yahweh's tenderness embraces all His creatures (Psalm 145:8-9). He waits for so long that some who've heard the rumors of a coming future judgment will begin mocking: "Where is this coming Judge we've been hearing about? Everything is going on just as it always has and will keep going on like this for a whole lot longer. There is no divine judgment looming on the horizon, you must be out of your mind!" (2 Peter 3:3-4, author's paraphrase). What such folk must be reminded of is not to take for granted the mercy, the patience, the goodness of the God who has declared the inevitability and the rightness of judgment.

Sometimes the punishment is delayed for so long that even we, who ought to know better, forget it is coming.

» » »

My childhood friend's father, Ted, was raised by a Polish grandma. He called her "Busha." Ted was a prankster and not overly compliant. Whenever he would step out of line, Busha would come after him waving some wooden implement. Because he was fleet of foot and she was out of condition due to an overabundance of latkes and pierogi, she was unable to make contact. She would stop the chase, catch her breath, and with spatula aloft, thunder ominously, "Just wait, Meester Big Shot, you just wait—next Toisday—eight o'clock!" She would leave the threat hanging and turn away. For the next few days, Ted would be in suspense but soon would forget entirely. Come Thursday he would be sitting at the table eating breakfast. Busha would walk up behind him and deliver a Polish slap to the back of the head. Ted would turn around in shock, and she, smiling grimly, would mutter, "Toisday—eight o'clock, Meester Big Shot!"

God is patient, and we forget.

Saint Peter tells us, "The Lord is not being slow to carry out His promises, as anybody else might be called slow; but He is being patient with you all, wanting no one to be lost and everybody to be brought to change his way." But he continues by assuring us that though He delays, "The Day of the Lord will come" (2 Peter 3:9-10).

In His inaugural address, quoting Isaiah 61, Jesus by omission lays stress on His mission strategy: He is coming first "to proclaim the Lord's Year of Favor" (Luke 4:19; Isaiah 61:2). The Day of Vengeance awaits His second coming.

Though some will mock, there are others who consciously and impatiently wait. These, unlike students dreading the sound of the headmaster's cane or a Polish hooligan held in suspense by his grandma's threats, wait for Father (and Son) to punish those who have not yet been punished.

What they wait for is justice.

Inevitably, there must be justice. Evil people—such as Idi Amin Dada, Hitler, Stalin, Mao, and their ilk—must have their due. The Janjaweed wreaking havoc in Darfur and the warlords behind them, the leaders of the Hutu militias—the Interahamwe and Impuzamugambi, who ordered the death by hacking into pieces of more than 800,000 Tutsis—the ruthless and brutal on all continents who keep back food so their political or tribal enemies starve by the millions, all of these must face the consequences of their terrible crimes.

Those who with impunity rape and pillage and crush and ruin human beings as well as the planet for power and profit are on a list that has not been erased. This is a matter of mere justice. The unrepentant serial killers who brutalize the weak and even feed on them await a day at the Bar of Divine Justice. As do those deviants who steal the innocence from innocents and leave them soiled, broken, and split. And along with them, the abusers who break the faces and the hearts of the defenseless, and the leaders of all time who have used their power to pervert the truth and wreak havoc to promote small, private, personal or nationalistic agendas.

God does not take kindly to those who do such terrible things to that which He made and those whom He loves. Though He waits, He does not forget.

But admittedly, and here is the difficult part. It's not just those big bad guys but all the rest of us nice little guys, whose only crime is murdering God (whether by aggressive rebellion or by mere apathy—passive disregard). Justice also waits for the rest of us, whose malfeasance gets no press but who persistently refuse to acknowledge and submit to the primacy of our Creator's claims on His creatures. These are the ones who disregard and dismiss and live as though they were not created to serve the One who laid down His life for theirs. They live their lives for themselves alone. These reject the Son through a thousand feints and dodges and silence the voice of Him who calls and woos and pleads. They turn their backs to the starry nights that trumpet the proclamation that God is God and He is worthy of worship—that there is more than pleasure and profit and power.

They shut their ears and their eyes to the persistent speech that pours down upon them that God is and that He can be known.

Paul strips away all defensive claims, for he exposes this silent but intentional activity as rebellion. He bluntly calls it "keeping the truth imprisoned in their wickedness" (Romans 1:18). Men's minds are dark, he tells us, and men walk about in ignorance, not innocently but purposefully: "Intellectually they are in the dark and they are estranged from the life of God without knowledge because they have shut their heart to it" (Ephesians 4:18).

The conclusion is a hard one, but it must not therefore be avoided: "That is why such people are without excuse: they knew God and yet refused to honor Him as God or to thank Him; instead they made nonsense out of logic and their empty minds were darkened" (Romans 1:20-21).

Therefore, it needs also to be said that, along with the notorious big bad guys, neither does God take kindly to those who quietly revel in His goodness, are ungrateful, and unwilling to glorify Him who is the Great Father, the giver of every good and perfect gift or to tremble and kiss His only Son who poured out His life's blood that they might be forgiven, restored, reclaimed, and renamed.

At the end of time, Jesus is depicted as the Lamb who is making war on the earth (Revelation 6:17). He is adored and praised as the only one worthy to open the seals of the scroll of divine judgment on the earth (Revelation 5:9-10). He breaks seven seals, each of which releases horrible devastation. At the conclusion of this outpouring of judgment, strangely, there is this hymn that erupts from those in heaven. What they are so glad about is that *finally* the time has come for God's anger to be released in full, for the dead to be judged, and for His children, the small and the great, to be rewarded. The song concludes with the exultant phrase "The time has come to destroy those who are destroying the earth" (Revelation 11:18).

Later, it is an angel who rejoices when water on the earth is turned to blood: "You are the holy He-Is-and-He-Was," he sings, "the Just One, and this is a just punishment: they spilled the blood of the saints and the prophets, and blood is what you have given them to drink, it is what they deserve" (Revelation 16:6). What we in the safe comfort and security of our western living rooms forget, because we have not felt the persecutor's machete or been forced to drink urine from horse troughs or watch as our daughters are brutalized and their babies are cut to pieces in front of them, is that there is a certain right and proper justice that awaits those who have spilled the blood of God's people. There is forgiveness for the repentant; for the others, according to the merciful and Just One who tells us that mercy triumphs over judgment, there is not: "There will be judgment without mercy for those who have not been merciful themselves" (James 2:13).

But for now, judgment waits.

And the waiting isn't calculated to heighten the intensity of the punishment.

The waiting is mercy.

It is the Favorable Year of God's long, patient kindness as He provides ample and repeated opportunity for salvation, deliverance, and reconciliation. It is mercy piled upon mercy, grace upon grace, kindness followed by more kindness. In another place it is called the Day of Salvation. It is not a psychological tool to cruelly raise the tension and heighten the fear.

It is not meant to break us but wake us.

Still, many have used this teaching to crush and frighten and horrify. It has been twisted in the hands of angry men to beat down, punish, and abuse. And though they have perverted God's gracious warnings of judgment into an excuse to become judges and judgers and condemners, the warnings still stand; they are still valid. Their abuse does not cancel out their good and proper use.

It was never meant to provide a justification for judgmentalism.

There is only one righteous judge, and it ain't us.

That's why Saint Paul turns the table on all us nice religious folks and tells us,

> So no matter who you are, if you pass judgment you have no excuse. In condemning others you condemn yourself, since you behave no differently from those you judge. . . . Or are you abusing His abundant goodness, patience, and toleration, not realizing that this goodness of God is meant to lead you to repentance? Your stubborn refusal to repent is only adding to the anger God will have toward you on that day of anger when His just judgments will be made known. He will repay each one as his works deserve. (Romans 2:1,4-6)

All those who out of gratitude and obedience seek to please their Lord by giving their lives away for others will enjoy life eternal. But for those who are "self-seeking and *who reject the truth* there will be wrath and anger. There will be trouble and distress for every human being who does evil" (2:8, NIV).

Punishment is real and it will fall on many who least expect it. But for now, it waits. The point is not the extent, the quality, or the location of the punishment, neither is it intended to give us a litmus test for predicting who goes in and who gets out. What we are meant to know is that it is real and it is very bad, so bad it's the last place on earth or away from the earth you would ever want to be. And it is the last experience you would want to ever undergo.

The good news is that there is yet time to accept the forgiveness and mercy Jesus offers. There is time to submit to Him as Lord and gratefully follow Him by living out His way of life. There is time to give yourself away in gratitude to the One who gave Himself away and held nothing back. There is time to repent of a proud, private pleasure-driven, self-aggrandizing, God-ignoring, selfish, grasping existence, focused on self-needs and ignoring the desperate needs of the truly needy. There is time to turn and let His love wash you, renew you, and empower you. Because the truth is, the merciful life He lived out and calls us to is impossible without that and without Him.

All this talk about hell is to highlight a truth: It has not yet come. Mercy triumphs over judgment and says, "Stop!"

But it will not wait forever.

We have His word on it.

Blessing

So may you rejoice in mercy granted and mercy received.
May the goodness of the Father
and His gentle patience
cause you to not be slack but sober,
cause you to be purposeful and productive,
cause your life to be a riotous garden filled,
whose good fruit brings healing to the nations and the neighbor.
May you give away the mercy you've received.
May your diligence be a warning to the careless.
May your gentleness and patience be a virtue that draws in
the impatient, the angry, the wounded, and the judged.
And may you not forget that though this is
the Year of the Lord's Rich Favor,
the gracious interlude of mercy,
there is a Day of Vengeance coming,
when Justice will have its way and all the wrongs will be made right;

all the selfish works exposed;
reality brought to light.
So may you live in grateful but reverential fear,
working out your salvation with thoughtful care,
not forgetting what is at stake.

15

LONGING FOR HOME

During our trip in 2000 to the orphanage in Mozambique, Africa, Patty was in charge of fun activities for the children. I was in charge of nothing. For whatever reason, over the years in "ministry" endeavors, I had usually been in some type of leadership role. When these activities were in an international setting, I could always communicate with the "nationals," since we were invariably in a Spanish-speaking context. This time around, I had no authority and minimal ability to converse.

As most of us know, if only intuitively, speaking is a means to power or can be. I had been stripped of verbal and positional strength. Portuguese is the national language and there were six tribal dialects, none of which I could spell, much less speak.

We had been met at the decidedly third-world airport in Maputo, a sprawling city of seven million, by Didi ("Gigi"), a Brazilian missionary in a white Land Rover who worked for Iris Ministries. An older orphan drove the other 4x4. Forty-five minutes later we were at the Machava orphanage. The property was a mostly flat plot of land, about twenty acres in size with several cement buildings and half a dozen houses made out of thin hollow canes known as canniso scattered randomly about. The perimeter was marked by a dilapidated barbed-wire fence. The ground was a rust red and ochre patchwork quilt.

Upon disembarking, we were surrounded by about sixty children, with a small herd of boys clamoring to assist in unloading the vehicles, which were now covered in a fine reddish dust. The orphanage directors, Jesse and Raquel Braga, were on a long-overdue vacation visiting their family in Brazil. They were physically and emotionally exhausted from the unrelenting pressure following the floods that had decimated the country and their orphanage earlier that year. Caring for almost a hundred children with only one missionary assistant had run them into the ground. Their youngest daughter was on her seventh bout with malaria.

As the flood waters slowly evaporated, the children had been reintegrated into the orphanage. By the time we arrived, more than eighty children had returned. We could see that construction was well underway on a new girl's dormitory and bathroom. The waters had receded, except for what looked like a large lagoon in the lowest corner of the compound. Several trees sprouted audaciously out of the placid water. At the very center was the church—a simple white-washed building with a corrugated metal roof. It could seat about 120 people. Sitting dejectedly in the middle of the quiet pond, it looked as forlorn as a bride abandoned at the altar.

The next morning and every day thereafter, we each received our own personal escort who, with remarkable self-confidence, would offer to take us by the hand and take us on a walkabout. The first day I was taken to visit the boys' dorms. For the most part, they were cement block with metal bunk beds lining the walls. Two unkempt and dirty canniso huts slept at least eight of the oldest orphans, ranging from fifteen to twenty-one years of age. The beds — actually foam pads wrapped in blue nylon — held a gray wool blanket. Some had pillows, most did not.

We inquired about buying pillows for the little ones who seemed to be consistently lacking them. We were told that pillows were prized items. These were invariably stolen from the youngest by the older orphans, who would sell them for candy and soda money. New clothes would usually travel the same path into the hands of street vendors.

That evening we began a ritual, one we would follow for the next twelve nights. At bedtime, between eight and nine o'clock, we followed pale flashlight circles and wended our tentative way to the children's sleeping quarters, where we split into three groups. One group headed toward the girls' dorm while the other two split off to visit the boys. When we arrived, the older children would still be awake, talking quietly among themselves, playing cards, or reading their tattered paperback school books by candlelight. Without exception, the little ones had shut out the world and were in a deep sleep.

We quickly discovered that the bedtime routine followed a predictable pattern: After supper, around seven o'clock, the youngest children would make their own way or be taken by an older orphan to the communal bathhouse, then after teeth were brushed, they would find their way to bed. Still wearing clothes, the little orphans would fold themselves into tight balls and, unless the heat was absolutely intolerable, pull the wool covering over their heads and be asleep in less than a minute.

This ritual was invariably followed night after night.

No one said goodnight.

No one gave them a hug.

There was no one to read a bedtime story.

No one prayed over them.

The closest thing to a parent's love was the feeling of being occasionally carried to a dark, lonely building and deposited on top of a nylon-covered mat. Every night, this quiet cycle of abandonment was repeated. No wonder they fell asleep so quickly. Where the older orphans had found anger to be their defense, the smallest escaped into the immediate oblivion and isolated safety of a heavy, sometimes troubled, sleep. So we would enter those buildings, illumined weakly by sporadic candlelight and our pale beams and lay hands on these little gray-wool bundles and pray God's favor, goodness, and joy into their lives.

We would pray for destiny and hope.

We prayed for mercy: that the God of the fatherless would extend His hands and provide for these who by any definition were among the most vulnerable, poor, ignored, and needy.

Not infrequently, we were at a loss for words. How do you pray for an abandoned, orphaned child, lying alone, huddled in a sweaty lump beneath a woolen blanket at the far reaches of the world? In a vast, cruel, and unjust world what real hope, what blessed future could they rightfully expect?

The questions reared up in front of us: What can we believe God for?

Sometimes, our empty hands outstretched, all we could do was cry.

Patty was busy and (mostly) happy and contributing. I had nothing to do to justify my existence. I am pathetic at just hanging out, plus my Spanish allowed me to converse in Portuguese only at about 25 percent efficiency. I felt inept and ineffective. I felt like a stupid Yankee, camera around the neck, making extravagant hand gestures at the natives trying to find his way to the nearest McDonald's.

This was a very odd sensation, since by the time I was in

seventh grade, I had gone to school on four continents. And when I graduated from high school, I had spent at most only five years in the United States. I loved relating across cultures. I was at home in the world. Or so I thought.

Then it slowly dawned on me. I was comfortable in the Spanish world, not the whole non-American world. For the first time in all my travels, I felt stranded—on a lonely island, alone, and cut off.

It kind of snuck up on me like a commando, grabbed me around the throat, and squeezed hard.

What I felt was . . . abandoned.

I wanted to cry.

I felt like a little baby.

I wanted my mommy.

It was the oddest feeling.

It was emotionally paralyzing.

I recall one particular evening. It was pitch-black. Electrical wires had not yet been provided to this country area less than an hour from the capital. I was sitting between two orphans, who were about thirteen years old. These two had latched on to me; I detected unspoken longing in their eyes and a competitiveness for my attention. Underneath their friendship was this hunger, this desperate wanting.

Just below the shy smile were the unspoken questions:

Will you take me home with you?

Will you be my father?

The terrible truth was that there was no way this would be possible.

I put my arms around their shoulders, and we stared up at the panorama overhead. I was trying to explain to them that God knows every star by name. I wanted them to know that they are more precious to Him than the stars and that even after I was gone, they could look up and know that their heavenly Father was there.

He was looking at them and knew them by name.

They were precious to Him.

They were not abandoned.

Although it really felt like it.

Somehow it dawned on me. This is how I had felt my whole life. I had felt alone. I had never paid it much attention. Here in this country orphanage in the middle of a devastated African country, surrounded by children whose hearts had been broken, who had been willfully abandoned or left parentless through a terrible disease, I had to stare it in the face. In theirs and in mine.

» » »

When I was quite small I was left in the care of an aunt. She watched over me while my folks were on deputation—raising support to go to South America as missionaries. I was too little to have conscious memory of it, but my mother has vivid recollections of that leave-taking.

I am screaming.

My arms are stretching out madly toward her.

She walks down the sidewalk and gets into the car.

She is sobbing.

This is what missionaries do.

This is the price they must be willing to pay.

I was barely six months old. I would not see my mother for two and a half months.

I was around one year old when my parents began language school in Costa Rica. A nanny was my surrogate parent most of the day. Again, I would stand at the door of our house and cry disconsolately. A few years later, when we were settled in Chile, my father would leave for months at a time on evangelistic campaigns. Every four years, we had to leave our home and friends and return to the United States, where we would begin establishing new friendships that would have to be abandoned a year later. Our first year in Spain, when I was twelve, my oldest brother and I were sent to a boarding school in Morocco. There were times we did not see our parents for four months.

My childhood was a series of long good-byes.

I never really thought about it much, but I grew up feeling kind of like an orphan. In Mozambique I was planted in the middle of almost eighty real orphans with their concentrated pain and my vulnerability.

I was exposed.

I felt emotionally torn open.

On one of the last nights at the orphanage, we had a devotional. It was about one of the names of God: El Shaddai. This, though translated as the Almighty, can also mean the Breasted One. This name is God telling us that He is to us not *only* heavenly Father. The comforting, satisfying breasts of a mother are a sacrament of the gentle, powerfully compelling, tenacious, and fierce devotion of our God. He protects us with mighty arms and suckles us with the nurturing care of a mother holding her infant in arms. We can feel alone and abandoned in the universe, but Shaddai holds us and is with us and will never leave us or forsake us, ever.

So has He promised.

» » »

Abandonment makes us hunger for home; it makes us long to be held.

When you are an orphan or feel like one, you know that you are not whole or complete or ever quite at home. No matter how many people circle about, how many happy, warm faces may surround you, there is a hole in your heart that cries out with longing to be filled by Mother and Father's saying you belong. It is a terrible aching and a long, dark, empty shaft that is hollow and bleak and leads to nowhere.

It leads to nowhere, that is, until you discover that it's a tunnel God has constructed for you to make your way down and through to Him. It is a path of dark grace that leads you to safety, to sanctuary, to a place where the only one who matters knows you by name.

Many look for meaning and fullness their whole lives. They try to flood the tunnel with noise, activity, shopping, or lovers. And the sad reality is that many never find out that the darkness is a channel and a pathway. Their ears are closed to the voice that resonates off the walls: "Come to Me all you who are exhausted by loneliness and burdened by despair, and I will give your heart rest. Come to Me. Come Home."

For those with eyes to see (and none of us can see without first having mud and saliva divinely daubed on our eyes), this deep hurt is a signpost showing us the way out or, better, the way in. It is a long, narrow, and painful wound inflicted by Love.

Like Cupid's arrows, God sends shafts to pierce and to wound us.[1] God is no sadist. He is speaking and wooing and reminding. And He will hurt us if He needs to. After all, the strongest and most powerful arrow He ever shot from His quiver was Jesus, and He did not shelter Him from pain. He has a million shafts to choose from, though some are subtle, even mute: those silent arrows that strike at the oddest moments.

Sometimes He takes away in order to point the way and sometimes He stabs by giving. Either way He wants us to pine for what is not here but there, in Him.

Sometimes it is the most familiar thing that somehow becomes transcendent and weightier than you can hold. You look up at a tree branch; it is bare, but it has an unearthly glow outlined against an early morning sky. You turn on the radio and hear the soft refrain of a song you've listened to a thousand times but never really heard. You're with old friends, and you turn to catch an expression on one of their faces, and it is haunting. Flipping through a magazine, you see a landscape that makes your heart almost stop. Or maybe it's a still life and the blue vase or clay bowl with pomegranates and ripe grapes cascading over the side makes you want to weep. At the movies, you watch a heroic act of devotion and courage and as the music swells, your heart is near to bursting.

It strikes you when you walk into the dimly lit room and look down at a stunning innocence shining off this chubby-cheeked infant with drool on his soft little lips, and you can barely contain the love and the pain. Then they get older and there is a shift, but that stab can still wound you when you least expect it. They wave as they walk out the door, but before they do, they look into your eyes, and you are so glad and so sad and so proud and you know there is something so holy here you almost quake inside.

You think you are just wishing that you could go back, but it's too weighty for that. You've caught a glimpse of something that is reminding you of Something, and it is more than the past; it's somewhere you've not been before. There is this almost flash of light or brilliance, and you understand for just this briefest second what the halos in medieval paintings are really all about.

For me, it strikes during the chorus of U2's "Still Haven't Found What I'm Looking For" or almost anywhere in Handel's *Messiah* or when I stand at the shore of the limitless ocean and the orange sun is cresting on the horizon and the tips of the waves are liquid gold.

Or when Patty looks at me a certain way, and she is just profoundly happy and content.

When these arrows find their mark, your throat and chest constrict and your heart burns and you suddenly want to cry.

What you are feeling is yearning.

It is deeper and richer and larger than the sexual. It is a craving for something you can't express, for something you've never really known, although it feels almost nostalgic. Sometimes you confuse it for nostalgia, but it really is not that, or if partly that, it is much more than that. It is a slow and secret and almost timid desire. It is a hunger of the heart that is somehow filled with twinges of joy and sorrow all wrapped up together. You don't ever want it to end, but you can't imagine surviving for long if it didn't.

The Germans have this kind of ugly word for it. They call it *sehnsucht*, and of all Christians to meditate and write on it, none has done it better than C. S. Lewis. He is worth reading if only for that. He winds up referring to this mysterious word as our inconsolable longing. He also calls it our lifelong nostalgia, the longing to be reunited with something in the universe from which we now feel cut off, to be on the inside of some door that we have always seen from the outside.[2] In another place he describes it as "spilled religion," whose drops are filled with blessing for "the unconverted who lick them up, and therefore begin to reach for the cup whence they were spilled."[3]

In his most popular book, *Mere Christianity*, Lewis speaks of it as "the desire for my true country."[4] And that is where the lifelong ache, the pain, the sorrow and unrequited joy, the hunger, and desire can begin to make sense.

All these arrows are postcards from home.

From the moment we are born, we face our true condition: We are helpless. And as soon as we are fully conscious, we discover something else: loneliness. We are not at home. As Lewis says, "Our whole being by its very nature is one vast need; incomplete, preparatory, empty yet cluttered, crying out for Him who can untie things that are now knotted together and tie up things that are still dangling loose."[5]

We were once at home in a Garden, and we were loved and in love with the Creator. We were at home in Shalom, and then it was shattered and we were expelled and everything began falling apart, including our bodies, and we shriveled up into shallow, selfish egotists bent on self-destruction. We fell out of love with the source of life and love and fell in love with ourselves. And death dropped over the entire world like this huge, musty diseased quilt.

It blocked the sun and killed the creation and infected us with a deadly plague. Like the survivors of the plague in *Twenty-Eight Days Later*, it filled us with an incoherent raging and insatiable hunger.

Where there was once only blessing, now curse reigned in its place.

So of course we feel lost and alone—we are not home. Of course we feel abandoned; the door has been shut tightly behind us. Of course we feel estranged from reality, from love; our Father's face is turned from us because we're facing the opposite direction. So we feel the haunting weight of a bleak, empty darkness because the curse reigns over us and the whole world.

This is why Jesus had to come to bear its full weight, break its power and throw it off. He came to pay the price to shatter death and release His creation from bondage. Which is why we and all creation with us groan and wait (Romans 8:22).

The stabs of longing are intended to remind us that this is not all that. He shoots an arrow or two our way to remind us that we were meant for something bigger, better, longer, deeper, and more real, more substantial, and more glorious than this finite, earthly, stuttering, spluttering, quavering little life. As Lewis puts it, "All joy (as distinct from mere pleasure, still more amusement) emphasizes our pilgrim status; always reminds, beckons, awakens desire. Our best havings are wantings."[6]

God knows we are temped to forget. Our Enemy wants us to forget. He wants us to think that what we miss is Mommy or the electricity of sexual desire. He wants us to think that what we are longing for is our father's approval, or beauty, or a comfortable retirement, or more chocolate.[7]

If we believe him, these fakes will break our hearts.

Satan wants us to look down and around and within (especially within) but not up.

There are those voices today that are countering the old-school "pie in the sky, by and by," and its emotional disconnect from creation with a plea to bring heaven on earth.[8] They are properly critical of an obsession with heaven and life after death that demeans the importance of this world and life *before* death.

While I have sympathy for this reaction against a fundamentalist, creation-dismissing, culture-hating worldview, the solution is not to squeeze hope into the size of a green and blue globe even if it is the size of our earth. Or, like radical chemotherapy, we will find that the proposed cure will be far worse than the disease.

This is where the proponents of "God is green" must tread carefully.[9] If you don't stay alert, you can be an unwitting accomplice in a dangerous (and I would say, demonic) scheme to steal real hope and silence a real voice and sedate a real longing. By repainting the biblical hope as a primarily this-worldly orientation, one can become an accessory to the Wicked Wizard's plot to cast a spell to muzzle the quiet whispers crying out for heaven.

This we must never do.

That road leads inevitably to an exhausted and a dreary despair. That path takes you deeper into the Dark Wood and leaves you lost, forever.

Infinitely better than the desire to bring heaven to earth is Saint Augustine's prayer that reminds us of a higher and deeper and more satisfying desire, a desire the creation was created to evoke: "Lead us, O Lord, and work within us: arouse us, and call us back; enkindle us, and draw us to you; grow fragrant and sweet to us. Let us love you, and let us run to you."[10]

When our heart leaps and burns with a jolt of stabbing joy and longing; when we pine to enter the beauty that beckons but rebuffs; when this world seems just not enough; when we hear a voice or a song that makes us ache with desire; when we know that this goodness, this satisfaction, this delight is good but not yet good enough; when the joy is slipping silently through our grasping fingers, we are being reminded to look up and away to where we belong.[11]

We are being invited to remember that we are strangers and aliens, that our true homeland, our real citizenship, is not in this world. Our loyalty is to another city, the City of God (Hebrews 13:14). We belong to another nation, the Israel of God (Galatians 6:16). We are members of a different race and order, a consecrated nation of royal priests (1 Peter 2:9). We are subjects of another realm, the Kingdom of God (Mark 10:14; Revelation 1:6). We are pursuers of a different dream, the kingdoms of this world becoming the kingdom of our God and of His Christ (Revelation 11:15), where we will dwell with Him in Shalom, in a new heaven and a new earth, and He will be our light. There sorrow, sighing, and sickness and death will flee away forever (Revelation 21:1-4; 22:3). And so we will be forever with our Lord, who is Lover and Friend and Father and Brother and Mother and all in all (1 Thessalonians 4:17).

The sobering reality is that having a longing does not mean that it will necessarily be fulfilled. As Lewis observes, simply because I get hunger pangs does not guarantee I will get to fill my belly. But what it does tell me is that I was created to eat. These inconsolable yearnings tell us that we are creatures who have been crafted to find fulfillment somewhere else. Lewis says, "If I find in myself a desire which no experience in this world can satisfy, the most probable explanation is that I was made for another world. If none of my earthly pleasures satisfy it, that does not prove that the universe is a fraud. Probably earthly pleasures were never meant to satisfy it, but only to arouse it, to suggest the real thing."[12]

Whether your wound was stuttering or losing or never having, or finding a door but discovering it to be the wrong one or having it slammed shut in your face, whether it was being betrayed or belittled or broken, the good news is that the beckoning, the longing, the hungering were not meant to lead us on and frustrate us. These desires were meant to be fulfilled. The yearning to belong, to be known and recognized, to be inside not outside, to be invited from the fringe into the inner circle, to be at home and at peace, are all messengers from our true country that tell us to seek our joy in Him.

We long for heaven because we were made for Him.

He is our heart's true home.

» » »

All of us can follow the desperate woman with the issue of blood into the inner circle and grab ahold of life. Sadly, some will choose to rage and flail and hunger forever. They will refuse to make their way home. Though it is within reach, there are many who will wake to find that because they failed to reach out like little children and take the hand their Daddy was offering, they have been left outside of the party forever. These are the words of Jesus. It was He who said that when He sits on His throne of glory judging the nations, He will tell many, "Go away from Me!" (Matthew 25:41). According to Him, many at that time will lay out their religious pedigrees, and He will shut the door to them with these words: "I have never known you; away from Me, you evil men!" (Matthew 7:23).

We were meant to be happy not sad, satisfied though not satiated, in not out, embraced not excluded, welcomed not cast away. The very good news is that there are good grounds to believe you can come home. The way through and out and in has already been prepared for you. That was the whole point of the cross: opening the door to the garden that had been shut tight in our faces, rescuing us from slavery to self and leading us through the dark tunnel into the light.

Some get confused when thinking about the incompatibility of the judgment and mercy of God. They think that the final word is just a word, like *grace* or *truth* or *reconciliation*.[13] But God's last word is actually the Word; it is a Person (Revelation 19:13). He is the one who has the last say. He is both the beginning and the end of the Great Epic. He explodes creation into existence with a word and again with His Word punishes, purifies, and restores creation into a new existence (Revelation 19:15; 21:5).

He sits on the throne and He says:

I am the Alpha and the Omega, the First and the Last, the Beginning and the End. Happy are those who will have washed their robes clean, so that they will have the right to feed on the tree of life and can come through the gates into the city. These others must stay outside: dogs, fortunetellers and fornicators, and murderers, and idolaters, and everyone of false speech and false life. (Revelation 22:13-15)

It bears repeating: These are the words of our gracious Lord Jesus, not some angry fundamentalist on the war path.

Jesus opens and Jesus shuts the gates. He holds the keys of heaven and hell, of "death and the underworld" (Revelation 1:18). Not we.[14] He is Sovereign King and the Righteous Judge, after all.

As Lewis describes it:

In some sense, as dark to the intellects as it is unendurable to the feelings, we can be both banished from the presence of Him who is present everywhere and erased from the knowledge of Him who knows all. We can be left utterly and absolutely outside — repelled, exiled, estranged, finally and unspeakably ignored. On the other hand, we can be called in, welcomed, received, acknowledged. We walk every day on the razor edge between these two incredible possibilities.[15]

The last words of the entire Epic are an invitation to choose the best of all possibilities: "Then let all who are thirsty come: all who want it may have the water of life, and have it free" (Revelation 22:17).

The gate has been opened, the banquet table set, the glasses filled, and whoever wishes to come are welcomed in.

And the word after that last word is a solemn guarantee that whoever adds or cuts off anything from the prophesies contained in the Epic's Final Word shall have his share cut off from the tree of life and of the holy city (22:18-19).

But then comes a gracious promise:

"I shall indeed be with you soon" (22:20).

And the last word of the Bride who yearns for her Royal Bridegroom with a longing that feels inconsolable but will one day find its eternal consolation is simply this:

"Amen; come, Lord Jesus" (22:20).

Blessing

"May the grace of the Lord Jesus be with you all now and forever."
Revelation 22:21

Epilogue

SHALL WE DANCE?

At the very beginning, I asked, Is the meaning of life war? *Ultimately?* I respond how I think Lewis just might if you asked him before he'd had his first hot cup of tea: "Absolutely not! Are you daft? Don't you know that the serious business of heaven is joy? I will tell you what is at the center, and you will hardly believe it. At the center is a God who blazes in a glorious dance, and we circle about Him in dizzying bands of light and color and laughter and music. And we not only circle about, but we enter in. All our lives we are fighting either to get in or to stay out of the dance.

"All may come, but many decline and choose instead to weave about forever in meaningless, empty futility. Their eyes burn, not with sorrow but with the brightness and sharp-edged reality of a joy that they hate as a rabid animal hates water. But it need not be that way. For from inside the circle comes a voice that shakes the stars, making the universe quake, but it is laughing even as it sears with razor-sharp, almost ferocious charity, and it says, 'Come and eat, come and drink, come and dance in the Wedding Dance of my Son who died that you might dance with Him forever. But if you say no, you will be banished not only from the dance but the universe, forever.'"

As G. K. Chesterton said, "Joy . . . is the gigantic secret of the Christian."[1] And as Peter Kreeft tells us, this joy of Christ *and* of the *Christian* "is the door out of the agonized world of spiritual darkness 'where ignorant armies clash by night.' This is the joy the New Testament speaks of in the strangest way anyone has ever spoken of joy. It is the joy of Christ, that came in the most unlikely place and time in all of history, Calvary. . . . This is the joy that conquered Hell on the Cross; the joy that was the door Christ saw behind the Cross, the cross-shaped door whose other side is a crown; the death-shaped mask worn by the Lord of life."[2]

The bottom line is not despair or dutiful struggle or even a battle against the powers—it is joy. And despite the idolatrous reduction of life to sex or death or, most currently, ironic despair, there are great grounds for hope, for "decadently apocalyptic ages elicit saints. Suffering elicits courage, compassion, heroism, and martyrdom."[3]

Dance around the burning effigy of man as the world shrivels and folds in on itself, or dance around the God who blazes and smokes and bring hope to the world. Paraphrasing Kreeft a bit, I would plead, Please love the Lord your God with all your heart, soul, mind, and strength. Please love Jesus by giving your life away for the life of the world and the joy of your God.

Please be a hero—be saint—and help save the world.[4]

NOTES

Prologue

1. Peter Kreeft, *Three Philosophies of Life* (San Francisco: Ignatius Press, 1989).

2. Kreeft, *Three Philosophies*, 85–86.

3. C. S. Lewis says, "It is a serious thing to live in a society of possible gods and goddesses, to remember that the dullest and most uninteresting person you talk to may one day be a creature which, if you saw it now, you would be strongly tempted to worship or else a horror and a corruption such as you now meet, if at all only in a nightmare. All day long we are, in some degree, helping each other to one or other of these destinations." Source: C. S. Lewis, *The Weight of Glory* (Grand Rapids, MI: Eerdmans, 1979), 14.

4. Kreeft, *Three Philosophies*, 85.

5. Kreeft, *Three Philosophies*, 85.

6. I am happy here to express my gratitude to an Orthodox brother into whose theological debt I am beginning to fall. It was he who finally pulled back the lattices and let the light shine on the real, sweat-and-blood Jesus I was encountering, almost for the first time, again, in the Gospels. It came in *Christ in the Psalms.* A perfect title for a book that is pungent and aromatic. It smells like Jesus after His anointing at Bethany.

Commenting on Psalm 76, which celebrates a resounding victory God has won over His (and Israel's) enemies, Father Patrick Reardon offers a brief critique of the classical western view of the atonement: Jesus came like a kind businessman offering His blood as the means of exchange to pay for the release of (to buy back) His kidnapped people. Whereas, Reardon tells us, the older, patristic view sees the cross in the context not of commerce but conquest. The death of Jesus is viewed "in terms of combat, defeat and victory." Thus, when we read that Jesus paid the price, we are to understand it as a warfare metaphor: "He did so as a warrior doing battle with the devil, sin, and death on our behalf. He willingly laid down His life, accepting suffering and death, but then descending into the nether regions victorious, as the very Giver of life whom neither the grave nor hell could hold, and rising again for our justification, having trampled down death by death. Thus Jesus defeated sin by His dying, and death by His rising again." Source: Patrick Henry Reardon, *Christ in the Psalms* (Ben Lomond, CA: Conciliar, 2000), 149.

Now that is hard not to like. Father Reardon, almost thou persuadest me to become Orthodox.

7. See note 1 of chapter 4.

Chapter 1

1. Rob Bell, *Velvet Elvis* (Grand Rapids, MI: Zondervan, 2005), 131.

2. Brian McLaren, *The Last Word and the Word After That* (San Francisco: Jossey-Bass, 2005), xiii.

3. The Christian, like Jesus, is both a friend and an enemy of the world. "Anyone who chooses the world for his friend turns himself into God's enemy" (James 4:4). The world returns the favor by hating those who follow in the way of Jesus. As David Wells notes, Paul exhorts us not only to turn away from our own sins, but also from following the "course of this world." Wells defines this as "our embeddedness in culture at the point of its fallen horizons, false belief structures, and misdirected devotions—all of which are kept in place by the powers of darkness (Ephesians 2:1-3). This is what gives to all culture its curiously ambiguous quality." Source: David F. Wells, *Above All Pow'rs* (Grand Rapids, MI: Eerdmans, 2005), 23.

4. C. S. Lewis, "The Decline of Religion," *God in the Dock* (Grand Rapids, MI: Eerdmans, 1970), 223.

5. According to Peter Forsyth, "Christianity is concerned with God's holiness before all else; which issues to man as love, acts upon sin as grace, and exercises grace through judgment. . . . We must take that view of Christ which does most justice to the holiness of God. This starting point of the supreme holiness of God's love, rather than its pity, sympathy, or affection, is the watershed between the Gospel and theological liberalism. . . . My point of departure is that Christ's first concern and revelation was not simply the forgiving love of God, but the holiness of such love." Source:

P. T. Forsyth, *The Cruciality of the Cross* (Eugene, OR: Wipf and Stock, 1997), viii.

Peter Forsyth, an English pastor and theologian, wrote this in a brilliant little book originally published at the beginning of the last century. In it he addresses the encroaching theological liberalism, which was emptying the gospel of its transformational power. Change the language a bit and he could be speaking to the church today, a hundred years later. It is an eloquent testimony to the Solomonic dictum that there is nothing new under the sun.

Chapter 2

1. I should make clear that, despite my rigid Baptist roots, I am no longer burdened with any real prejudice against that foamy beverage. Just because every time my sons open a can, I see this image of a corpulent, sweaty guy in a wife-beater bragging about his bowling scores and spitting brown streams of tobacco does not necessarily mean I believe they are on a slippery slope to perdition. I've given it a serious try, but there is less chance of my developing a taste for beer than President Bush's memoir becoming a bestseller in Iran.

2. I should probably also make clear that I don't take exception to Rob's questions. I have great respect for his communicative gifts and find him to be a thoughtful, highly articulate young pastor who has his finger on the pulse of an important demographic—which contains, to date, four of the most important people in my life: my three oldest sons and my only daughter. So I care a lot about what he has to say. I take him seriously. I also happen to agree wholeheartedly with his call to integral mission.

3. Rob Bell, *Velvet Elvis* (Grand Rapids, MI: Zondervan, 2005), 10–12.

4. Bell, 27–28.

5. This statement was part of a sermon delivered by Mark Driscoll (who also pastors Mars Hill Church, but in Seattle, at a conference hosted by John Piper in 2006. The conference was titled "Above All Powers: The Supremacy of Christ in a Postmodern World" (kudos on a very heady but compelling title), and the sermon is titled "The Supremacy of Christ and the Church in the Postmodern World" (no kudos for originality).

6. Bell, 27–28.

7. I found support for this statement in an unexpected place. An "ordinary radical" named Shane Claibourne, whom Rob Bell endorses strongly, wrote a compelling autobiographical book about the genesis of The Simple Way in inner-city Philadelphia. In one of his best chapters, Shane discusses the economics of the call to simplicity. He states that, first of all, it must be rooted in love. He then makes a significant observation: "I am convinced that most of the terribly disturbing things that are happening in our world in the name of Christ and Christianity are primarily the result not of malicious people but of bad theology. (At least, I want to believe that.) And the answer to bad theology is not no theology but good theology." Source: Shane Claibourne, *Irresistible Revolution* (Grand Rapids, MI: Zondervan, 2006), 169.

I would add that bad theology convinced otherwise well-intentioned champions of the poor in Central America to take up machine guns instead of laying down their lives and their guns. Bad theology turns you into a revolutionary Marxist while good theology makes you an Oscar Romero.

It can lead you to take life or give life.

8. This position is argued forcefully and in a nontechnical manner in Gregory A. Boyd, *God of the Possible* (Grand Rapids, MI: Baker, 2000).

9. Back in the day, the prophets would have used the term *shofar*, the ancient near-Eastern version of the electronic gizmo used for crowd control and ear-splitting declarations of all kinds. Rob Bell, in the NOOMA DVD titled *Bullhorn*, takes a bit of a jab at the guy bellowing out amplified warnings about hell. He implies, at least, that there is something *inherently* repugnant or laughable about raising your voice to warn people of eternal danger. The Old Testament prophets were not so categorical or absolutist. They would not get the joke.

   The ancient means of getting the public's undivided attention was the ram's horn, or *shofar*. In many versions, it is translated as "trumpet." It alerts Israel that the Jubilee Year has begun (Leviticus 25:9) and calls warriors to come to battle (Nehemiah 4:20). Prophets are to shout out warnings of judgment like a ram's horn blast (Isaiah 58:1; Jeremiah 4:5; Hosea 5:8; Joel 2:1). The watchman is obligated to blow the horn when danger is imminent. If he fails, he becomes personally responsible for all who are killed (Ezekiel 33:2-3,6). Saint Paul asks the searching and timely question: "If the speaker, clever and culturally sensitive though he be, fails to blow the bullhorn of warning loud and clear but instead puts a sock in it to muffle the sound and nuance the sharp edge, who will get ready for battle?" (1 Corinthians 14:8, author's paraphrase). Who indeed?

10. The Bible is immensely important, for without it we are making up our own stories about God, rather than listening

to Him tell it for Himself. Karl Barth makes this point when he says that theology "is itself a word, a human response; yet what makes it theology is not its own word or response but the Word which it hears and to which it responds. Theology stands or falls with the Word of God, for the Word of God precedes all theological words by creating, arousing, and challenging them." Source: Karl Barth, *Evangelical Theology: An Introduction*, trans. Grove Foley (London: Weidenfeld and Nicholson, 1963), 16–17.

Take away the Bible and theology joins the rank of fantasy: creative (but at a fundamental level) merely a spiritually impotent invention.

Chapter 3

1. Politics used to matter a lot to me in the early eighties, but the crash and burn of liberation theology, along with the Sandinistas (defenders of the people) in Nicaragua, kind of did me in. Liberation theology rose out of Central America and raised the consciousness of the evangelical church to the biblical "option for the poor." But it went astray in its frustration against economic and social oppression, advocating and justifying violence very much like the biblical Zealots.

I have this innovative idea that power corrupts and absolute power corrupts absolutely — which being interpreted means: Politics, given a fallen world, will eventually eat your soul. Too much is at stake. Too much money is on the line. Nowadays, the left and the right seem to me to be pseudonyms for social-ethical variants that exist, at the very core level, to perpetuate their power above all else. That is not to say there is an absolute equivalence between these politico-economic polarities, but that the differences, behind the rhetorical facade, are grossly exaggerated. I feel more comfortable casting my vote for Jesus as Lord of all and swearing allegiance to His party and His kingdom. Yeah, I know, I sound cynical. I may still vote, but I'm not sure I'm really happy about it. If I manage to talk myself into it I will be grumbling truculently all the way to the booth.

2. Not surprisingly, the Old Testament prophets are no strangers to this response of anger mixed with incomprehension. Jeremiah moans, "You have seduced me, Yahweh, and I have let myself be seduced; you have overpowered me: you were the stronger (Jeremiah 20:7). Rabbi Abraham Heschel was the one who first brought this haunting verse to bear on my consciousness. The good rabbi, being Jewish, is not as dainty as the Catholic translators of the above Scripture, the latter portion of which he tells us "misses completely the meaning of the text." According to him, it should more properly be rendered, "Thou hast raped me and I am overcome." Source: Abraham Heschel, *The Prophets: An Introduction* (New York: Harper & Row, 1962), 113.

   While *seduced* denotes enticement, *rape* conveys a sense of violence. The prophet Jeremiah felt the paradoxical tension of being wooed and of being set up, coerced, told to jump, and then dropped on his head. He is not the only one.

3. Christian Smith, a sociologist at the University of North Carolina, conducted face-to-face and telephone interviews with thousands of American teens. In his book *Soul Searching*, he describes his findings. He coins a phrase for what he believes is the de facto dominant religion among American youth. He calls it "Moralistic Therapeutic Deism." Its creed sounds something like this:

- A God exists who created and orders the world and watches over human life on earth.
- God wants people to be good, nice, and fair to each other, as taught in the Bible and by most world religions.
- The central goal of life is to be happy and to feel good about oneself.
- God does not need to be particularly involved in one's life except when God is needed to resolve a problem.
- Good people go to heaven when they die.

Source: Christian Smith, *Soul Searching: The Religious and Spiritual Lives of American Teenagers* (Oxford, 2005), 156–158.

4. According to Greg Boyd, the sooner we get rid of "any lingering suspicion that evil somehow fits into the eternal purposes of God," the better. Boyd says, "Jesus spent his entire ministry revolting against the evil he confronted. He never suggested that any of the physical or spiritual afflictions He confronted somehow fit into His Father's plan. Rather, He confronted these things as coming from the devil . . ." Source: Gregory A. Boyd, *God of the Possible* (Grand Rapids, MI: Baker, 2000), 102. One is left to wonder what was Jesus saying when He tells His disciples that the death of Lazarus was for His Father's glory (John 11:4).

5. Augustine, *The Confessions of St. Augustine* (Garden City, NY: Doubleday, 1960), 43.

6. Peter Kreeft, *Three Philosophies of Life* (San Francisco: Ignatius, 1989), 92–93. I am hugely indebted to this very

smart and very wise Catholic brother for insights on Job and on life that I could never have gotten on my own. One could do much worse than read everything Dr. Kreeft has written. To get started, read this little gem of a book.

7. As Peter Kreeft notes, most philosophical answers to the meaning of life or the problem of evil "ignore the grubby little question that nags us . . . How is this dwarf to fly like that eagle? How can I get from cretin to Christ? [We were made] to become a shining, radiant, strong, noble creature that can endure the perfect light of Heaven, a veritable god or goddess.

"So how are we to get from here to there? The wise and honest answer is that it will take some doing. What is remarkable is not that God hits us with so many blows of the sculptor's chisel but that He manages with so few. What is remarkable, once you see the distance between where you are now and where you are destined to be, is how God's mercy succeeds in bringing us there with so little trouble, so little pain. What is remarkable is not how many bad things happen to good people but how many good things happen to bad people." Source: Kreeft, *Three Philosophies of Life*, 86.

Chapter 4

1. Whereas the term *story* is by far the most commonplace contemporary term to use about the Bible, *epic*, for a variety of reasons, seems to me to be preferable. *Story*, particularly in an ancient Middle-Eastern context, brings to mind what the glib of tongue do to entertain those around a campfire. It is something creatively spun and elaborated upon over time for the delight and instruction of one's listeners. That does not quite match what the Bible says about itself. Plus, bedtime

stories are cute. That is the last thing we would say about the Bible—or about an epic, for that matter. An epic has about it the weight of tragedy, the sound of steel against helmet, the screams of dying animals, the bluster of storms, and the brutality of mythic warriors. An epic contains catastrophe, disaster, and hairbreadth escapes. It is all about a hero. It also weaves through the sweetness and hope of romance and unrequited or requited love. It also covers much ground and takes a lot of time and pages. This is why I opt for the latter term in referencing the Scriptures.

2. Due to the influence of C. S. Lewis and a bit of Frank Peretti, I wrote a fantasy novel titled *The Paladins*. The book is a spiritual-warfare thriller for late teens/early twenties. When I completed the manuscript, it had to buck the anti-Harry Potter, anti-fantasy backlash, so the major publishers kindly pulled back from it. The small publishing house that took it on, due to insufficient capitalization, almost went bankrupt within months after my book's release in 1997. To my dismay, the marketing support quickly waned and withered away. My book succumbed to a slow, and to me, painful asphyxiation.

3. Peter Kreeft, *C.S. Lewis for the Third Millenium* (San Francisco: Ignatius, 1994), 32.

4. An example of a forced dichotomy is seen in McLaren's commentary on the work of Jesus on the cross. He is contrasting how the Romans exerted power and how Jesus established His—not by killing His enemies but by letting them kill Him. "The *pax Christi* (Christ's peace) is not the peace of conquest but rather the peace of true reconciliation." Source: Brian McLaren, *The Secret Message of Jesus* (Nashville, TN: W, 2006), 99. Here we are being required to decide between the warrior Jesus and the pacifist Jesus.

Chapter 5

1. Sources for the material on anger include *The Zondervan Pictorial Encyclopedia of the Bible*, ed. Merril C. Tenney, "Anger" article by D. G. Stewart and "Wrath" article by W. White Jr. (Grand Rapids, MI: Zondervan, 1978); *Theological Workbook of the Old Testament*, ed. R. Laird Harris, Gleason L. Archer Jr., and Bruce K. Waltke (Chicago: Moody, 1980); *The Strong's NIV Exhaustive Concordance* (Grand Rapids, MI: Zondervan).

2. Just to show you how utterly unembarrassed they are, the poet Asaph, reciting the less-than-stellar history of the Jewish nation, describes how God finally rouses Himself to beat back His enemies (and those of His people). But the image he uses is almost hilarious. It sounds like he's talking about Ulysses or some other pagan champion. "Then, like a sleeper, like a hero fighting-mad with wine, the Lord woke up to strike His enemies on the rump and put them to everlasting shame" (Psalm 78:65-66). Granted, this is from a Catholic translation (*The Jerusalem Bible*). One could not imagine a staid, teetotaling Protestant linguist coming up with that. So let's raise a glass to gutsy and earthy honesty and laughter. Maybe what our theology needs is a nice sweet snifter of humor to shake us all loose just a bit. Perhaps we need to confess that at times we just might possibly take ourselves (and perhaps God, too) a little *too* seriously. I think about the platypus and some of those insanely quirky tropical birds that puff and prance and preen and just know that they're God's inside joke. He laughs too.

3. Patrick Henry Reardon, *Christ in the Psalms* (Ben Lomond, CA: Conciliar, 2000), 10.

4. The book of Wisdom is found in the Apocrypha, the books that pod the Catholic Scriptures. It is attributed to Solomon. Though not in the Jewish canon, the New Testament authors make use of it. It is like a hybrid of Ecclesiastes and Moses' recapitulation of Israel's history.

5. In Exodus and Deuteronomy, which are the books that depict Israel's betrothal and marriage to Yahweh, God's people are told six times that their King is jealous. Twice it is God Himself who is speaking: "For I, Yahweh your God, am a jealous God and I punish the father's fault in the sons, the grandsons, and the great-grandsons of those who hate me. But I show kindness to thousands of those who love and keep my commandments" (Exodus 20:5-6). This He repeats in the injunction against making images (Deuteronomy 5:9-10).

   In Exodus 34:14, Moses tells Israel twice that the name of their divine Husband is "Jealous," and lest they miss the point, he lets them know that this God is a jealous God. He repeats this in Deuteronomy 6:15. When Moses is reminding the Israelites about what occurred on Mt. Sinai the day God appeared in smoke and fire and thunder, He tells them that "Yahweh your God is a consuming fire, a jealous God" (Deuteronomy 4:24).

   God wants His people to know that (like a husband) He desires and (like a king) He demands their exclusive love and devotion. His jealousy burns so strongly that His people beg that the ardor be turned aside just a little. It is not always pleasant to be the focus of distilled, unrelenting divine love. "How much longer will you be angry, Yahweh? For ever? Is your jealousy to go on smoldering like a fire? Pour out your anger on the pagans, who do not acknowledge you" (Psalm 79:5-6).

6. The prophet Nahum reports that God thunders against Israel's mortal enemy, Nineveh, known as one of the most cruel of ancient nations. "Yahweh is a jealous and vengeful God, Yahweh avenges, He is full of wrath; Yahweh takes vengeance on His foes, He stores up fury for His enemies. Yahweh is slow to anger but immense in power. Most surely Yahweh will not leave the guilty unpunished" (Nahum 1:2-3). Yahweh's jealousy is not only stirred up against His people's adultery; it burns against those who have the temerity to lay their hands on her.

7. These apparent opposites are rarely ever mentioned in the same breath. I found a helpful treatment of this seeming paradoxical claim in George MacDonald's collection of sermons, a book to which C. S. Lewis claims a debt that "is almost as great as one man can owe to another." Source: *George MacDonald: An Anthology*, edited and with a preface by C. S. Lewis (New York: Macmillan, 1978), xxx.

   In his sermon "The Consuming Fire," MacDonald writes, "Love has ever in view the absolute loveliness of that which it beholds. Where loveliness is incomplete, and love cannot love its fill of loving, it spends itself to make more lovely, that it may love more; it strives for perfection, even that itself may be perfected—not in itself, but in the object. . . . Therefore, all that is not beautiful in the beloved, all that comes between and is not of love's kind, must be destroyed. And our God is a consuming fire." Source: George MacDonald, "The Consuming Fire," *Unspoken Sermons* (Whitethorn, CA: Johannesen, 2004), 18–19.

8. Father Reardon clarifies the distinction between God's and man's anger. "The divine wrath is not some sort of irritation; God does not become peeved or annoyed. The wrath of

God is more serious than a temper tantrum. It is a deliberate resolve in response to a specific state of the human soul." Reardon, 11.

9. Rob Bell, *Velvet Elvis* (Grand Rapids, MI: Zondervan, 2005), 34.

10. Father Reardon comments on Psalm 76, which recounts God's victory over Sennacherib. With characteristic pungency, he brings together what few current theologians dare to, using as his point of reference the first two verses, which allude to God's tent being pitched in Salem (based on *shalom*—peace), Jerusalem's ancient name: "One rarely hears modern Christians speak of Christ's redemptive work as an outpouring of the divine anger, but most assuredly it was. True combat always involves anger, and the redemptive deeds of Christ were the supreme and ultimate war ever waged in this world. Indeed, this truly was a war to end all warfare, for it graced human history with the key to its final peace." Source: Patrick Henry Reardon, *Christ in the Psalms* (Ben Lomond, CA: Conciliar, 2000), 150.

The death of Jesus is not a choice between reconciliation or conquest or an antithesis between redemption and victory over the powers. It is not about giving away and lying down rather than taking up and smashing through (nice, pacifist Jesus versus angry, aggressive Jesus). The cross involves it all. Let's be very cautious about forcing unnecessary choices between mutual exclusives that really aren't.

Chapter 6

1. Brian McLaren, *A New Kind of Christian* (San Francisco: Jossey-Bass, 2001).

2. Rob Bell, *Velvet Elvis* (Grand Rapids, MI: Zondervan, 2004), 21.

3. Pastor Dan, the fictional protagonist of *A New Kind of Christian* and *The Last Word and the Word After That*, explains that his discomfort with the traditional view of hell is because it seems so exclusive. Whereas "everything about Jesus' life and message seemed to be about inclusion, not exclusion." Source: Brian McLaren, *The Last Word and the Word After That* (San Francisco: Jossey-Bass, 2005), 35.

According to this line of thinking, categorizing people as saved or not, believer or nonbeliever, is to be avoided. These terms are offensive and "work against Jesus' teaching about how we are to treat each other." Source: Bell, 167. By unofficial calculation, I have a list of almost fifty references where Jesus stereotyped or used polarizing language that overtly "in-grouped" and "out-grouped."

4. McLaren, *A New Kind of Christian*, 65.

5. This is a list of those whom we are told Jesus specifically scandalized:

- The Pharisees (Matthew 15:12)
- The hometown crowd (Matthew 13:57)
- His followers (John 6:61)
- John the Baptizer (Matthew 11:6)
- The twelve disciples (Matthew 26:31)
- Those who claim to believe in Him (Matthew 24:10)
- We should not forget his immediate family who thought he was insane (Mark 3:31)

6. Dorothy Sayers said, "I believe it to be a great mistake to present Christianity as something charming and popular with no offense in it. . . . We cannot blink at the fact that

gentle Jesus meek and mild was so stiff in his opinions and
so inflammatory in his language that he was thrown out
of church, stoned, hunted from place to place, and finally
gibbeted as a firebrand and a public danger. Whatever his
peace was, it was not the peace of an amiable indifference."
Dorothy C. Sayers, *Creed or Chaos?* (Manchester: Sophia
Institute Press, 1949), 56.

Chapter 7

1. I am indebted to Ray Vanderlaan with That the World May
   Know Ministries for this Jewish perspective on the Seder
   (www.followtherabbi.com).

2. Rob Bell, *Velvet Elvis* (Grand Rapids, MI: Zondervan,
   2004), 83, 125.

3. Gregory A. Boyd, *God of the Possible* (Grand Rapids, MI:
   Baker, 2000), 56–59.

4. In his extremely insightful book on postmodernity, David
   Wells provides what I believe is a biblically informed
   approach to culture: "It is impossible to live with any degree
   of authenticity as a Christian unless the modern world is
   understood to be what, in fact, it is: delicious but dangerous,
   like the Turkish delight that proved so irresistible and so
   lethal to one small boy in C. S. Lewis's *The Lion, the Witch
   and the Wardrobe.*" Source: David F. Wells, *Above All Earthly
   Pow'rs* (Grand Rapids, MI: Eerdmans, 2005), 16. (This is
   not a reactionary repugnance and repudiation of culture.
   It is sanity.) Wells continues by explaining what it is about
   culture that the Christian must beware: "its fallen horizons,
   false belief structures, and misdirected devotions—all of
   which are kept in place by the powers of darkness (Ephesians
   2:1-3). This is what gives to all culture its curiously

ambiguous quality. . . . We have to be redeemed from sin and uprooted from what is dark in culture, from what in the Bible is called 'this world,' for Satan's captivity is exercised through the instrumentality of sin and that of 'the world.' It therefore becomes a matter of no small moment to be able to discern what in our culture is good, what is simply innocent, and what is neither" (Wells, 25).

Chapter 8

1. A quarter century later, the CIA conceded what everyone (except me and my staunchly proestablishment evangelical community) knew: It had purposefully *destabilized* (the word that had been newly coined for that venture) the Chilean economy after spending millions attempting to prevent Allende's election. Following his election, Nixon's famous words to CIA chief Richard Helms were, "Make the economy scream!"

   America's collusion with the Chilean military was such that it is impossible to know who was directly responsible for Allende's death. What is clear is that Nixon and Henry Kissinger let it be known that an assassination would not be looked at unfavorably. U.S. support for the military was overt and intense. The CIA admitted knowing about the plot. As it turned out, the approved and hand-picked successor, General Augusto Pinochet, slid into power, which resulted in the gruesome deaths of thousands of political prisoners. He became such an international black eye that twenty-five years later, he was arrested in Spain and convicted of torture and genocide. His economic legacy was such that, at the time of his arrest, Chile had one of the most extreme and inequitable distributions of income on the planet. Source: Robinson Rojas, *The Murder of Allende* (New York: Harper & Rowe, 1975). Also see "Chile and the United States: Declassified Documents Relating to the Military Coup, September 11, 1973," http://www.gwu .edu/~nsarchiv/NSAEBB/NSAEBB8/nsaebb8i.htm.

2. On this I was influenced by Anabaptists like Vernard Eller, *Christian Anarchy: Jesus' Primacy over the Powers* (Grand Rapids, MI: Eerdmans, 1987); Donald B. Kraybill, *The Upside-Down Kingdom* (Scottdale, PA: Herald, 1978).

On the subject of patriotism, Paul S. Minear, who taught biblical theology at Yale Divinity School, quotes William Stringfellow, who writes, "A biblical person is always wary of claims which the State makes for allegiance, obedience and service under the rubric called patriotism. Such demands are often put in noble or benign or innocuous terms. But in any country the rhetoric and rituals of conformity and obedience to a regime or ruler latently concern idolatry of the Antichrist, even though that name is not generally invoked except where the explicit and blatant deification of the State occurs. . . . The American vanity as a nation has, since the origins of America, been Babylonian — boasting, through Presidents, often through pharisees within the churches, through folk religion, and in other ways, that America is Jerusalem. This is neither an innocuous nor benign claim; it is the essence of the doctrine of the Antichrist." Source: William Stringfellow, *An Ethic for Christians and Other Aliens in a Strange Land* (Dallas: Word, 1973), 114, quoted in Paul S. Minear, *I Pledge Allegiance: Patriotism and the Bible* (Philadelphia: Geneva Press, 1975), 132–133 .

It's no wonder I was conflicted reading such subversive propaganda issued from the liberal fringe while sitting alone inside the thick walls of an uncritical, patriotic evangelicalism.

3. See John Howard Yoder, *The Politics of Jesus* (Grand Rapids, MI: Eerdmans, 1972); John Howard Yoder, *The Priestly Kingdom: Social Ethics as Gospel* (Notre Dame, IN: University of Notre Dame, 1984); and non-Anabaptists like Jean-Michel Hornus, *It is Not Lawful for Me to Fight* (Scottdale, PA: Herald, 1980).

4. Ava Garber Exhibit, in New York City, 1993, and the "Sensations" Exhibit, 1999, artist Chris Ofili.

5. This detachment was aided by my dawning realization that there was very little support for American folk religion's conviction that America is a truly Christian nation, or ever truly was one. Not in authentically and honestly biblical categories at least. See Mark Noll, Nathan O. Hatch, and George M. Marsden, *The Search for Christian America* (Westchester, IL: Crossway, 1983).

6. Tom Sine, *The Mustard Seed Conspiracy* (Waco, TX: Word, 1981). This book did for evangelical social activism what Shane Claiborne's *Irresistible Revolution* (Grand Rapids, MI: Zondervan, 2006) is doing for the new monastic movement.

7. It can be accessed on our ministry's website at www.orphan-justicemission.net.

8. Orphan Justice Mission is partnering with Glory of Christ Church in Uganda to provide education, food, and (hopefully) employment for hundreds of AIDS orphans in the district of Rakai, ground zero for the AIDS pandemic. This small church is feeding and educating more orphans than they can fit inside their building. There are more than four

hundred students attending, most of whom have lost both mother and father to AIDS. A larger number than I care to think about are in child-headed households — that's little kids raising little kids. The goal is to advocate and be a partnership link to connect the church here with the church there to place orphans on a path of hope that leads to a productive future. The website is www.orphanjusticemission.net.

9. Rob Bell in the NOOMA DVD *Rhythm* states it this way: "As you live in tune with the song written on your heart [living in truth, love, mercy, compassion, grace], in tune with the Creator of the Universe, may you realize that you are in relationship with the Living God." Source: Rob Bell, NOOMA *Rhythm* DVD (Grand Rapids, MI: Zondervan, 2005).

The conclusion is almost inescapable that "doing good things" is synonymous with pleasing God (being in relationship with God or playing in tune). And this despite what Paul declares: "There is no good man left, no not one. . . . [This] is meant to silence everyone and to lay the whole world open to God's judgment, and this is because no one can be justified in the sight of God by keeping the Law [doing nice, kind, compassionate deeds]" (Romans 3:10,19-20).

10. As Neo fulminates in *A New Kind of Christian*, "The only kinds of sin we want to focus on as modern Christians are the isolated individual sins committed by isolated individual monads: lying, having an abortion, indulging in pornography, taking drugs, saying naughty words. Not to minimize those things in any way, but that is far short of a fully biblical understanding of sin, and it leads to dangerous truncations of justice and compassion. . . . Modern Christianity

has too often acted as if the only kind of righteousness that mattered was the kind of righteousness of the scribes and Pharisees—the righteousness of nice, clean, legalistic monads who managed to stay disconnected and disinfected on the other side of the street." Source: Brian McLaren, *A New Kind of Christian* (San Francisco: Jossey-Bass, 2001), 100–101. While true, there is an equal danger of truncating social justice from ethical righteousness: God cares about the boardroom not the bedroom.

Chapter 9

1. John the Baptizer's father, Zechariah, on the eighth day when John is to be circumcised, launches into an ecstatic, prophetic song. The Messiah, he proclaims, whose way his son, John, will prepare, is coming as "the rising Sun to visit us, to give light to those who live in darkness and the shadow of death, and to guide our feet into the way of peace" (Luke 1:78-79). What provoked the confrontation was not the tolerance of Jesus but the intolerance of the darkness.

   It is Jesus, looking toward the near future, who gives the whole plot away at the beginning of His ministry. He gives us the motive and then pronounces the basis for the final judgment on the perpetrators: "On these grounds is sentence pronounced; that though the light has come into the world men have shown they prefer darkness to the light because their deeds were evil. And indeed, everybody who does wrong hates the light and avoids it, for fear his actions should be exposed" (John 3:19-20).

   But there is good ground for hope nonetheless. Isaiah prophesies of a future that is partially fulfilled during Jesus' first advent, though it waits on His return to be completely fulfilled. "Arise, shine out, for your light has come, the glory of Yahweh is rising on you, though night still covers the earth and darkness the peoples. Above you Yahweh now rises and above you His glory appears. The nations come to your light and kings to your dawning brightness" (Isaiah 60:1-3). At this sight the people of God will "grow radiant, their hearts throbbing and full" (60:5). While the darkness hates the light, it can never overcome it.

2. On the day Jesus was dedicated, Simeon, a very old man with a prophetic streak, takes the infant in his arms. Looking down at a chubby baby boy, he warns His mother that she is in for a terrible ordeal—a sword would pierce her heart. Jesus was not coming on a sweet errand of mercy that would win Him accolades and guarantee Him the Nobel Peace Prize. There was a dangerous edge to this man's calling. It would cause pain to those closest, frustration to those on the fringe, and ultimately provoke fury on all sides. Simeon prophesies that Jesus would cause the rise and fall of many in Israel "so that the secret thought of many may be laid bare" (Luke 2: 35). Sweet little Jesus boy had come to lift up the rocks and show everybody what was underneath. It was not pretty, and it would not end pretty.

3. "Jesus didn't get crucified for being exclusive; he was hated and crucified for the reverse—for opening the windows of grace and the doors of heaven to the tax collectors and prostitutes, the half-breeds and ultimately even Gentiles." Source: Brian McLaren, *A New Kind of Christian* (San Francisco: Jossey-Bass, 2001), 127.

4. Here's Lewis's thinking on the matter: "I thought I saw how stories of this kind [fantasy] could steal past certain

inhibitions which had paralyzed much of my own religion in childhood . . . supposing that by casting all these things into an imaginary world, stripping them of their stained-glass and Sunday school associations, one could make them for the first time appear in their real potency. Could one not thus steal past those watchful dragons?" Source: C. S. Lewis, "Sometimes Fairy Stories May Say Best What's to Be Said," *On Stories* (New York: Harcourt Brace Jovanonich, 1982), 47.

5. David Wells writes that the television series *Seinfeld* is an example of how our "sense of internal loss and disorientation had been turned into a brilliantly acted but completely banal sitcom." The western world has exchanged its clothing from a melancholic black overcoat to the clown's suit. "Now we are no longer serious enough to do anything but smirk. The journey into the postmodern world, from the writers of this literature of bewilderment into television shows like this, is one from darkness in the depths to mockery on the surface, from suicide to shallow snickers." Source: David F. Wells, *Above All Earthly Pow'rs* (Grand Rapids, MI: Eerdmans, 2005), 188.

6. In a letter to a Sister Penelope, Lewis lets us in on this little literary subterfuge. "Any amount of theology can be smuggled into people's minds under the cover of romance without their knowing it." Source: Lewis, *On Stories*, xvii. Let the reader beware.

7. Peter Kreeft, *C. S. Lewis for the Third Millennium* (San Francisco: Ignatius, 1994), 133.

8. Rob Bell, *Velvet Elvis* (Grand Rapids, MI: Zondervan, 2004), 168.

9. Bell, 167; Brian McLaren, 104.

What these writers really want to say is better articulated

by Chuck Smith Jr. when he states that "the type of evangelism that is concerned *only* about winning souls, while neglecting the needs of individual men, women, and children, is a contradiction of Scripture, which tells us that God made humans in his image and that salvation means wholeness as well as rescue." Source: Chuck Smith Jr. and Matt Whitlock, *Frequently Avoided Questions* (Grand Rapids, MI: Baker, 2005), 69. But Smith also asks, "If we have an agenda, does that not invalidate the 'friendship'" (Smith, 187).

10. See note 5 in chapter 6.

11. The artist, not unlike her Savior, can also say, "The Spirit of Lord Yahweh has been given to me, for Yahweh has anointed me. He has sent me to bring good news to the poor, to bind up hearts that are broken; to proclaim liberty to captives, freedom to those in prison; to proclaim a year of favor from Yahweh, a day of vengeance for our God, to comfort all those who mourn and to give them for ashes a garland, for mourning robe the oil of gladness, for despondency, praise" (Isaiah 61:1-3).

Chapter 10

1. C. S. Lewis, *The Weight of Glory* (Grand Rapids, MI: Eerdmans, 1979), 11. If you were to read no other book this year or the next, other than the Bible, it would be sufficient if you simply read the title essay. It should be on everyone's top-ten-things-to-read-before-I-die. As Dr. Hoch, my seminary Greek professor, would frequently tell us (though never about Lewis), "Sell your shirt and buy the book!"

2. Lewis, *The Weight of Glory*, 11.

3. Lewis, *The Weight of Glory*, 11. Lewis continues in one of his

sweetest sentences, "At present we are on the outside of the world, the wrong side of the door. . . . But all the leaves of the New Testament are rustling with the rumour that it will not always be so. Some day, God willing, we shall get *in*" (Lewis, 13).

4. C. S. Lewis, "Christianity and Literature," *Christian Reflections* (Grand Rapids, MI: Eerdmans, 1967), 7.

5. According to Peter Kreeft, "Glory is greater than we can contain, comprehend, or control. It ravishes us right out of our skins, out of our selves, into an ek-stasy, a standing-outside-the self, and out-of-body-experience; and we tremble in fear and delight. It is not in us, we are in it, like being 'in love': 'it's bigger than both of us'. Thus it does not enter into us, we enter into it. 'Enter into the joy of thy Lord.'" Source: Peter Kreeft, *Heaven: The Heart's Deepest Longing* (San Francisco: Ignatius, 1980), 236.

6. The difference in literature, Lewis comments, is exposed by a simple question: Do I have any desire to ever read this again? Whereas I have read Umberto Eco's *The Name of the Rose* three times, and hope to do so again, thrillers and mysteries (unless written by Dorothy Sayers or perhaps Laurie King) are tolerable once and once only. The former has weight; the latter, none.

7. Hypocrites do their rituals publicly to be "honored" (glorified — *doxa-sowsthin*) by men (Matthew 6:2). Fearful disciples fail to confess Jesus publicly because they value man's praise (*doxan*) rather than the doxan of God (John 12:42-43). Jesus received honor and glory (*doxan*) from His Father (2 Peter 1:17). Our afflictions "which weigh little, train us up for the carrying of a weight of eternal (*doxys*) which is out of all proportion to them" (2 Corinthians 4:17).

If these aren't enough, read Lewis's *The Weight of Glory*, from which this quotation is taken: "It is written that we shall 'stand before' Him, shall appear, shall be inspected. The promise of glory is the promise, almost incredible and only possible by the work of Christ, that some of us, that any of us who really chooses, shall actually survive that examination, shall find approval, shall please God. To please God . . . to be a real ingredient in the divine happiness . . . to be loved by God, not merely pitied, but delighted in as an artist delights in his work or a father in a son — it seems impossible, a weight or burden of glory which our thoughts can hardly sustain. But so it is" (Lewis, 10).

8. The psalmist writes, "You the Terrible! who can oppose you and your furious onslaught? When your verdicts thunder from heaven, earth stays silent with dread; when God stands up to give judgment and to save all the humble of the earth, man's wrath only adds to your glory" (Psalm 76:7-10).

The incongruity of the mention of a chuckle is an allusion to something that C. S. Lewis explains suddenly came to him following his wife's death: "That impression which I can't describe except by saying that it's like the sound of a chuckle in the darkness. The sense that some shattering and disarming simplicity is the real answer." Source: C. S. Lewis, *A Grief Observed*, quoted in Peter Kreeft, *C. S. Lewis for the Third Millennium* (San Francisco: Ignatius, 1994), 187. It is also derived from G. K. Chesterton (whom Lewis deeply admired), who wrote, "Joy, which was the small publicity of the pagan, is the gigantic secret of the Christian. . . . Jesus never restrained His anger. . . . Yet He restrained something. I say it with reverence: there was in that shattering personality a thread of what must be called shyness. There was something that He hid from all men when He went up a mountain to pray. . . . There was some one thing that was too great for God to show us when He walked upon our earth; and I have sometime fancied that it was His mirth." Source: G. K. Chesterton, *Orthodoxy*, quoted in Kreeft, *C. S. Lewis for the Third Millennium*, 188.

The psalmist David also alludes to this. He tells us that God is not only angry, but that He "sits laughing" at the raging and muttering, the plotting, scheming, and rebellion of the pagan nations (Psalm 2:4). Perhaps so can we.

9. Timothy Kallistos Ware quoted in Madeline L'Engle, *Walking on Water* (Colorado Springs, CO: Shaw, 2001), 25.

10. "[Glory] means profundity, significance, importance, greatness, enormousness, something immeasurably bigger than we have ever met, something that catches us up into it rather than down." Source: Peter Kreeft, *Heaven*, 237.

11. C. S. Lewis, *Christian Reflections*, "Christianity and Literature" (Grand Rapids: Eerdmans, 1967), 6-7.

12. Lewis, *Christian Reflections*, 9.

Chapter 11

1. The psalms, which are an amazing window into reality, contain scores of prayers about and against enemies. Perhaps the most common foe is the wicked liar, "champion in villainy, all day plotting destruction. Your tongue is razor sharp, you artist in perfidy" (52:1-2). This evil destroyer and his insidious weapon of deceit are mentioned directly at least thirty-four times and indirectly many more. David calls him a "frightening enemy," who sharpens his tongue like a sword, "shooting bitter words like arrows, shooting them at the innocent from cover, shooting suddenly, without warning

(64:3-4). Solomon, David's son, explains the effect of these deceptive barbs: "a deceitful tongue crushes the spirit" (Proverbs 15:4, NIV). And so it does.

While personified in the Wisdom Literature, for the Christian, the liar represents not so much people but the more brutal enemies of our soul who are sent from their father, the Devil, whom the Messiah tells us is a murderer, a liar, and the father of lies (John 8:44). That is ultimately where the lies originate, and it is he whom we must resist. If we do so, we are told on good authority that he will flee from us (James 4:7). Eventually. Thus is the power of the lie broken over us.

2. "The writer does want to be published; the painter urgently hopes that someone will see the finished canvas (Van Gogh was denied the satisfaction of having his work bought and appreciated during his lifetime; no wonder the pain was more than he could bear); the composer needs his music to be heard. Art is communication, and if there is no communication, it is as though the work had been stillborn." Source: Madeline L'Engle, *Walking on Water* (Colorado Springs, CO: Shaw, 2001), 30.

According to Thomas Wolfe, "I wrote always because I knew my writing must be read, and yet I never knew its public. . . . But this great flame of energy and wild creation kept burning for two years or more, and I knew that *they* must take it, read it, like it, hold me in esteem — not knowing all the time who 'they' might be. I am certain it must have been this way with every writer who ever lived, who ever began to write, who ever wrote his first book in utter obscurity, but who was sustained all the time by the flame of this wild and burning and indestructible hope, and the reason I am telling it to you is that you, if you have never written and published your first book before, must know it, too, because it is the first, the essential, and the incomparable experience that goes with the making of a writer." Source: Thomas Wolfe, *The Autobiography of an American Novelist* (Cambridge, MA: Harvard University Press, 1983), 9.

3. C. S. Lewis, *The Weight of Glory* (Grand Rapids, MI: Eerdmans, 1979), 14.

4. Paul tells us that when the Lord comes, He will judge us, will bring to light what is hidden, and will expose the motives of men's hearts. "Then will be the time for each one to receive his praise from God" (1 Corinthians 4:5). The word *praise* is from *epainon*, which can be translated as approval, delight, or applause.

5. See chapter 10, note 7.

6. While this sounds self-seeking, Paul tells us that we are to long for and live our lives purposefully to please our Daddy. He says, "In our present state, it is true, we groan as we wait with longing to put on our heavenly home over the other. . . . This is the purpose for which God made us. . . . Whether we are living in the body or exiled from it, we are *intent on pleasing Him*." (2 Corinthians 5:2,5,9, emphasis added). This last phrase comes from an amazing Greek word: *philotimoumetha*. It is a compound made up of *phileo*, to love or enjoy, and *timaw*, honor or praise. In its intensive form, it means to be passionately ambitious of honor. This is a good thing, Paul tells us, if the source of the honor you crave is your Father.

Note also Romans 2:7-8: "To those who by persistence in doing good seek glory [*doxa*], honor and immortality he will give eternal life. But for those who are self-seeking . . .

there will be wrath and anger" (NIV). It is those unconcerned and disinterested in receiving their Father's approval who are truly self-seeking.

As Lewis comments, Jesus tells us that we have to become like little children to enter the kingdom of God, "and nothing is so obvious in a child — not a conceited child, but in a good child — as its great and undisguised pleasure in being praised. . . . With no taint of what we should now call self-approval she will most innocently rejoice in the thing that God has made her to be." Source: C. S. Lewis, *The Weight of Glory*, 9.

Chapter 12

1. Gregory Boyd believes that "a God who knows all possibilities, experiences novelty, and is willing to engage in an appropriate element of risk is more exalted than a God who faces an eternally settled future." Source: Gregory A. Boyd, *God of the Possible* (Grand Rapids, MI: Baker, 2000), 15.

   Boyd comes to this conclusion because Old Testament writers use words about God like "ask, forget, repent." He takes these to mean that (just like us, when we use those words about ourselves) God does not know, does not remember, and makes dumb mistakes. This is a failure to rightly understand symbolic language; it is to drain the life out of metaphor. When you step into the pages of the Bible, like the children walking through the wardrobe into Narnia, you are being invited into mystery, replete with symbol and metaphor. That is, in fact, the function of metaphoric language; it is an invitation to go further up and deeper in. Like Hansel's breadcrumbs, they make a path that tantalizes us to move deeper into the magical forest where eternal happiness and sanctuary can be truly found. Figures of speech are less than they represent, not greater. They point to something beyond themselves and in the case of God, to Someone transcendent. They give us a choice — we can make the dog's mistake and sniff at the outstretched finger or turn and look to where it is pointing. Open Theism stares at the hand, oblivious to its real significance.

2. Paul is writing about the importance of learning to keep control of our bodies in a way that is holy, "not giving way to selfish lust like the pagans who do not know God. He wants nobody at all ever to sin by taking advantage of a brother in these matters" (1 Thessalonians 4:5-6).

Chapter 13

1. Nobody writes more powerfully or honestly about this bondage of the human will to sin than Saint Augustine, who battled with sex addiction for many years. As John Piper notes, he had "analyzed his own motives down to this root: everything springs from delight. He saw this as a universal: 'Every man whatsoever his condition, desires to be happy, there is no man who does not desire this, and each one desires it with such earnestness that he prefers it to all other things. . . .' So saving grace, converting grace, for Augustine is God's giving us a sovereign joy in God that triumphs over all other joys and therefore sways the will. The will is free to move toward whatever it delights in most fully, but it is not within the power of our will to determine what the sovereign joy will be." Source: John Piper, *God's Passion for His Glory* (Wheaton, IL: Crossway, 1998), 87, quoting Augustine's *Confessions*. That is the biblical context in which to speak honestly and accurately about man's "freedom."

2. It is possible that an obsessive commitment to conversion can be an imbalance that "prostitutes the friendship and invalidates the evangelism." Source: Brian McLaren, *A New Kind of Christian* (San Francisco: Jossey-Bass, 2001), 104. This is a valid criticism of an accepted manipulative mindset: "I will pretend to like you so I can ram the Four Spiritual Laws down your throat just as quickly as possible." But sadly, it is being twisted by many young followers to mean any desire for conversion is loathsome and inauthentic. Thus, the corrective becomes worse, in many cases, than the original error. Manipulative conversions "whether from false motives or true," according to Saint Paul himself, is to be preferred over no conversions (Philippians 1:18, NIV). I take it that this even covers the cynical desire to add "scalps" to the evangelist's belt.

Chapter 14

1. William L. Lane, *Mark, New International Commentary on the New Testament* (Grand Rapids, MI: Eerdmans, 1974), 68.

Chapter 15

1. Augustine, *The Confessions of St. Augustine* (Garden City, NY: Doubleday, 1960), 206.
2. C. S. Lewis, *The Weight of Glory* (Grand Rapids, MI: Eerdmans, 1979), 4, 12.
3. C. S. Lewis, "Christianity and Culture," *Christian Reflections* (Grand Rapids, MI: Eerdmans, 1967), 23.
4. C. S. Lewis, *Mere Christianity* (New York: Macmillan, 1977), 120.

5. C. S. Lewis, *The Four Loves* (New York: Harcourt Brace Jovanovich, 1960), 13–14.
6. C. S. Lewis, *Letters*, 5 November 1959 (Fort Washington, PA: Harvest Books, 2003).
7. This is the testimony of a brilliant and hungry soul who for many years sought his comfort in the addicting arms of beautiful women but, at long last, found the true and the beautiful one, and freedom, too, thrown in for the bargain:

> Too late have I loved you, O Beauty so ancient and so new. Too late have I loved you. Behold, you were within me, while I was outside; it was there that I sought you, and a deformed creature, rushed headlong upon these things of beauty which you have made. You were with me, but I was not with you. They kept me far from you, those fair things, which, if they were not in you, would not exist at all. You have called to me, and have cried out, and have shattered my deafness. You have blazed forth with light and have shone upon me, and you have put my blindness to flight! You have sent forth fragrance, and I have drawn in my breath, and I pant after you, I have tasted you, and I hunger and thirst after you. You have touched me, and I have burned for your peace. Source: Augustine, *The Confessions of St. Augustine*, 254-255.

8. For instance, Rob Bell says in *Velvet Elvis*, "For Jesus, this new kind of life in him is not about escaping this world but about making it a better place, here and now. The goal

for Jesus isn't to get into heaven. The goal is to get heaven here." Source: Rob Bell, *Velvet Elvis* (Grand Rapids, MI: Zondervan, 2004), 148. Also see, Brian McLaren's *A New Kind of Christian*, 82–83, 129.

Bell and others wishing to push the creational pendulum to an opposite pole fail to take seriously the cataclysmic impact of both the Fall *and* the Crucifixion. Brother Schmemann, former professor of Liturgical Theology at Saint Valdimir's Orthodox Seminary, from a tradition that eulogizes, without deifying, creation, strikes the balance. "In this world Christ was rejected. He was the perfect expression of life as God intended it. The fragmentary life of the world was gathered into His life; He was the heart beat of the world and the world killed Him. But in that murder the world itself died. It lost its last chance to become the paradise God created it to be. . . . While [the world] can be improved, it can never become the place God intended it to be. Christianity does not condemn the world. The world has condemned itself when on Calvary it condemned the One who was its true self." Source: Alexander Schmemann, *For the Life of the World* (Crestwood, NY: Saint Vladimir's Seminary Press, 1973), 23.

9. The title of a sermon series preached at Mars Hill Church in Grand Rapids, Michigan, in 2007, by Rob Bell.

The more orthodox and biblically balanced cosmology alert to creation's seductive claims to idolatry is presented by Orthodox priest Father Patrick Reardon, who says, "Inasmuch as 'the form of this world is passing away' (1 Corinthians 7:31), then, a certain measure of detachment is necessary to prepare ourselves for the wedding feast of the King's Son, a certain using of this world as though not using it, a refusal to take seriously its unwarranted claims on our final loyalty." Source: Patrick Henry Reardon, *Christ in the Psalms* (Ben Lomond, CA: Conciliar Press, 2000), 88.

10. Augustine, *The Confessions of St. Augustine*, 187.

11. Peter Kreeft who is the author who, for my money, most approaches Lewis, whom he has studied long and hard, describes this with Lewisian beauty: "We meet the glory in great art, when a picture becomes no longer an object in the world but a magic window opening up on to another world for us, a hole in our world. . . . Or we know it in the electric shock of an absolutely perfect flower, or in the high, clear, crystal glass of winter night, or in the seagull's haunting, harking call to return to Mother Sea. . . . Some of us, any of us who really chooses to put their trust wholly upon Christ, will know it full in the face when we die; we shall be hailed by the Angel of Death with the same lightsome glory with which Mary was hailed by the Angel of Life, because Christ has made Death into life's golden chariot, sent to fetch His Cinderella bride out of the cinders of this fireplace of a world, through a far midnight ride, to his very own castle and bedchamber, where Glory will beget glory upon us forever." Source: Peter Kreeft, *Heaven* (San Francisco: Ignatius, 1989), 233–234.

12. Lewis, *Mere Christianity*, 120.

13. Brian McLaren, *The Last Word and the Word After That* (San Francisco: Jossey-Bass, 2005), 101, 166.

14. McLaren, *The Last Word and the Word After That*, 187–188. This is one of those places that even Lewis gets it wrong. Saint John tells us that the door is locked not from the inside but the outside and Jesus has the keys in His hands.

15. Lewis, *The Weight of Glory*, 12.

Epilogue

1. G. K. Chesterton, *Orthodoxy*, quoted in Peter Kreeft, *C. S. Lewis for the Third Millennium* (San Francisco: Ignatius, 1994), 188.
2. Kreeft, *C. S. Lewis for the Third Millennium*, 188, emphasis added.
3. Kreeft, *C. S. Lewis for the Third Millennium*, 188.
4. Kreeft, *C. S. Lewis for the Third Millennium*, 189.

ABOUT THE AUTHOR

TIMOTHY J. STONER grew up in Chile and Spain, where his parents served as missionaries. He attended Grand Rapids Theological Seminary before going on to law school. He has been practicing law for twenty years and lives in Grand Rapids, Michigan, with Patty, his wife. They have five children. Timothy is also founder of Orphan Justice Mission, which exists to enable U.S. churches to establish and maintain healthy partnerships with the African church so both can establish justice by caring for orphans in their distress. When not reading, he is doing other things, like working on his next book, which asks, What's a nice Jewish boy like you doing on a cross like that?

For more information, go to w .rw.tjstoner.com.

Check out these other titles from NavPress Deliberate.

Dangerous Faith
Joel Vestal
ISBN-13: 978-1-60006-197-4
ISBN-10: 1-60006-197-4

In *Dangerous Faith*, the idea of knowing God and spreading His matchless good news is challenged on the anvil of action: Will we simply talk about matters of compassion and justice on behalf of the world's marginalized people, or will we unite and become part of the Christ-hope and relief that changes the world one life at a time?

Free to Be Bound
Jonathan Wilson-Hartgrove
ISBN-13: 978-1-60006-190-5
ISBN-10: 1-60006-190-7

Jonathan was a product of the new South: color-blind and culturally sensitive. Yet despite his progressive worldview, he was unaware of the invisible borders separating neighborhood churches. *Free to Be Bound* chronicles Jonathan's experience as he crosses color lines that fragment the church. With an honest heart and passionate voice, he delivers a call for true unity within the church that will inspire every believer.

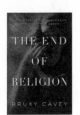

The End of Religion
Bruxy Cavey
ISBN-13: 978-1-60006-067-0
ISBN-10: 1-60006-067-6

In *The End of Religion*, Bruxy Cavey contends that the Jesus described in the Bible never intended to found a new religion; instead he hoped to break down the very idea of religion as a way to God. With a fresh perspective on biblical stories, Cavey paints a picture of the world God originally intended and still desires: a world without religion.

To order copies, visit your local Christian bookstore, call NavPress at
1-800-366-7788, or log on to www.navpress.com.
To locate a Christian bookstore near you, call 1-800-991-7747.